1000 HOURS OUTSIDE

ACTIVITIES TO MATCH SCREEN TIME WITH GREEN TIME

GINNY YURICH

CONTENTS

CHAPTER THREE

SUMMER

CHAPTER FOUR

FALL

INTRODUCTION

There was a time, years actually, when I felt very lost as a parent. The needs of small children feel endless and they are endless—often until we step outside.

Nature is the antidote to many modern parenting problems. Time outdoors gives us all reprieve from the expectations that loom over us and the plates we are spinning. It gives us a moment to catch our breath and remember to be present during the fleeting childhood years. Play in nature smooths out the rough edges of daily family life. Plus, it helps children to develop in a whole-self way: cognitively, emotionally, socially, and physically. The benefits abound as we connect with our children and find joy out in the open air.

I started the 1000 Hours Outside movement as a blog in 2013. From a small grassroots idea, it has expanded across the globe and now includes a lifestyle brand, a top-rated podcast, and a top-ranked mobile app.

The premise here is simple, though the execution is harder. Our aim is to be intentional about nature time, to fill our year with hands-on living (1000 hours of it, to be exact), and to balance out an increasingly pervasive screen culture. The number of hours itself isn't so important—it's the intentionality that counts. In generations past, a goal like this wasn't needed because play was woven through the landscape of childhood. But with changes

My family and I live in Michigan in the US.

in society, there is now a need to protect the time and space that kids need for optimal development and that we all need for a rich family life.

"Where do I begin?" is a question many parents and caregivers ask, and this book is an answer. The ideas here are a reminder that simple joys still hold the ability to create fulfillment. Written for parents, grandparents, caregivers, and kids themselves, these year-round ideas will help you balance out the virtual and the real.

I was thrilled to be able to reach out to the 1000 Hours Outside community around the world and ask for pictures—and they came pouring in by the thousands. Sadly, there's space only for a fraction of them here.

If you're on a path of slowing down, of leaving some white space in your calendar, know that you are not alone. And know that with each touch of the earth, each daisy chain woven, and each bird observed, you are impacting our world for generations to come.

Ginny Yurich

CHAPTER ONE

WINTER

30 mins –3 hrs

HOT CHOCOLATE HIKE

When the temperatures drop, the winds are whipping, and it's cozier to stay inside, a little treat can go a long way in helping us get out the door. Hot chocolate is easy to bring along, it keeps our insides warm, and there are a lot of ways to give your drink extra flair that will make winter hiking more memorable.

SUPPLIES

- Thermos
- Hot chocolate mix (store-bought or homemade)
- Warm water
- Mugs
- Hot chocolate toppings (optional)

INSTRUCTIONS

1. Ask an adult to help you fill your thermos with warm water and add your hot chocolate mix according to the packet instructions or your homemade recipe. Thermoses can be larger than a standard mug so be sure to get your ratios correct. If hot chocolate isn't your drink of choice, you could fill your thermos with a different drink or even some warming soup.
2. Make sure the thermos lid is on securely. Pack any fun, tasty toppings such as mini or jumbo marshmallows, freeze-dried strawberries, cream, crushed candy canes, chocolate syrup, pieces of candy bars, or cinnamon sticks.
3. Head out on your hike. Take care pouring your drink because it will be hot. Drink along the way (be careful not to spill!) or make a stop to enjoy your surroundings while you sip.

Hot chocolate tastes better outdoors!

EXTRA TIME

- Hot chocolate isn't just for hikes. Take it with you all season long when you're trying to increase your time outside. If you're going to be in a stationary location, you could set up a **hot chocolate bar** for serving friends, with containers of all your toppings.

TRY THIS!
Toppings like this marshmallow snowman look cool but help keep you warm.

45 mins active time

SALT DOUGH SHAPES

One way to preserve your favorite little bits of nature is by using salt dough—which has a simple recipe with common ingredients. Making salt dough is a great hands-on activity for working on large and fine motor skills as well as some real-life mathematics. Add in some paints and this could turn into a full day of creating!

SUPPLIES

- Little bits of foraged nature
- Mixing bowl
- 2 cups (250g) flour
- 1 cup (125g) salt
- Natural spices (optional)
- Food coloring (optional)
- 1 cup (240ml) water
- Rolling pin
- Parchment paper
- Baking sheet
- Cookie cutters (optional)
- Oven (optional)
- Paint and paintbrushes (optional)
- Ribbon (optional)

INSTRUCTIONS

1. Go on a hunt for nature treasures like leaves, flowers, grasses, or seeds.
2. If using an oven, preheat it to 250°F (120°C) or its lowest setting.
3. Mix the flour and salt. You can add spices for a delicious scent.
4. If you want colored dough, add food coloring to the water.
5. Gradually add the water to the mix, stirring it until it's no longer sticky.
6. Knead your dough for five to ten minutes until it's soft and pliable.
7. Shape the dough by hand or, on a lightly floured surface, roll it out to half an inch (1.5cm) thick and then shape it with cookie cutters.
8. If you want to hang your shapes, poke a straw-size hole in each one.
9. Gently press your nature items onto the shapes. You can keep them there or remove them to leave behind an impression.
10. Place your shapes on a lined baking sheet and put it in the oven for about three hours. Ask an adult to help with the oven. Or your shapes can dry in the open air for 48 hours. Flip them over halfway through.
11. Once your shapes are dried and cooled, paint them and hang them with ribbons.

You can use cutlery to **engrave** patterns and details on your dough shapes.

TRY THIS!
Make shapes that link to the season and hang them up every year.

SNOW PAINTING

30 mins –2 hrs

Spring, summer, and fall are ablaze with color, but aside from the occasional cardinal flying by or red berries, winter can be void of color. Painting snow is a vibrant way to add color to the lackluster winter landscape. If it's too frigid outside, you can do this activity inside using your bathtub or a plastic bin.

SUPPLIES

- Snow
- Small bowls or squirt bottles or squeeze bottles
- Water
- Food coloring
- Paintbrushes
- Eyedroppers (optional)

INSTRUCTIONS

1. For fluffy snow, pat it down to create a canvas that is easier to paint on.
2. Fill small bowls, squirt bottles, or squeeze bottles with water and a few drops of food coloring. Stir or shake to combine. Be careful because food coloring can stain your clothes.
3. Using paintbrushes or squirt bottles, create your art. You could paint a picture or add color to something you've already built out of snow. How about a snow turtle? Or an oversize snowball that you paint like a mosaic? You could paint a treasure map in the snow or write messages for your friends and neighbors.

As well as food coloring, you can use **nontoxic paint**.

MORE IDEAS

- Add a little extra fine-motor skill work by using **eyedroppers** to add color.
- Use a spray bottle to soak your colored areas with water. Watch the colors **run and blend** together!
- Work with only the **primary colors** red, yellow, and blue, and see what colors you can make by mixing them.

TRY THIS!

Brighten up your snowpeople and make them stand out with splashes of color.

INVENT A CONSTELLATION

Thousands of years ago, the ancient Greeks saw pictures connecting stars in the sky and gave them names based on their mythology. But how fun would it be to make up your *own* constellations?

STAR SPOTTING

Head outside with an adult and look up at the night sky. Scan for star patterns that remind you of shapes. Perhaps you can see animals, people doing activities, or your favorite characters?

TIP

- **Chilly**, **cloudless** nights are the best time to see stars, but wrap up warmly.

On a perfectly clear night, you might be able to see up to **6,000** stars.

SIGNS OF THE ZODIAC

Which stars you see depends on the time of the year and where you are in the world. The northern and southern hemispheres have different views of the night sky. These constellations are four of the 12 signs of the zodiac, whose origins are thousands of years old.

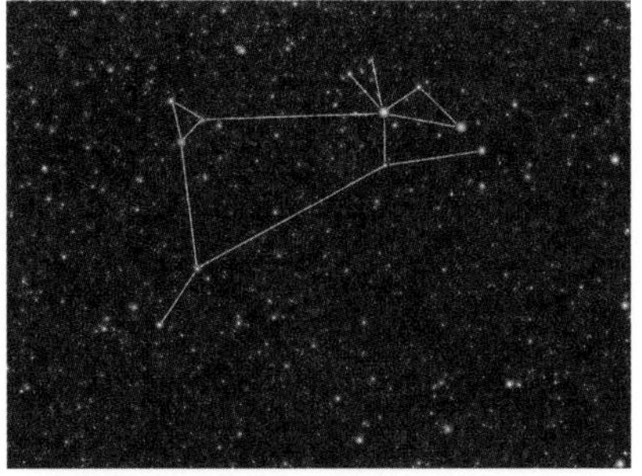

Ares: This constellation was thought to look like a sheep with curled horns.

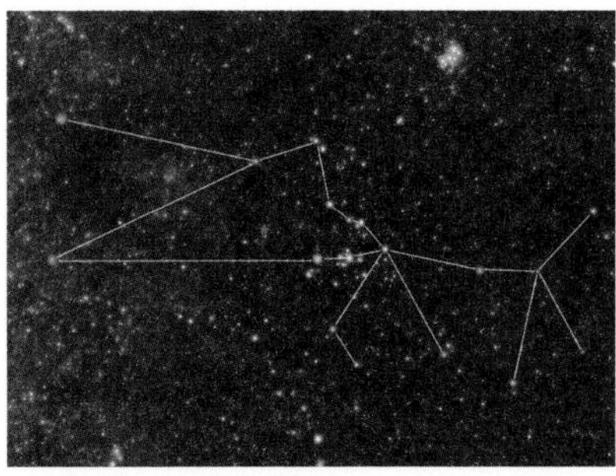

Taurus: Thousands of years ago, people saw a bull in this group of stars.

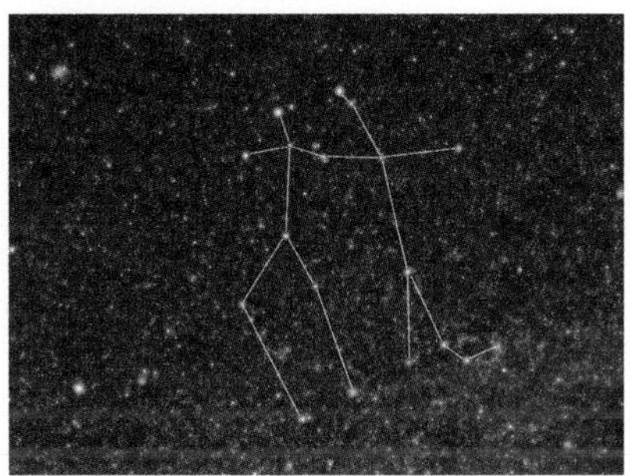

Gemini: Gemini was named long ago for a pair of twins. Can you see them here?

Cancer: The name of this pattern of stars is Latin for "crab." Does it look like a crab to you?

EXTRA TIME

- Create themes (sports, animals, tools, famous people, etc.) and see who comes up with ten new **constellation names** first!
- Have everyone create five constellations and **vote** for which is the best.

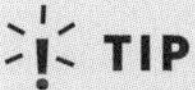

TIP

- The best time to go stargazing is right before or right after a new moon. The moon's surface is very dark at those times so it reflects less light, making the sky darker and stars appear **brighter**.

ICE BRICK TOWER

2–3 hrs

Make your own colored ice bricks and stack them into a rainbow tower. You can add to and play with your cool creations all season long—as long as the temperature stays low. But if your tower does melt, don't worry. You can always build a new one during the next freeze—or with the help of a freezer.

SUPPLIES

- Cardboard milk containers, rectangular plastic tubs, or aluminum trays
- Water (tap temperature)
- Food coloring (optional)
- Flower petals or citrus slices (optional)
- Warm water
- Tray big enough to fit each of your containers

INSTRUCTIONS

1. Fill your containers with water.
2. Add food coloring, flower petals, citrus slices, or a mix to some or all of your containers, if you'd like. However, food coloring can stain, so be careful not to get any on your clothes.
3. Set them to freeze outside or in a freezer. Freezing times may vary.
4. Place the bottom of your container in a tray of warm water momentarily. This will loosen your bricks so that you can gently remove them.
5. Then your bricks are ready to stack into an ice tower. You could use a slushy snow mix as a mortar and wet it down afterward with a spray bottle or a hose to add even extra reinforcement. If you don't have snow, use a spray bottle or a hose to wet the bricks. It might take a few soaks to get the bricks to freeze together.

MORE IDEAS

- Make **mini towers** using ice cubes. This is a great option if you don't have a big freezer or cold temperatures. Follow the steps above, but use an **ice cube tray** as your ice brick container.

Freeze water in **balloons** for round bricks with flat bottoms.

TRY THIS!

How high can you stack the ice bricks without knocking any down?

TRY THIS!
Start a snowball fight from the safety of your fort!

2–5 hrs

STAINED ICE FORT

If you've been to a very cold place, perhaps you've seen igloos made with blocks of snow in someone's yard or at a park. Traditionally, igloos and snow forts are white. Spice up your snow-brick building and add some color to your life and your yard with rainbow bricks, even in the midst of a cold, drab winter.

SUPPLIES

- Snow
- Water
- Bread loaf pans
- Food coloring
- Spoon

INSTRUCTIONS

1. Once you're sure you have several below-freezing days coming, make a lot of colored ice bricks (see page 16).
2. Clear some flat ground and mark out the shape for your build.
3. Stack your blocks. You could make a fort with battlements, a curved igloo, or any construction you like.
4. As you stack each layer, pack snow between the bricks to act as "mortar" and hold them together. Place rectangular bricks at an angle to each other for a curved wall. Continue building up layer after layer and don't forget to leave a space for the door!
5. Once you have your fort or igloo, you could use it as a base for an adventure game—perhaps take turns to attack and defend it with snowballs. If it gets damaged, it's simple to rebuild.

Once it's dark, use a flashlight so your bricks shine like **stained glass windows**.

MORE IDEAS

- Pour a little water over your structure so it freezes overnight, **strengthening** it for the next day.

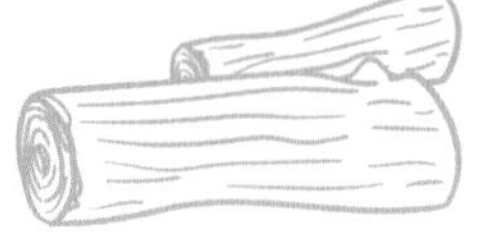

WINTER FIRE

30 mins –3 hrs

Bonfires are common in the height of the summer: long, warm days lead us to campsites or neighborhood celebrations where the flames dance high and we roast marshmallows, sing songs, and tell stories into the night. But winter is also an excellent time for bonfires—they draw us out and help us spend more hours in chilly conditions.

SUPPLIES

- Rocks
- Dry kindling
- Fire-starting log (optional)
- Matches or a lighter
- Firewood
- Dry seating (optional)
- Blankets or quilts (optional)
- Marshmallows and long skewers or sticks (optional)

INSTRUCTIONS

1. Find a flat spot away from any low-hanging branches that is big enough for both your fire and for you to move around it safely. Stomp down the snow.
2. Build a platform with rows of logs or rocks.
3. Place a ring of rocks around the platform to limit the fire.
4. Place a small amount of dry kindling (such as pine needles, twigs, newspaper, or cardboard) in a tepee shape on top of your foundation. Fire-starting logs make the process a little quicker and easier.
5. With adult supervision, use matches or a lighter to start your fire. As it gets going, add kindling as well as larger and larger sticks and logs.
6. During the day, your fire is a place to warm up between activities. In the evening, it's a cozy gathering place in the cleansing air.
7. At the end, douse the fire with water and make sure it's completely out.

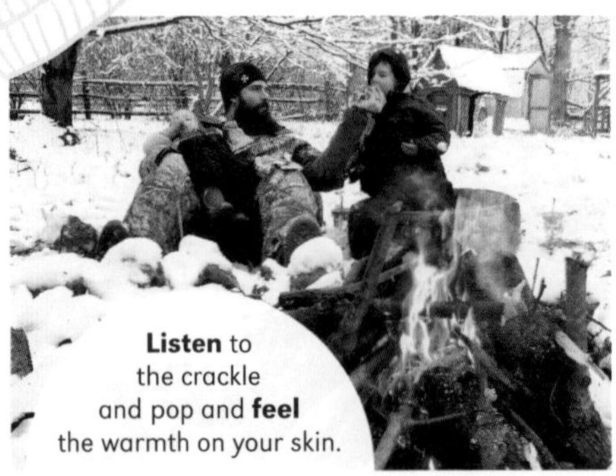

Listen to the crackle and pop and **feel** the warmth on your skin.

⚠ SAFETY FIRST!

- Always make sure you follow local **regulations**.
- Make fires only with **adult supervision**.
- Don't make fires on **windy** days.
- **Never** play with matches.
- Never leave the fire **unattended**.

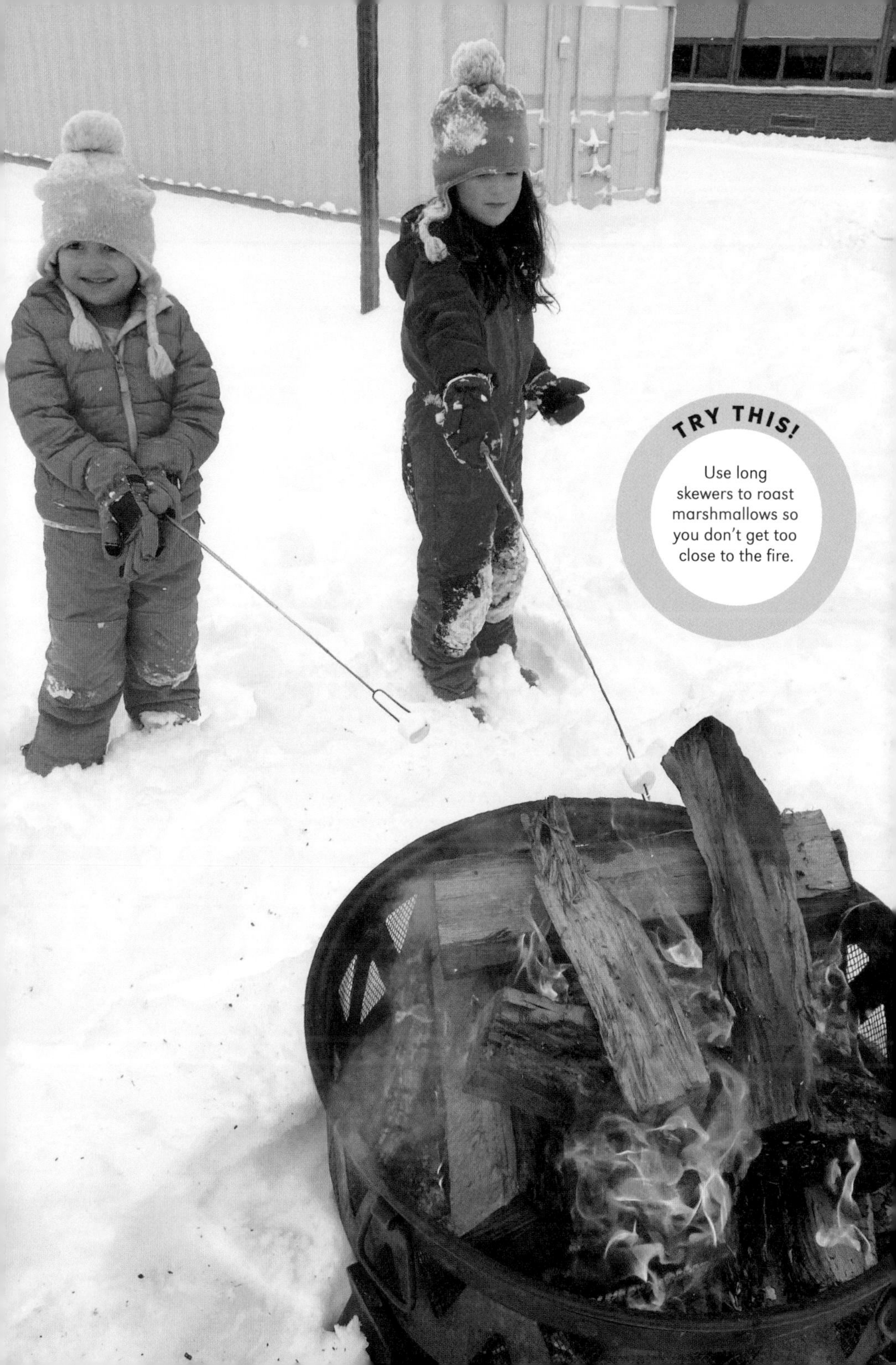

TRY THIS!

Use long skewers to roast marshmallows so you don't get too close to the fire.

45 mins
–2 hrs

SNOW CAKE

Beautiful snow cakes come in all different shapes and sizes and are a great way to add color and creativity to a winter backdrop. Even better, you can decorate your cake creation so that it becomes a tasty treat for the birds and animals in your area during the depths of winter.

SUPPLIES

- Snow
- Snow cake toppings such as berries, nuts, seeds, corn, fruit, vegetables, or birdseed.
- Molds or containers (optional)
- Cake-decorating tools such as levelers (optional)

INSTRUCTIONS

1. First of all, collect snow into the basic shape of your cake. It could be square, rectangular, or circular, and it could have many tiers like a wedding cake. You could also freeze snow in a mold or container to shape it, like the top two tiers of this tall cake.
2. Smooth the top of your cake with a leveler, a shovel, or your mitten.
3. Decorate your snow cake with the materials you have on hand. Get creative! Use your decorations to make patterns, leaves, stars, hearts, or other designs.
4. Once your cake has been standing for a few days, scout the tracks around it to figure out which animals or birds may have visited.

EXTRA TIME

- Make different kinds of snow cakes: perhaps the **biggest** one you can without it tipping over or a **tiny** one perfect for little mice.
- Host a **snow cake party** with neighborhood friends and end it with a real cake for all of you to enjoy!

TRY THIS!

Carefully cut decorative shapes out of orange peel—but don't eat them!

WINTER WALK

Taking a walk might not be the first activity you think of during winter, but the winter months offer unique opportunities to see and do things you can't during the other seasons—even if you live somewhere without snow.

LAYER UP

When it's coldest, it may take longer to get dressed for the elements than the time you get to spend outdoors, but it's worth it. Layering helps hold in heat. For the layer closest to your skin, choose a material that will help you stay dry.

BRING A FRIEND

Take your walk with a friend, sibling, or pet for companionship. Stomp in the snow together. Swipe the snow off tree branches together. And when your legs get tired, sit and listen to the birds and watch the gentle falling snow together.

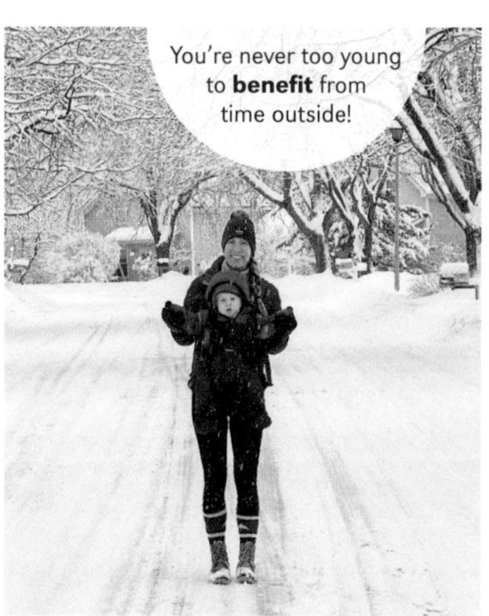

You're never too young to **benefit** from time outside!

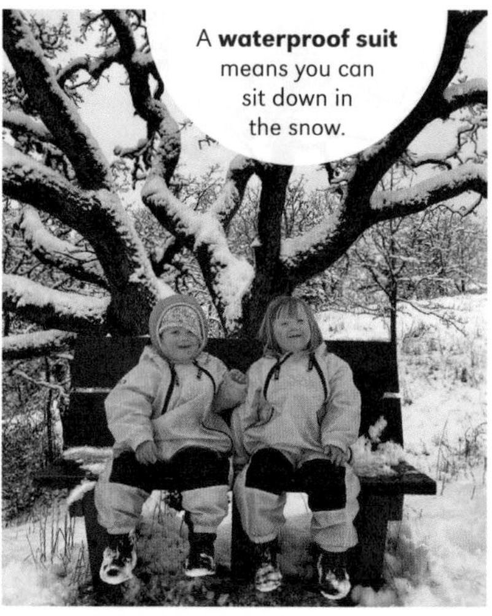

A **waterproof suit** means you can sit down in the snow.

FIND FASCINATION

Each season offers its own mysteries. Take some time to look for those unique parts of the season. You probably won't have to walk very far to find wonder. If you pass the same point regularly, look for changes—like measuring icicles to see how much they grow.

Take a **magnifying glass** along on your walk to take a closer look at what you find.

ICICLE HUNT

Some icicles grow like upside-down cones but others form interesting shapes because of differences in the wind and water quality. For a short while, icicles can capture your imagination and be used for pretend play, especially if you find one that's an interesting shape!

How many **nonconical icicles** can you find?

ALONG THE WATER

Take your winter outing along a body of water. If the water isn't frozen, watch for wildlife. Are there ducks around? Swans? Can you see any fish below the surface? If the water is frozen, don't trust that it's strong enough to step on.

TIP

- Head outside, even when it's cold, and allow the natural light to help **improve your mood**.

Return to the same water several times to see if it has **frozen** over.

30 mins active time

EGGSHELL CRESS

This is a delightful activity with a lot of creativity and learning! Using the eggshells leftover from cooking, you can create eggshell people who grow their own green "hair!" They will produce different looks depending on the seeds you use. Give them a "haircut" and use the trimmings for salads, soups, or sandwiches.

SUPPLIES

- Clean, empty eggshells
- Permanent markers, paint pens, or googly eyes and glue
- Seeds (such as arugula, cress, radish, chia, mung bean, alfalfa, oregano, basil, or thyme)
- Cotton balls or potting soil
- Egg carton or an item that holds your eggshells upright, such as a flat tray filled with small rocks
- Pan of boiling water (optional)

INSTRUCTIONS

1. You will need at least half of an eggshell intact so try to crack your eggs near the thinner end. Use the contents to cook something delicious!
2. Gently clean the shells inside and out. You could even ask an adult to help you boil them for one minute to make sure they're completely clean.
3. Decorate your shells with markers, paint pens, or googly eyes and glue.
4. Add damp cotton balls to each shell or fill them two-thirds with potting soil. If you do the planting outside, then you won't make so much mess. Wash your hands after handling soil.
5. Place the seeds on the cotton balls or just under the soil's surface.
6. Carefully put your eggs back in the egg carton or on your tray with rocks.
7. Place them somewhere sunny and keep them moist but don't overwater them because the shells don't have drainage holes. Sprouts should appear after three to five days.
8. When your sprouts are long enough, give your egg heads haircuts. Some sprouts will continue to grow.
9. If you want your seedlings to grow more, gently crack the eggshell in a few places, then plant the whole thing directly into the ground outside or in a larger pot of soil. Eggshells contain calcium so they are a great addition to garden soil.

TRY THIS!
Make funny eggshell faces with googly eyes.

30–90 mins

BEESWAX LUMINARIES

None of your beeswax! Have you ever heard that saying about minding your own business? It's kind of silly! Beeswax is very useful and once you have some, hang onto it because you can melt it down and reuse it over and over. Instead of a flame, these beeswax luminaries have a battery-operated tealight.

SUPPLIES

- Beeswax
- Double boiler (bain-marie)
- Balloon or orange
- Pressed flowers (optional)
- Construction or tissue paper
- Scissors
- Watered-down glue
- Battery-powered tealight

INSTRUCTIONS

1. Ask an adult to help you melt down your beeswax in a double boiler (bain-marie) on the stove. The bowl with the wax could get damaged, so don't use a special one. Be very careful because the wax will be hot.
2. Blow up a balloon to about the size of a softball and secure it with a knot. Or you can use a large orange instead.
3. Carefully dip the balloon into the melted wax so it's submerged at least halfway, but not to the top. If you're using an orange, don't dip it more than halfway so you'll be able to remove the orange.
4. One dipped, place the object on a flat surface until it dries and hardens.
5. Once the wax is dry, carefully dip it again and again until you've added enough layers of wax to make the luminary strong.
6. When the final layer of wax is completely dry, pop the balloon and pull it out or carefully remove the orange.
7. Go outside to find leaves or pine needles to press (see page 132). Glue them or pressed flowers saved from summer or tissue-paper cutouts onto your luminary for decoration.
8. After dark, find a safe place outside, such as a deck or balcony, to display your lantern. Place a battery-powered tealight inside it and enjoy the glow.
9. Gather everyone together and share a warming outdoors bedtime story.

TRY THIS!
Group several beeswax luminaries together for a greater glow.

TRY THIS!

Check out local resale stores for novelty shaped muffin pans like hearts or stars.

ICE ORNAMENTS

30 mins active time

Maximize the winter sun with these gorgeous ice ornaments, which sparkle and capture the light. Our brains are wired for novelty, and these ornaments bring a lot joy during the long, winter months. It's exciting to see how they turn out once they are frozen, and if they melt, you can make them over and over again.

SUPPLIES

- Muffin or bundt pans
- Water
- Colorful bits of nature such as petals, berries, leaves, or seeds
- Thin citrus slices (optional)
- String or twine
- Scissors
- A freezer or freezing weather

INSTRUCTIONS

1. Add a thin layer of water to your pans—enough to hold your items in place but not so much that the ice will be too dense to capture light.
2. Add your nature items. Where there is space between them, more light will shine through.
3. Unless your pans have a natural hole (like a bundt pan), drape a piece of string in each one so both ends are in the water and there is enough length out of the water to hang up your ornaments.
4. Set your ornaments to freeze outside or in a freezer. It will take 12 to 24 hours. Make sure they're not in a spot where they'll get covered with snow.
5. Once the ice is frozen, remove it from the container. If it doesn't come out easily, set it for 15 or 20 seconds in a shallow pan with a layer of warm water. This will loosen your ornaments and they will easily slide out. Be careful not to drop them or they might shatter.
6. Hang your ornaments outside and watch as they sparkle in the sunlight. Decorate a tree with them or clip them to string to make an icy garland.

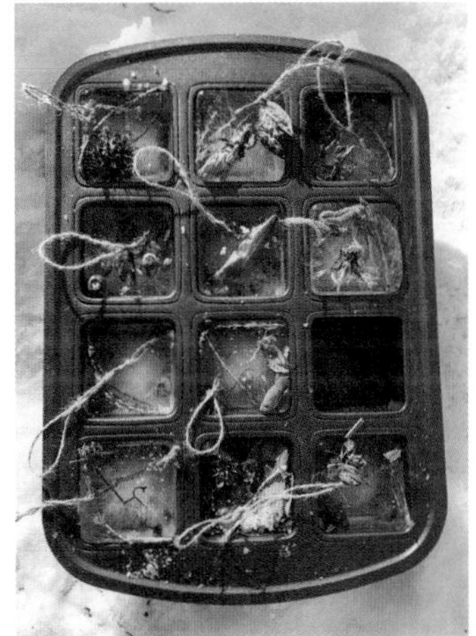

The less water you use, the **more the sun** will shine through.

MAKE SOME MUSIC

45 mins

The outdoors is the perfect place for children to release their need to be loud. The sensory experience of banging on a variety of household items teaches you about how vibrations make sounds. This is a great open-ended activity for infants who can sit independently all the way up through older children.

SUPPLIES

- Household items that could make noise such as a colander, a cooling rack, wind chimes or dangling metal spoons, cans, buckets, muffin pans, pots, or pans
- Drumsticks—choose from wooden sticks, metal or wooden spoons, whisks, potato mashers, etc.
- Container to hold your "drumsticks" (optional)

INSTRUCTIONS

1. Ask an adult to gather whatever supplies they have on hand and set them out for you to explore all the different sounds they can make.
2. Include any other musical items you might have on hand such as a children's xylophone.
3. Strike up the band and make some noise! Play two or three different instruments all at once or in succession with drumsticks or your hands. Experiment with the types of sounds you can make by hitting items with varying pressure or in different places.
4. When you're finished, keep all of your drumsticks and instruments organized so that you can use them over and over again. If they're stored properly, this activity can last for many years.

An adult could make a **music wall** by screwing items on a fence at varying heights.

MORE IDEAS

- Create a **junkyard band**. Give each member of the family an "instrument" to play and see what songs you can come up with.
- Play music from a speaker and **tap along** to the **rhythms**.

GO WILD
TRY THIS!
String up household items on paracord and play them as they hang.

CAFE PLAY

Setting up little pretend restaurants or cafes is fun all year round. Whether you serve up fluffy snow or mud pies baked in the hot sun, there are so many great ways to be a top-rated outdoor chef, no matter the season!

WINTER WONDERS

Gather natural items from outside or bring out indoor toys to help create the ultimate outdoor dining experience. Use an old baking sheet to make snow pizzas or muffin pans to make scrumptious baked goods.

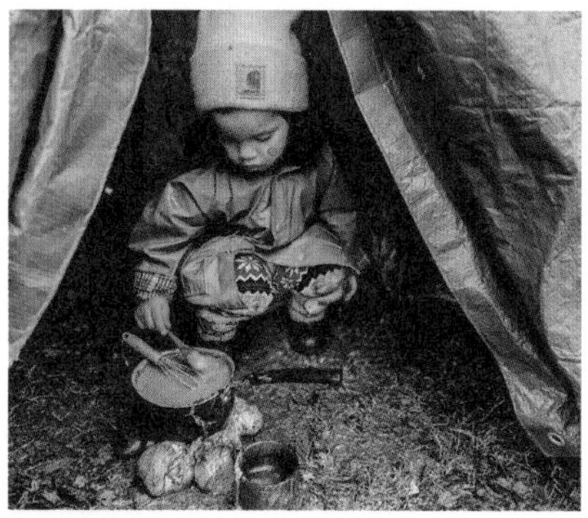

Set up a **simple tarp tent** for a rugged camp cookout in winter.

A quick trip to a **thrift store** can produce all sorts of fun kitchen utensils!

SPRING SUPPERS

Spring typically offers one main ingredient in great abundance—mud! Take advantage of the winter thaw and the spring rain to concoct delectable mud soup in a large bowl, or water it down even more and fill a pitcher with refreshing mud juice.

Don't be afraid to get messy. Cooking in the **mud** is the best!

SUMMER SIZZLERS

The summer brings all sorts of new life—flowers in bloom, saplings, and even weeds. Collect a basketful of beautiful ingredients and use them to make a colorful pie or perhaps a bowl of pretend pasta.

Make the most of the **bright colors** of summer's bounty while you can.

TIP

- Take advantage of what each season has to offer. The uniqueness of each one helps expand your creativity!

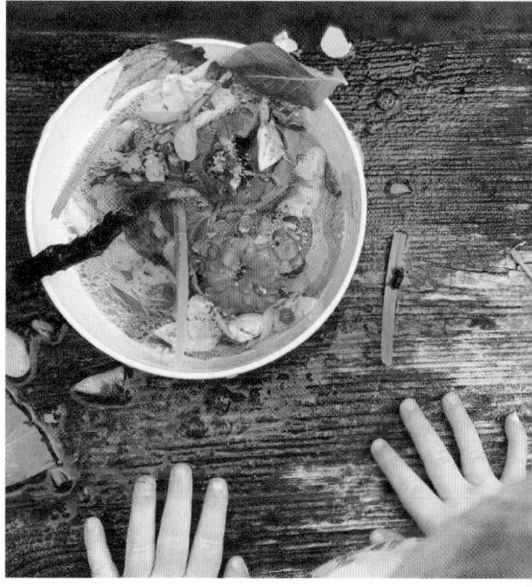

FALL FEASTS

When the leaves start to turn brown and fall from the trees, you know there will be a lot of special things to bake with! A leaf and acorn entree, complete with a side of tree bark bread, is sure to get rave reviews from anyone who tries it!

Have any old kitchen gear like a sink? Set it up outside for a **professional** looking kitchen.

30 mins

SNOW VOLCANO

Winter and science combine in this explosive activity that's fun for all ages! It's great for taking a class of kids outside, for a scout group, or even at a snowy, outdoor party. And if you don't have snow, this experiment still works really well with just the jar, or you could construct a volcano from sand or *papier-mâché*.

SUPPLIES

- Large pile of snow
- Glass jar or plastic cup
- 1 tablespoon dish soap
- ¼ cup (60ml) warm water
- 1 cup (240ml) vinegar
- ¼ cup (58g) baking soda
- Food coloring
- Small shovel (optional)

INSTRUCTIONS

1. Smooth a large pile of snow into a volcano shape.
2. The middle of a volcano is called the "central vent." With your hands or a small shovel, carve out a crater to be the central vent in your volcano. It needs to be large enough to fit your jar or cup.
3. Carefully place your jar or cup inside the volcano. Alternatively, you can place your jar in the snow first and then build the volcano shape around it. Pack the snow tightly so it supports the jar.
4. Mix the dish soap, baking soda, and warm water in your jar.
5. Add food coloring to your mix, but be careful because it can stain clothes and skin. This is a great time to experiment with color combinations!
6. Now it's time to add the vinegar, step back, and watch the volcano erupt! The more vinegar you add, the larger the eruption. Also, the smaller the hole at the top of your jar, the higher the eruption will go. Keep back if you're wearing clothing that you don't want to get ruined.
7. You can make repeat volcanoes in the same spot and watch how the colors run together. Or make a bunch of volcanoes next to each other.

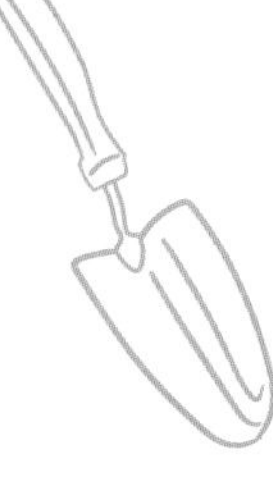

MORE IDEAS

- Try dividing your jar with a piece of cardboard down its center. Add **different colors** of food coloring to each side and watch what happens. Red on one side and yellow on the other will look like lava!

TRY THIS!
Create a row of volcanoes and then see how quickly you can make them all erupt.

1–2 hrs

STORY STONES

Story stones are great prompts for both children and adults to work on their creativity and storytelling. The first part of the activity is creating beautiful stones, then you can use them to tell stories, either on your own or collaboratively. Each new stone can spark a new twist in the tale—and the possibilities are endless!

SUPPLIES

- Smooth, flat stones of different shapes and sizes—larger stones will be easier for younger children
- Permanent markers, paint pens, or acrylic paint and paintbrushes
- Watered-down craft glue and stickers, magazine clippings, or fabric scraps (optional)
- Basket, bag, or other container

INSTRUCTIONS

1. Draw or paint objects, scenes, or patterns on your stones.
2. You could also add magazine clippings or stickers and cover them with a thin layer of watered-down glue. Possible ideas for story stones include:
    - **Food items**—raw ingredients such as fruits and vegetables as well as finished meals such as a plate of spaghetti
    - **People**—real friends or family or fictional characters
    - **Animals**—farm animals, zoo animals, dinosaurs, or even fantastical creatures or aliens
    - **Places**—a field of wildflowers, a cabin, or a tent
    - **Clothing**—different seasonal items such as rain boots or mittens
    - **Weather**—clouds, wind, sun, snow, etc.
    - **Fairy-tale elements**—draw on classic stories for inspiration.
3. Once your stones are dry, gather them in a container.
4. Pull them out one at a time and come up with a story that connects them.
5. Alternatively, play in a group. Each person takes it in turns to pull out a stone and then adds to the story.
6. Try to give your stories a beginning, a middle, and an end, but they can be as wacky as you like!

EXTRA TIME

- When you reach the end of your story, **write it down** or **record** yourself telling it so you can remember it.

TRY THIS!
Use bright colors for striking stones that will spark your imagination.

FROZEN BUBBLES

45 mins

Bubbles are a hit with kids year-round, but when the temperatures dip well below freezing, we can aim for frozen ones! You can use a simple bubble solution to make these, while others swear by a few special ingredients. Become a frozen-bubbles scientist—try out different bubble formulas and predict which will work the best and why.

SUPPLIES

- Below-freezing temperatures
- Bubble wand

Option 1:

- Store-bought bubble solution

Option 2:

- 1 part water
- 4 parts dish soap
- Dash of light corn syrup

Option 3:

- 1 cup warm water
- 2 tbsp sugar
- 2 tbsp light corn syrup
- 2 tbsp dish soap

INSTRUCTIONS

1. Choose a very cold day that isn't very windy. Be very careful in the frigid temperatures, and make sure you dress accordingly.
2. Follow one of the bubble solution recipes (or experiment with all three!) The dish soap creates the bubbles, the corn syrup adds thickness to your mixture, and the sugar helps with crystallization.
3. Cool your bubble solution(s) down in the fridge for around 30 minutes.
4. Find a sheltered spot outside and start blowing your bubbles. If they have a soft spot to land on, like snow, they are less likely to break.
5. Admire your bubbles as they freeze! But be patient—it could take several attempts to get a good one.

Every bubble has a unique frozen pattern.

MORE IDEAS

- Try to get some **slow-motion video** footage of the incredible process of your bubbles freezing.
- If the bubbles are working for you, see how many you can **stack** on top of each other.

TRY THIS!

Experiment with different sizes of bubble wands. Do they affect how the bubbles freeze?

TRY THIS!

Instead of wool yarn, use tinsel with stars attached to make a handle.

2 hrs

LANTERN

Hiking at dusk or into the night opens up a whole new world of exciting adventure (see page 44). As opposed to a flashlight, a homemade lantern gives off a minimal circle of light, allowing your eyes to really adjust to the darkness. Hanging up several of these makes an outdoor space very cozy and they also make unique gifts.

SUPPLIES

- Heavyweight watercolor paper approx. 8 x 20in (20 x 50cm)
- Watercolor paints or crayons
- Paintbrushes
- Olive oil
- Scissors
- Stapler and staples
- Cardboard
- Glue
- Tissue paper
- Hole punch
- Wool yarn
- Battery-operated tealights
- Long stick (optional)

INSTRUCTIONS

1. Paint one side of your watercolor paper and allow it to dry. Alternatively, you could color it with crayons.
2. Once the paper is dry, paint it with a thin layer of olive oil. This will make your paper semitranslucent so light shines through it beautifully.
3. Along one long side of your paper, carefully cut slits about 4 inches (10cm) in length every 2 inches (5cm).
4. Carefully cut shapes out of your paper, such as a moon, heart, or star, and glue tissue paper behind each hole.
5. Roll your lantern into a cylinder or fold it perpendicular to the long side in three equally spaced places to make a rectangular prism.
6. Ask an adult to help you staple your lantern shut.
7. Glue the tabs down and glue cardboard to the base to hold it all together.
8. Punch two holes at the top, and tie each end of a piece of wool through the two holes.
9. Tie your lantern to a long stick.
10. Finally, put battery-operated tealights inside your lantern.

Jam jars and **tissue paper** also make good lanterns. Use the lids to secure string handles.

NIGHTTIME HIKE

Hiking at dusk or into the night opens up a whole new world of sights, sounds, and smells. You can even walk the exact same trail or path at night versus the day and have a completely different experience.

SNOW AT NIGHT

Whether you're cross-country skiing or simply hiking in the snow at night, a lighted path makes the snow glitter and glow as you make your way. Also, the crunch of the snow seems extra loud in the still and quiet of the evening.

TIP

- Hiking at night takes a little extra planning, but it's totally worth it. Always have a backup flashlight with you and go with an adult.

Just a single light can **brighten** up a large stretch of dark trail.

LANTERN HIKE

Make your nighttime hike extra special with a homemade lantern to light your path (see page 43 for how to make one). A flashlight can guide your way, but a lantern gives a softer, magical light, creating a more atmospheric nighttime experience.

Homemade lanterns make an outdoor space very **cozy**.

GLOW HIKE

Make your night hike a glowing good time by using glow sticks to wrap around your wrists or ankles, or make necklaces out of them. You could even tape them to your clothes to make a glowing skeleton!

Make a video on your hike of **skeletons** moving about in the dark!

SPARKLER HIKE

Sparklers brighten up the dark with a dazzling array of light. But be sure to wear gloves because sparklers can burn skin, and don't wave them near anyone else. Only adults should light sparklers.

How many **letters** or **numbers** can you draw before the sparkler goes out?

30 mins

HOOP ART

There's just something wonderful about catching sunlight. These pieces of nature art framed in embroidery hoops are gorgeous to hang on any window so you can watch the light stream through. This is an open-ended project that can be completed year-round, highlighting the seasonal nature items in your area.

SUPPLIES

- Embroidery hoop
- Pencil
- Contact paper
- Scissors
- Natural materials that are mostly flat like leaves, grasses, or pressed flowers (see page 132)
- Ribbon or twine

INSTRUCTIONS

1. Trace around the inner ring of your hoop on contact paper and carefully cut it out.
2. Carefully cut a rectangular shape that's slightly bigger than the inner ring.
3. Peel the backing off the rectangular piece and lay the clear side on a table with the sticky side facing up. Place the inner ring onto the sticky paper.
4. Press your natural materials onto the sticky paper, inside the hoop.
5. Peel the backing off the circular piece. Press it firmly, sticky side toward your natural materials, into the inside of the small hoop—essentially sandwiching your design between the two pieces of contact paper.
6. Add the outer ring of the hoop to the inside ring and tighten the screw. Carefully trim off any excess contact paper.
7. Tie twine or ribbon around the screw and hang your creation up so it can catch the light.

EXTRA TIME

- There are **three common sizes** of embroidery hoops: 4 x 4in (10.2 x 10.2cm), 5 x 7in (12.75 x 17.75cm), and 6 x 10in (15.25 x 25.5cm). Use one of each to make a **trio of art**.

MORE IDEAS

- Instead of natural objects, you could use **tissue paper** to make your hoop art. Cut it into different scenes and let the light shine through.
- Make one hoop art **per season** and notice how the materials change.

TRY THIS!
Layer up objects to create darker patches of color where items overlap.

5–10 mins

SNOW ANGEL

There's something about laying your body completely out on the peaceful snow on a cold winter day, flat on your back, with your eyes up to the sky. While you're enjoying the sensation, follow the steps below to create a gorgeous imprint in the snow that will looks as though a beautiful angel has been to visit!

SUPPLIES

- Snow that's deep enough that you won't see the ground or grass beneath it.
- Waterproof clothing that will keep you dry and warm.

INSTRUCTIONS

1. Find an area with undisturbed snow. It's best if the snow is at least 4 inches (10cm) deep and has a layer of powdery snow on the top. Heavy snow makes it difficult to move and make the right shape.
2. Sit in the snow first, then lay down and stretch out your arms and legs. If the snow is deep enough, you can also jump backward from standing.
3. Swing your arms and legs out and back several times as if you're doing jumping jacks. This creates an impression in the snow that looks like angel wings and an angel's gown.
4. Press your head back into the snow to leave a print of the angel's head.
5. Escaping from your creation without disturbing its beauty is the most difficult part. Get up slowly and try not to step down into any part of the gown. Jump away if you can to avoid leaving footprints.

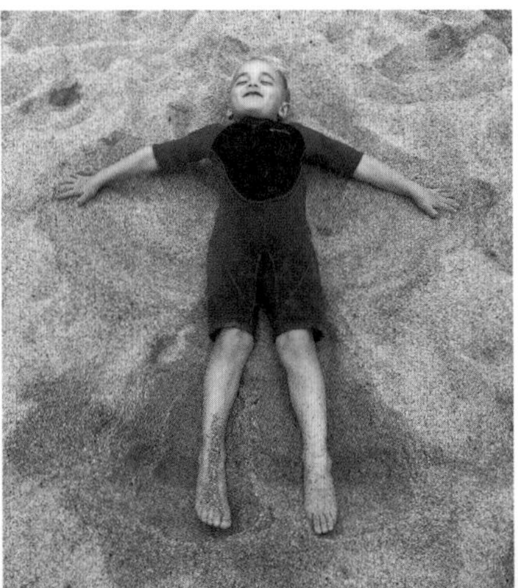

You don't need snow—use **sand**, **leaves**, or **long grass** instead.

MORE IDEAS

- Add natural materials such as **walnuts, acorns, or sticks** to give your snow angel a **face**.
- Try **painting** your snow angel with ideas from pages 12 and 13.
- See **how many** angels you can make in a set amount of time.

TRY THIS!

Wave your arms—but don't bring your arms right up to your head.

MOON CYCLES

The moon never changes shape, but to us on Earth, it looks like it does. We see only the part of the moon that reflects the sun's light, and that changes as the moon orbits around Earth each month.

THE HARVEST MOON

Sometimes the moon looks really small and is high in the sky. But have you ever seen one so big and low, you almost felt you could reach out and grab it? That was probably a Harvest Moon. It occurs only once a year, but there are eight moons you can spot every month.

MORE IDEAS

- Most years there are **12 full moons**, but every two and a half years there are 13. Plot them on your calendar for this year.

A **Harvest Moon** over Washington, DC in the US.

MOON PHASES

Paying attention to the shape of the moon will help connect you with the rhythms of nature. Each month the moon follows the same eight moon phases.

It takes **29 and a half days** to go through an entire moon cycle.

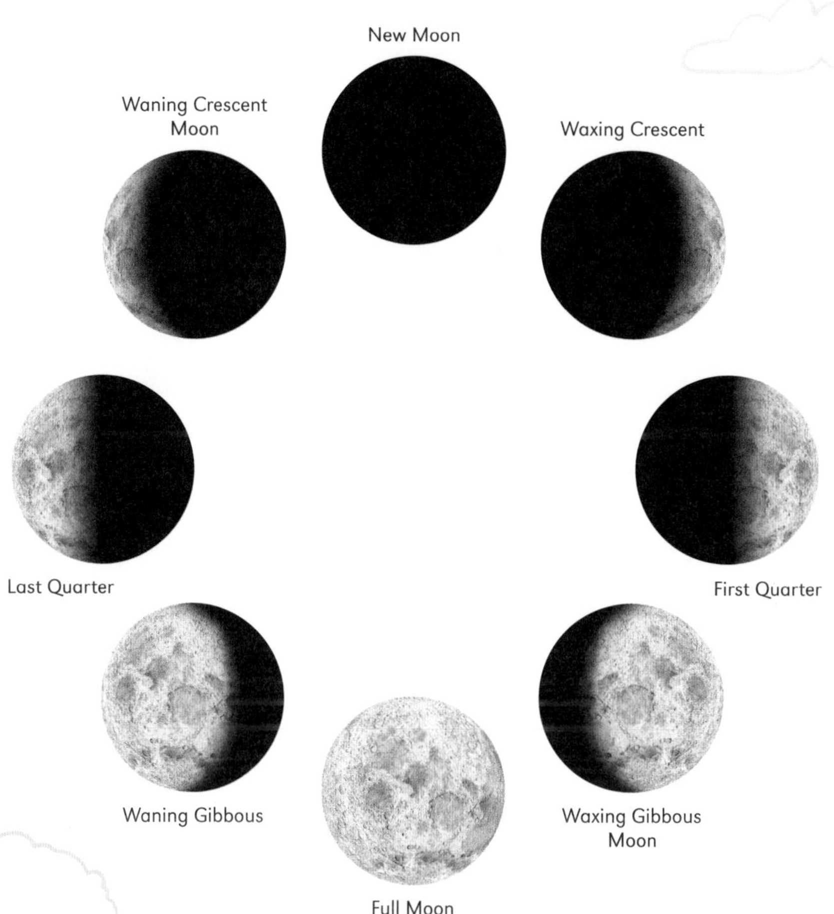

FUN FACTS

- If you looked at the **Earth from the moon**, it would go through phases as well, following the pattern of how much light from the sun hits it.
- During the new moon and full moon phases, the **sea's high tides** will be at their highest, and low tides will be at their lowest.

45 mins active time

BIRD FEED SHAPES

The chirps and melodies of birdsong help our bodies relax, so why not return the favor and feed the birds in your area? It will also help you connect with nature. This is an activity you can do year-round, but it's especially fun to attract birds in winter to see their color and watch their movement against a barren landscape.

SUPPLIES

- ½ cup (120ml) water
- Saucepan
- Stove top
- 2–3 cups (280–420g) of birdseed
- 2 oz (60g) of powdered gelatin
- Spoon
- Cookie cutters
- Parchment paper
- Paper straws cut into 2in (5cm) pieces
- String, twine, or ribbon

INSTRUCTIONS

1. With adult supervision, bring your water to a boil on the stove top.
2. Remove the pan from the heat and add the gelatin. Stir until dissolved.
3. Pour in two cups (280g) of birdseed and stir. If the mixture is still runny, add more birdseed, a little at a time.
4. Arrange your cookie cutters onto parchment paper.
5. Fill the cookie cutters with the mixture and press it down firmly.
6. Insert pieces of straw wherever you want your ribbon holes to be.
7. Allow your bird feeders to dry overnight.
8. Gently remove your feeders from the cookie cutters, remove the straw pieces, and tie ribbon through the holes. String them up outside.
9. Remember to retrieve your ribbons once all the food has been eaten.

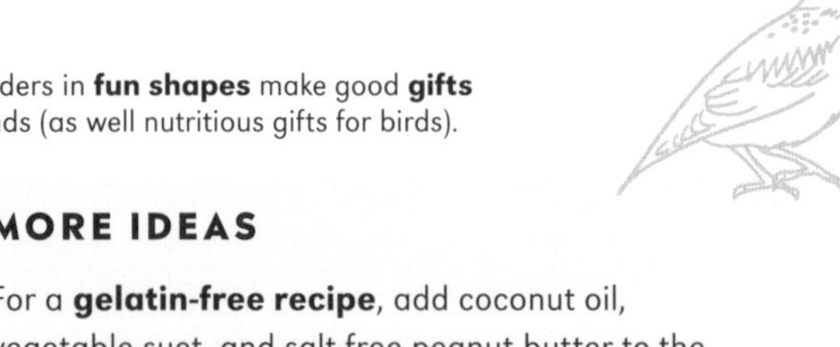

Bird feeders in **fun shapes** make good **gifts** for friends (as well nutritious gifts for birds).

MORE IDEAS

- For a **gelatin-free recipe**, add coconut oil, vegetable suet, and salt-free peanut butter to the mix instead of gelatin. It holds its shape best in really cold weather. Alternatively, try the suggestion on the opposite page.

TRY THIS!

Stick seeds to cardboard with salt-free nut butter and attach a clothespin.

FEEDING BIRDS

Have you heard the phrase, "eating out of the palm of your hand"? Perhaps it came from someone who fed birds! Feeding birds is a thrilling way to get up close and personal with nature. It just takes a little patience and persistence! Always wash your hands after contact with wildlife.

QUIET AND STILL

Once you have some birdseed in your hand, it's super important to stay very still and very quiet! Birds will get scared and won't come close if you're moving or are making a lot of noise.

SEEDS ON YOUR HAT

Sometimes birds won't land in your hand, but they will land on your head! Placing some seeds on top of your hat might be just the trick to lure a tentative bird in for a snack.

Have your **camera ready**. Birds don't stay long!

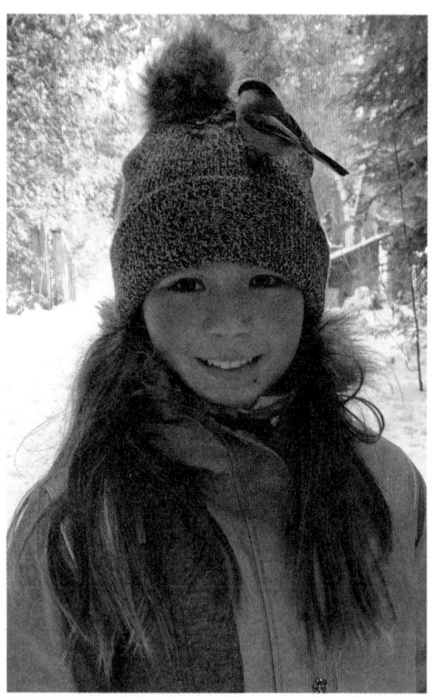

A **hat** can hold seeds to attract a bird—and it helps protect your head.

EXTRA TIME

- Take a hike with friends and see who can **attract the most birds** with food. Whoever gets the most birds to land on them wins!

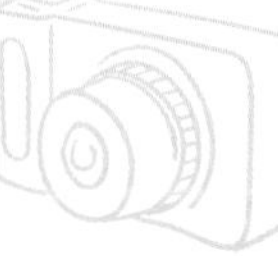

HOMEMADE BIRD FEEDER

Perhaps the birds near you are too shy to eat out of your hand, so you can make a feeder for them instead. You can put a bowl of food out for them, but incorporating it into a snowman is a particularly neat idea.

TIP

- Make your own **birdseed**. Black oil sunflower seeds, chopped peanuts, and striped sunflower seeds are a great mix.

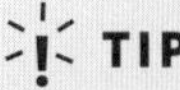

A **snowman seed dispenser** will also attract squirrels and other wildlife.

HUMMINGBIRD NECTAR

If you have hummingbirds visit where you live, you can hang up nectar for them. Add one cup of sugar to four cups of water and let it dissolve. These birds flap their wings 10 to 15 times a second, so they need a lot of energy.

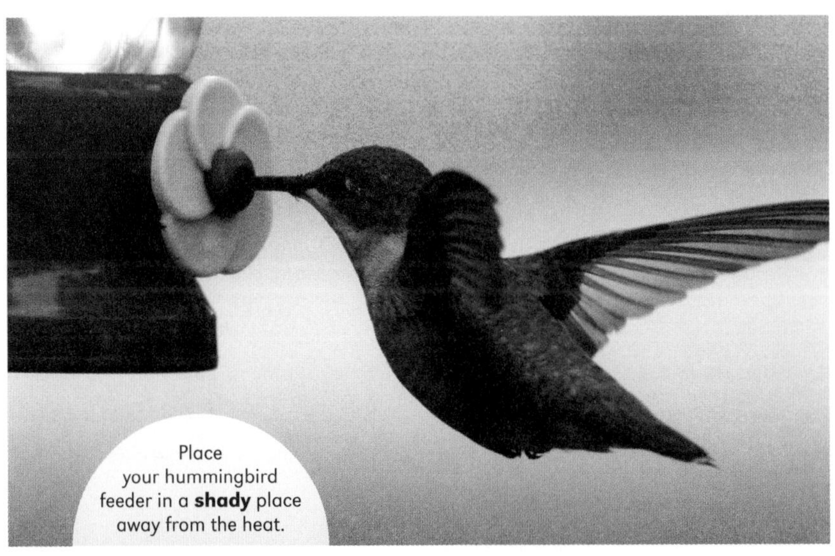

Place your hummingbird feeder in a **shady** place away from the heat.

SNOWFLAKE STUDY

20–30 mins

Did you know that no two snowflakes are alike? There are seven general "types" of shapes, but each individual flake is unique. If you're someone who likes to see the evidence yourself, here's a great way to test it out, so wait for snow and get investigating! If you don't have snow, you could check out frost particles from your freezer.

SUPPLIES

- Snowflakes
- Black or very dark blue paper

INSTRUCTIONS

1. Once snowflakes start falling, grab some of your dark paper and head outside.
2. Wait about 10 minutes for your paper to cool down outside after being in your cozy home.
3. Place the paper on a flat surface, ideally in a somewhat dry spot so it doesn't get wet immediately.
4. Let the snowflakes fall on the paper. You should be able to clearly see the different types of shapes—plates, stellar crystals, columns, needles, spatial dendrites, capped columns, and irregular forms.

Out on the ice is a good place to find **patterns** to study.

MORE IDEAS

- If it's not snowy where you are, you can make **fake snow** to play with. Set up somewhere outside where you can get messy. Mix 1 pound (450g) baking soda in a container and slowly knead in foamy shaving cream until you have a snowy consistency.

TRY THIS!
A dark background shows up snowflake details best.

TRY THIS!
Add a garnish of colorful berries, but never eat them. Wild berries can be poisonous!

MUD PIES

30–60 mins

***Apple, peaches, pumpkin pie, who likes mud pies, holler "I"!* Well, that's not how that actually goes, and while you can't eat them like you can the others, mud pies are deliciously fun! Playing with mud helps you develop your fine motor skills and gets you used to different textures. More than anything else, it's just a good time!**

SUPPLIES

- Smooth dirt
- Water
- Bucket for mixing
- Muffin or bread loaf pans
- Buckets and shovels (optional)
- Natural materials for decoration such as rocks, flowers, leaves, berries, and sticks

INSTRUCTIONS

1. Get your mostly smooth dirt and put it in the bucket, mixing it with equal amounts of water.
2. With your hands, make sure to mix it around well until it feels like raw pizza dough.
3. If it's too wet, add more dirt, and if it's too dry, add more water.
4. Mix it in your hands until it's solid enough to hold its shape.
5. If you want, you could mix more dirt and water with varying consistencies in other containers. You could even make mud sauce for drizzling over your pies.
6. Get ready to shape the mud in pans and start fake baking!

Pack your mix in old pans to **bake in the sun**. You just might be able to pull out perfectly formed desserts!

MORE IDEAS

- Tired of pies or don't like them? What about **mud cookies**? Just make them smaller and add the most delightful toppings you can find.
- Can you make a **double-decker pie**? Place a layer of sticks in between two pies to offer two pies in one!

15 mins

PAINTING ICE SHEETS

Some of the greatest artists ever used canvas for their paintings: Vincent van Gogh, Pablo Picasso, and many others. But what about using ice instead of canvas? Watercolor paint can be used outside to create beautiful art that will brighten up and decorate your yard—at least until the sun comes out!

SUPPLIES

- Sheets of ice
- Watercolor paint (don't use other kinds)
- Paintbrushes of varying sizes
- Cups for paint
- Water pot for cleaning brushes

INSTRUCTIONS

1. Head outside and hunt for recently frozen puddles or other areas where you can gently break off sheets of ice.
2. Carefully place the ice sheets somewhere safe and stable.
3. Start painting! Pay attention to how the watercolor paint changes its color and texture as it drips down and mixes with the ice.
4. Take a photo of your masterpiece before it melts.
5. If you live somewhere warm and never have ice outside, put a container of water in the freezer. Once it's ready, pop the frozen water out of the container, place it on a tray, and paint the homemade ice instead.

Ice freezes with different patterns that can add **texture** to your art.

MORE IDEAS

- Paint small pieces of ice and create little colorful ice "**stones**" to mark a footpath through your yard.
- How **large** of a piece of ice can you keep intact and paint?

TRY THIS!

Prop your ice sheet up in a snow pile so you can paint it upright.

DECORATE A TREE

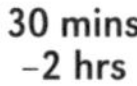

30 mins –2 hrs

There are endless ideas for decorating an outside tree. You can use items from the indoors such as ornaments or you can make edible ones, which are great for working on fine motor skills and will be beloved by your neighborhood critters. Make sure that everything you use is safe for wildlife in case it blows out of the tree.

SUPPLIES

- Durable ornaments that can be exposed to the elements
- Raisins, figs, or prunes
- Large sewing needle
- Thread
- Scissors
- Pipe cleaners
- Cereal pieces
- Citrus slices (can be dehydrated ahead of time; see below)
- Popcorn
- Cranberries

INSTRUCTIONS

1. Carefully string together raisins, figs, or prunes with a sewing needle and thread to look like long, yummy icicles. Younger children can thread pieces of cereal onto pipe cleaners to make a different icicle treat.
2. Sew thread through each citrus slice (see page 66). This will be less messy if you dehydrate them ahead of time (see below).
3. String together popcorn and cranberries to make long garlands. Or use them to make shorter, vertical hanging ornaments.
4. Gather your bought, found, and homemade ornaments and get decorating! Don't stand on anything to reach high branches without adult supervision.

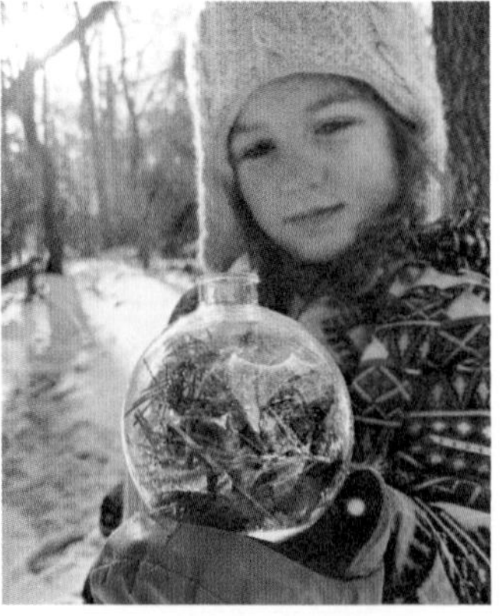

Collect natural items to hang inside **clear baubles**, which can be split in half.

EXTRA TIME

- For **dried citrus slices**, set your oven to its lowest temperature, around 170–200°F (70–90°C). Cut slices ¼ inch (0.5cm) thick and lay them on a baking sheet with foil and lightly misted with cooking spray. Dry them for 3–4 hours, turning them every 30 minutes.

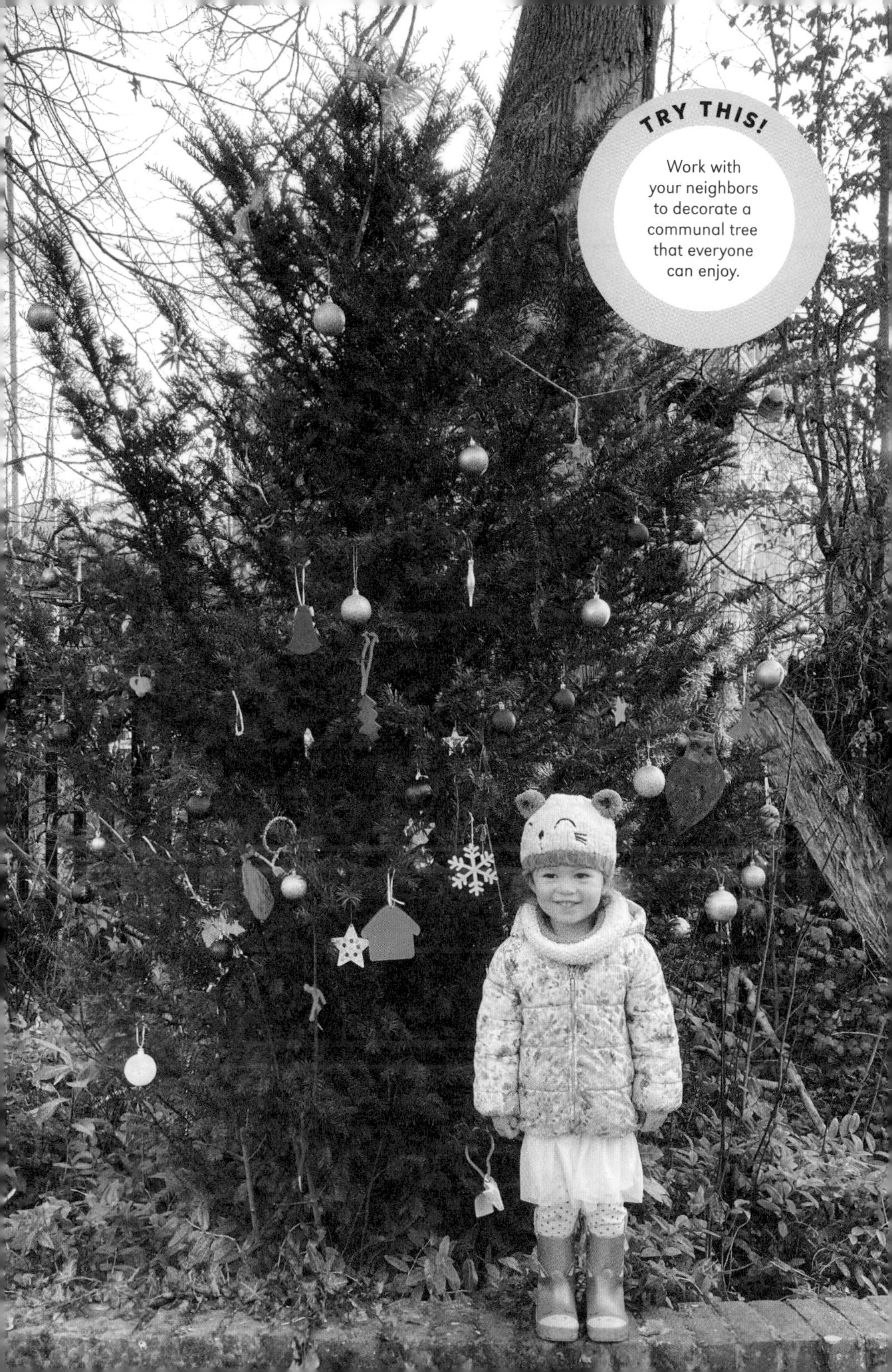

TRY THIS!

Work with your neighbors to decorate a communal tree that everyone can enjoy.

FROST WALK

The very first frost brings with it the end of the gardening season and an invitation to slow down. Any frost is beautiful, but it's especially beautiful if you can catch the very first frost early in the morning.

FUN FACT

- Frost occurs only when the days are warm enough to have moisture in the air and the nights are cold enough for that water vapor to freeze overnight.

WINTER BIRDS

During the coldest months of the year, many birds migrate to warmer locations (see page 262), but not all birds do. When the trees are bare, it's the best time to search for your local birds that have stuck around.

Two **waxwings** on the frosty branches of a mountain ash.

THINK AHEAD

If you think frost might be due, check the weather before you go to bed at night. You are looking for low winds (less than 10 miles per hour) and temperatures below 32°F (0°C). This combination could lead to a morning frost cover, and if you live in a foggy area, it will be more prone to frosts!

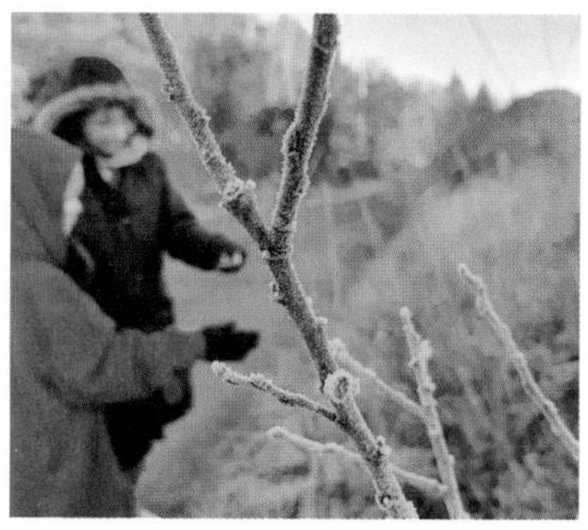

The **morning frost** covers tree limbs in ice.

EXTRA TIME

- Search for the rare: **Frost flowers** are completely white and made from frost. They form when plant stems push out thin layers of ice, which curl into patterns that look like flowers.

GO EARLY

If you're expecting a frost, set your alarm clock relatively early so you can catch the frost before all of the ice crystals melt again as the day warms up. Get dressed in your cold-weather clothes and head outdoors with an adult.

FROST FEATURES

See if you can identify different types of frost on your walk. Hoar frost looks like hairs or spikes. Rime frost is like a crust that accumulates around the edges of leaves and petals. Fern frost is what you see on windows.

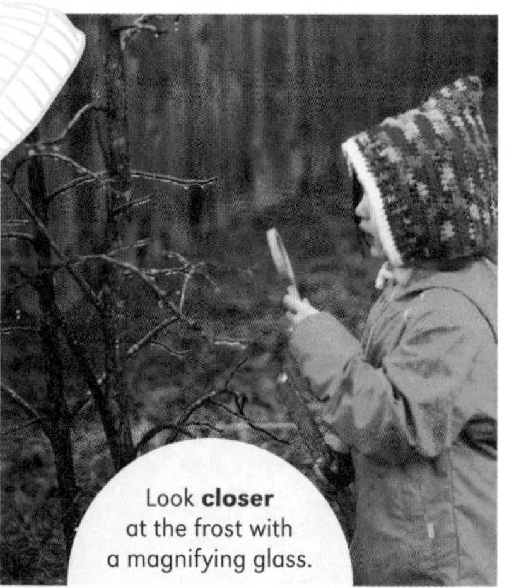

Look **closer** at the frost with a magnifying glass.

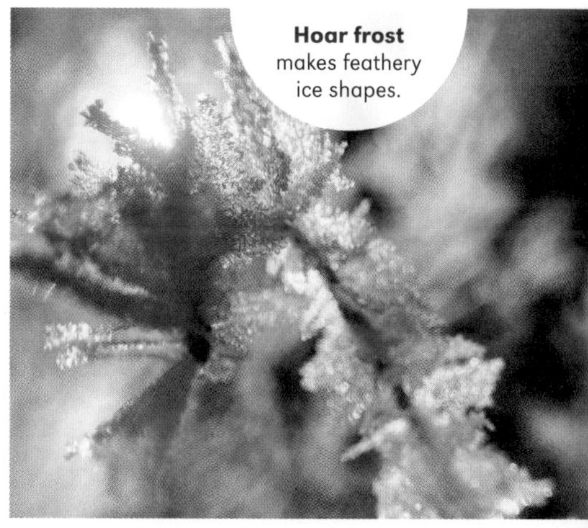

Hoar frost makes feathery ice shapes.

30–60 mins

FRUIT FEEDER

Did you know that some birds really enjoy eating fruit? Robins, bluebirds, woodpeckers, jays, and many others like the types of fruits that you may have in your kitchen such as apples, pears, oranges, grapes, and berries. Instead of putting fruit out whole, why not turn it into beautiful feeders for your neighborhood birds?

SUPPLIES

- Pieces of fruit—cut pieces of apples or pears, slices of citrus, whole grapes or berries, etc.
- Thick thread, string, or twine
- Scissors
- Large sewing needle

INSTRUCTIONS

1. Tie a large knot in one end of the string and then thread the other end through the needle.
2. Carefully thread your fruit onto the string. For grapes, berries, and pieces of apples or pears, poke the needle straight through the middle of the fruit. For citrus slices, push the needle through the flesh near the rind and then out the other side near the opposite rind. You could alternate fruit to make a pattern.
3. Once you have threaded all the fruit, remove the needle and put it somewhere safe. Tie a large loop at the end of your feeder.
4. Hang the feeder outside and set up an observation area so you can see which species of birds come to dine.

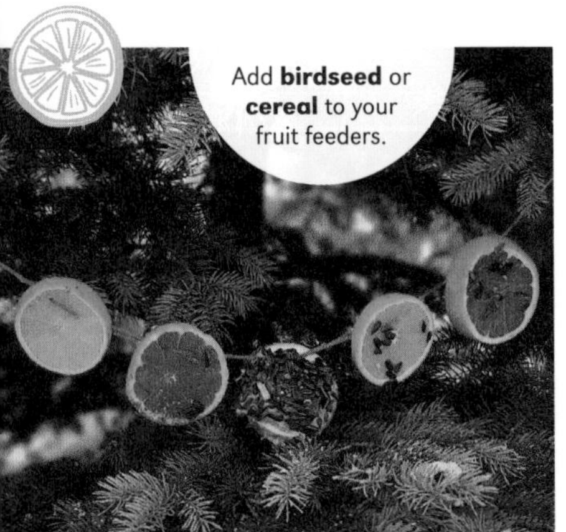

Add **birdseed** or **cereal** to your fruit feeders.

MORE IDEAS

- Instead of sewing the fruit together, you could thread it onto **wooden skewers** and tie them up outside.
- Keep a **nature journal** of the birds who come to feed. Look online to find out more about their preferred diets.
- Monitor which fruit in your **bird buffet** gets eaten first, so you know which to make more of next time.

TRY THIS!
You could twist two threads together to make your feeder stronger.

SNOW ANIMALS

1–3 hrs

We love Frosty the Snowman—he's a true legend. We also love decorating our yards with other snowmen and snow women. But what about other creatures? Forest friends, swamp dwellers, safari roamers, and more can all be created out of that fresh snow that just blanketed your yard. They'll soon be the talk of the neighborhood!

SUPPLIES

- Snow
- Shovel
- Yard items like sticks, leaves, rocks, pine cones, trash can lids

INSTRUCTIONS

1. Take the same approach as for building a traditional snowman—roll up balls of snow and pat them together into shapes. But instead of only building Frosty, you can make animals too. Possible ideas include:
    - **Snow Turtle**—sculpt a turtle in the snow using a trash can lid to form the shell. Then use a stick to create lines in the "shell."
    - **Snow Elephant**—make the biggest snowballs you can and use downed branches for a trunk and tusks.
    - **Snow Reindeer**—look for branches that mimic antlers.
    - **Snow Seal**—make the shape of the seal, being sure to make it skinnier at one end with flippers. See if you can balance a giant snowball on its nose like a ball at the circus!

Can you make a **handheld** mini snow animal?

MORE IDEAS

- Create a **mini herd** of snow animals around your yard.
- Surround a traditional snowman with **forest friends** also made out of snow.

TRY THIS!

Give your snow animals facial features, whiskers, and a tasty snack!

SNOW HOT TUB

15+ mins

Have you ever been outside in your bathing suit in the snow? Well, now you can! Believe it or not, snow is a very good insulator because of all the pockets of air in it—this is why people can survive blizzard conditions by digging into a snowbank. It keeps the temperature above freezing even though outside it might be 30 degrees colder.

SUPPLIES

- Clean, plastic tub that is big enough to sit in
- Snow shovel
- Several large pots of warm water

INSTRUCTIONS

1. If the snow is deep, use your shovel to dig out a spot for your tub. If the snow isn't so deep, use the shovel to build snow up around the tub so it covers the walls on the outside.
2. Ask an adult to help you warm up pots of water in the house and then fill the tub. You could use bath-temperature water from the tap or an adult could boil hot water and add it to cold water to make a cozy temperature.
3. Get on your most beach-friendly bathing suit, run out to your new hot tub, and prepare to relax!
4. As soon as you start to feel cooler, get out, wrap up in a towel, and go straight inside to warm up properly. If you get too cold, you can risk getting hypothermia.

Add **birdseed** around your tub and enjoy the show as birds swoop in for a snack.

MORE IDEAS

- **Invite some friends** over and enjoy doing this together with multiple tubs.
- Bring some **snacks** out and pretend that you're at a spa, relaxing and snacking in the open air.
- Get help from an adult to build a fire at night and enjoy a **moonlit soak** under the stars!

TRY THIS!
Add bath toys to your hot tubs to play with.

A glove on your **nondominant** hand is a smart way to avoid injury.

WOODCRAFT

Woodworking is quite a skill set that takes years to master, but there are plenty of things you can do now to practice and get comfortable making things out of this abundant, natural resource.

SPLITTING WOOD

Often you need to make a piece of wood smaller—this is where splitting comes in! Various tools can split wood, but a neat thing to do is carve a small log into the shape of a mallet, then use it to hammer your wood splitter. Goggles are a good idea in case of any flying fragments.

SAWING WOOD

There are numerous types of saws, and each of them serves a different purpose, but use one only with adult supervision. For fine cutting on wood that requires accuracy, a bow cut saw can prove to be the perfect tool. It's lightweight and easy to maneuver for delicate cuts.

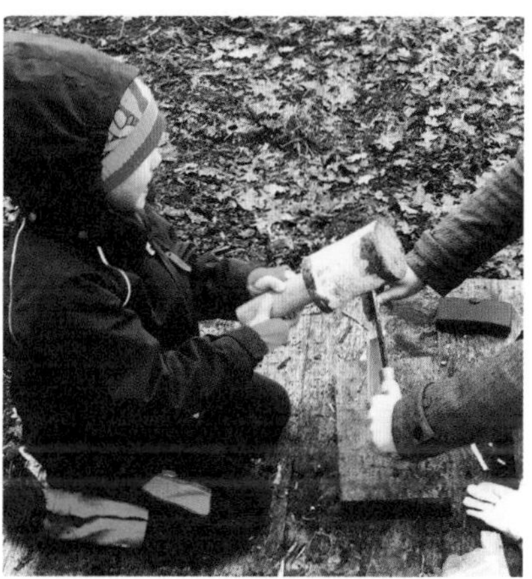

Make sure the wood is **held firmly** in place—and that no fingers are in the way!

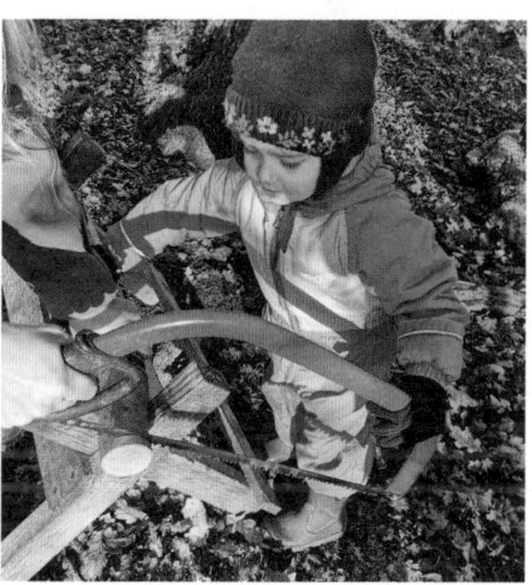

Simple **camping saws** are a versatile type of saw to have, and they are very inexpensive.

WHITTLING

Whittling is a way to carve and shape wood with a blade. People often use pocket knives, but using a vegetable peeler on softer woods is safer. Once you've mastered whittling sticks into a point, practice more complicated shapes. Fresh, smooth wood works best.

SCRAP WOOD

Always save any leftover pieces of wood, however small. You can use them for mini projects, whittling practice, or for making blocks to play with. Even wood shavings can be used for crafts. If you don't have any other need for spare wood, it's useful for starting fires.

SNOW LANTERN

1–2 hrs

Whenever you have packable snow, you can make these glowing lanterns to brighten up the wintry landscape. In Sweden, they're called *snölykta*. Experiment with lantern heights and shapes to add time to your outside hours. There's also a lot of geometry going on—you can learn through living as your pyramid lanterns take shape.

SUPPLIES

- Snow, lots of snow
- Battery-operated tealights

INSTRUCTIONS

1. Find or create a flat area in the snow large enough for your lantern.
2. The final shape of your lantern will be a pyramid. To estimate how many snowballs you will need, make an initial ring of snowballs on the ground and then count how many snowballs you used. Each higher ring will be one or two snowballs less.
3. Then make your snowballs—lots of snowballs! Try your best to keep them all approximately the same size and as round as you can make them.
4. Make a ring of snowballs that will be the base of your lantern.
5. Make a second ring on top of your base that is slightly smaller and then continue up until you reach the very top. Leave a space large enough in the back to be able to reach your hand through and place your tealights.
6. Place the tealight on a waterproof surface to keep the battery dry.
7. If you are using a tealight candle (instead of a battery-operated one), be sure to light and place your tealight with adult supervision.

EXTRA TIME

- **Line a path** with lanterns or frame your front door with them.
- Make a snow lantern out in the **woods** or build several in the middle of a **flat field**.
- Instead of a pyramid, you can also make these in a shape where the width of each ring is fairly similar until the very top. This method uses more snowballs, but it's fun to **experiment** with lantern shapes.

TRY THIS!
Use multiple tealights to make your snow lantern brighter.

CHAPTER TWO

SPRING

CALENDAR OF FIRSTS

Year after year, the rhythms of the seasons bring delight and we can begin to build traditions around nature's cues. "Phenology" is a word that describes the cycle of natural events that occur every year.

FIRST SNOWDROP

In many places, the arrival of the snowdrop brings the promise of a long-awaited spring. You can find snowdrops in fields, in gardens, and in woodlands, and they often look like a white carpet or a white blanket spread along the ground.

There are more than **2,500 varieties** of snowdrops.

FIRST BLACKBERRIES

There's nothing quite like foraging for berries. When they appear, you'll know you have a few months of returning to pick their ripened goodness. Look for them along fence lines or the edges of wooded areas. Be careful of thorns and wash any fruit before eating it.

Blackberries start green, turn to pink or red, and then to **dark purple** when fully ripe.

FIRST FALLING LEAF

Leaves mean shade for warm picnics and they make a beautiful rustling sound in the breeze, but many species of tree drop their leaves in the fall in order to survive winter. When they start changing color and fluttering to the ground, it marks the coming of cooler days.

Pay attention to which trees have **color-changing leaves** and what hues they are.

Enjoy all seasonal firsts, including blowing **dandelion clocks**.

FLOWER MANDALA

30–60 mins

Mandalas are circular designs that radiate symmetrically out from a central point. In nature, they can be seen in seashells, spiderwebs, snowflakes, and tree rings. They are fun to create with different sizes, shapes, and colors of flowers, and this activity is also an introduction to the math concepts of patterns and symmetry.

SUPPLIES

- Scissors
- Small basket
- Access to a variety of flowers, petals, and leaves

INSTRUCTIONS

1. Using your scissors, carefully cut a variety of flowers and leaves and collect them in your basket.
2. Choose something to be the central piece of your mandala. It could be a large whole flower, a beautiful rock, or anything else that catches your eye.
3. Find a suitable spot to lay out your mandala.
4. Place your central piece first and then arrange pieces emanating out from it in a symmetrical pattern. For instance, if you place a yellow flower to the left of the center item, be sure to also place a yellow flower to the right of the center as well. Think about your mandala as being like a bicycle wheel, with lines of flowers coming out from the center, like wheel spokes.

A pale **sand backdrop** really makes bright colors stand out.

EXTRA TIME

- Put your flower mandala between two pieces of **contact paper** to preserve it.
- Make or print a **template** to fill in for different mandala ideas.
- Try making **duplicate mandalas**. Is it easy or hard to make a replica of a mandala that's already been created?
- Add **fresh herbs** to your mandala design for an amazing scent.

TRY THIS!
Use bright green grass for a lush backdrop for your mandala.

HUNT FOR ANIMAL HOMES

INSECT HOME HUNT

Insect homes are all around you wherever you live! Take a walk and see how many you can spot. Which ones you find will depend on where you live, and be careful if you're in an area with any dangerous creatures.

SPIDERWEB

Webs are especially easy to find when the sunlight hits them from certain angles. Once you've found a spiderweb, notice what activity is going on around it. Can you find the spider? What does it look like? Is it colorful or drab? Are there any other insects stuck in the web? What do those look like?

ANT HILL

Ant hills often look like small volcanoes coming out of the cracks in the sidewalk. These hills lead to elaborate systems of tunnels and chambers underground. If you want to watch a lot of ant activity, put a small piece of candy or a scoop of jam near an ant hill and then wait to see what happens.

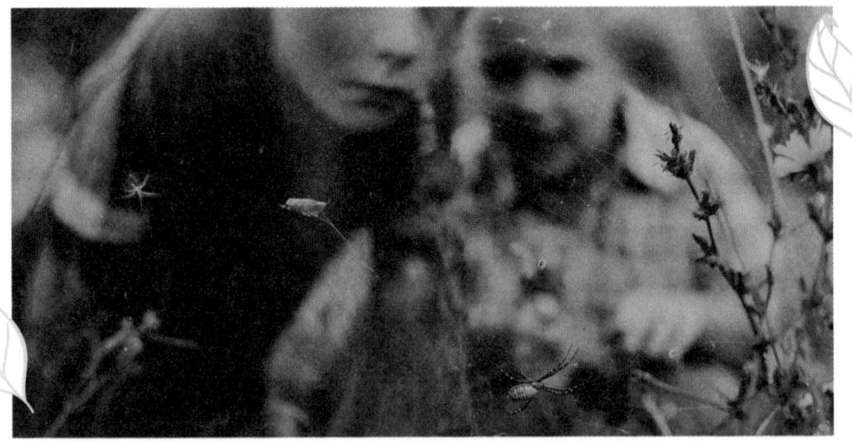

Webs come in different shapes. Round webs like this one are known as **orb webs**.

EXTRA TIME

- As you go on your insect home hunt, count how many homes you find. Keep a running tally and see whether you can beat your numbers on your next hunt for insect homes.

ANIMAL HOME HUNT

BIRD NEST

If you come across a bird's nest, you can use many clues to figure out what type of bird it belongs to. Does the nest you found have any eggs in it? What materials is it made of? Look closely but be careful not to touch the nest. Can you hear any bird calls nearby?

SQUIRREL NEST

Squirrels live in nests called dreys. They can be tricky to spot because squirrels often build their nests on tree branches that are high off the ground. If you see one, compare how it's different from a bird's nest. How big is it? What materials has the squirrel used to build it?

BEAVER LODGE

You might find a beaver lodge near a pond or a lake. Look closely to find out what materials the dome-shaped home is made from. You'll be able to see part of the home, but unless you brought your goggles, the entrance will be hidden—those are underwater!

MORE HOMES

You might find other homes along the way. What types of insect and animal homes can you find where you live? Which kind of animal home would you prefer to live in? How do you think these animals use their homes to protect themselves?

EXTRA TIME

- Look closely at the homes you find. Then gather natural materials and try to create your own version of an animal home such as a bird's nest.

MORE IDEAS

- Why not note down or draw what you observe about insect and animal homes in a notebook or a journal?

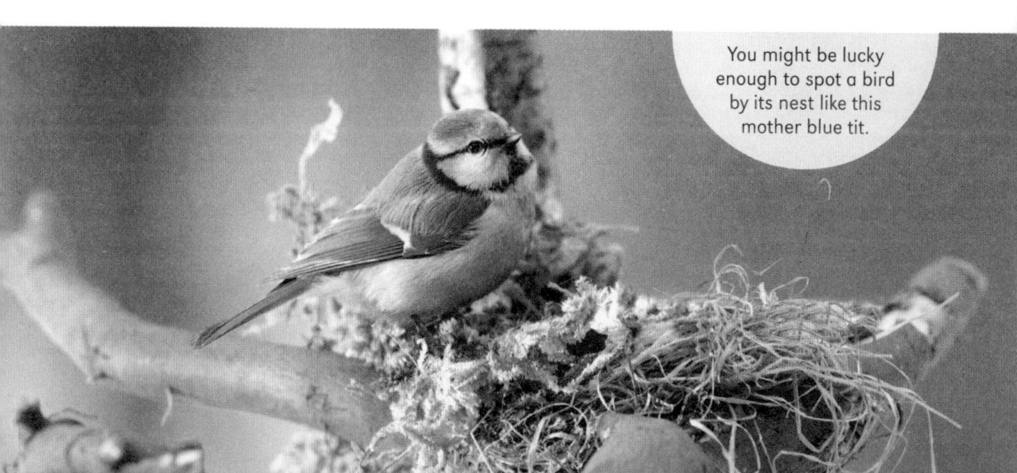

You might be lucky enough to spot a bird by its nest like this mother blue tit.

20 mins active time

COLOR-CHANGING FLOWERS

Beautiful daffodils signal that winter is coming to an end and spring is on its way. You might see these popular flowers in shades of yellow, pink, orange, and white. These are all very pretty, but you can do something interesting with food coloring to turn daffodils into colors you won't find on a stroll or at the local nursery.

SUPPLIES

- White daffodils
- Food coloring
- Clear glass jars
- Water
- Spoon

INSTRUCTIONS

1. Trim your daffodil stems so they are 4 to 6 inches (10 to 15cm) long.
2. Fill each jar two-thirds with water, add 10 to 15 drops of food coloring, and stir. Be careful because the coloring can stain.
3. Place the daffodils in the jars, stem first, and make sure the flower heads aren't in contact with the water.
4. Leave your flowers. After a few hours, you should see them starting to change color. The daffodils are sucking up the water and transporting it around their flowers in tiny tubes in a process called capillary action. The food coloring travels with the water and means we can see where it goes.
5. Keep checking during the next day or two to see the colored petals get darker the longer the flowers are in the water.

MORE IDEAS

- This experiment also works with **carnations** and **stalks of celery**—just make sure the leafy ends are still on the celery.

TRY THIS!
Do you like purple? Or blue? Maybe even a green daffodil? The choice is yours!

TRY THIS!

Pull apart pine cones and use their scales to tile your roof or wall panels.

1–2 hrs

FAIRY HOME

Fairy houses and gardens have become so popular that you can go to a store and buy whimsical woodsy cottages. But many of these are made of plastic and covered in fake moss, bark, and acorns. Nature creates the best materials, and making a fairy house out of items you find outside will suit fairies much better than plastic.

SUPPLIES

- Old birdhouse or log (optional)
- Sticks
- Stones and pebbles
- Moss and grass
- Acorns
- Tree bark
- Pine cones
- Glue (wood glue works best but should be used only by an adult)
- Outdoor paint

INSTRUCTIONS

1. First, decide what type of structure you'll build. A hut with a pine-cone roof? A home made from a hollowed-out log? Or a bungalow with an arched roof? Whatever you choose, start with a stable, solid base. An old bird house is a great starting point. Or you could glue sticks together for a frame and then build walls with small pieces of wood or rocks.
2. Once you have your main structure, hunt out materials for decorating it with fairy-size details. Do you want a roof of moss or tiny pine cones? Do you want stones and pebbles or tree bark stuck to your walls? Let your imagination take over, just make sure you use enough glue to hold it all together! If you're using wood glue, ask an adult to do the gluing for you. Once your house has dried, you could add some colored paint.

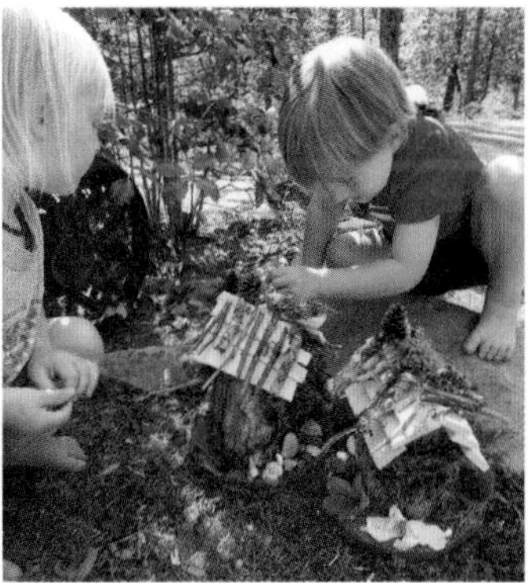

Pine cones make lovely, natural plump **chimney stacks**.

EXTRA TIME

- Once you have a lovely, cozy home ready for a fairy, why not build neighboring houses? You could keep going until you have a **whole village** for sociable fairies to move in to.

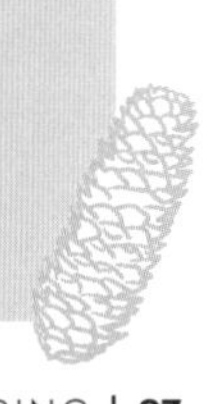

INSIDE OUTSIDE

Time inside with favorite toys and games is fun, but have you tried taking your inside activities outside? It might seem silly at first, but it's a fantastic way to get fresh air and sunlight, while doing the things you already love!

BLANKET TIME

Sitting on the carpet and playing with toys in your bedroom is great, but try taking a soft, cozy blanket out onto the porch or deck instead, and play with those same toys outside. Also, everyone can join in—the family pet can come and the baby can nap in the fresh air, too.

Spreading loose parts out on a **blanket** keeps everything clean and contained.

TRAIN YARD

Building train tracks can sometimes be a challenge due to a lack of space. But that's not a problem outside! Bring all your track pieces to the backyard where there's plenty of room to build extra-long sections of track. And if there's a small hill, your train will go even faster!

How **long** can you make your train track now that there are no walls in the way?

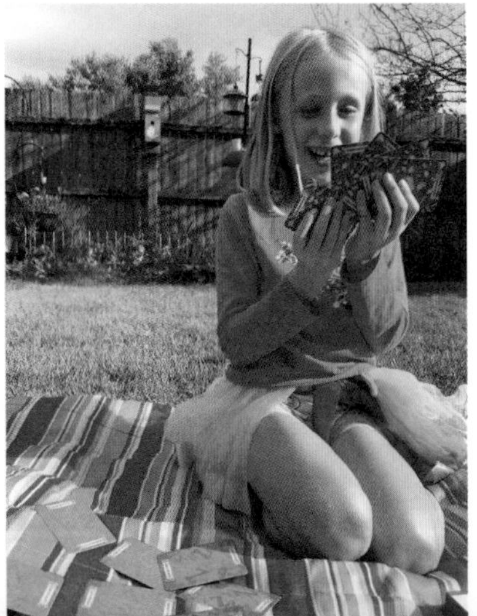

When playing outside, you don't have to be quiet so be as **loud** as you want!

BORED GAMES?

It's impossible to play board games outside and be bored! A board game or a game of cards under the open sky is a great change of pace. Just make sure you have something to hold down the cards or papers if it's breezy out!

Be sure to bring out some **tape** to secure your drawings to the easel so they don't blow away.

ART OUTSIDE

When painting inside, there's sometimes pressure to not make a mess on the floor or tabletop. But that doesn't matter when you're outside! So bring your paint, markers, paintbrushes, and easel outside to create art free of worries!

 TIP

- Bringing out some snacks or **eating a meal** together outside is a sure way to prolong the time you spend in the great outdoors.

CONSTRUCTION SITE

Massive pile of dirt on the living room floor? Not a good idea. Massive pile of dirt outside? Perfect! Perhaps no other toys are better suited to be outside than construction vehicles. Take them where they belong and where you'll have the most fun with them—outside!

 MORE IDEAS

- Take your **dress-up clothes** or play silks outside for a change of scenery.
- Plan, rehearse, and then perform an **outdoor play**.

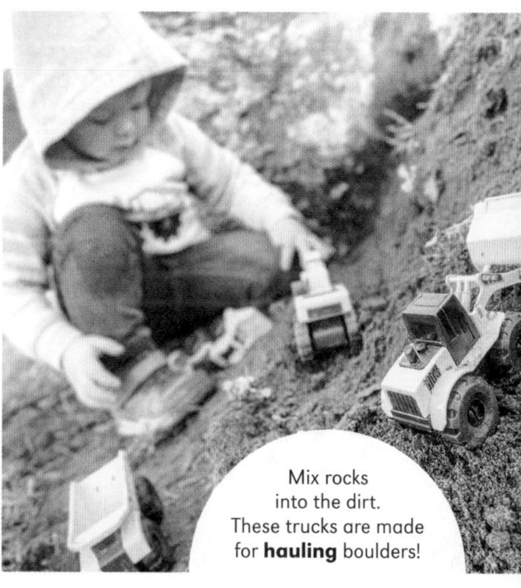

Mix rocks into the dirt. These trucks are made for **hauling** boulders!

INSECTS

Insects are everywhere, wherever you live. Many people take them for granted, but stopping to identify and observe them in their habitat is definitely awesome and you should try it! If you touch any, then wash your hands.

BEETLES

Beetles have hard wing cases, and many of them are brightly colored. There are more than 400,000 types of beetles, and they comprise almost 40 percent of known insects and 25 percent of all known animal life-forms.

CICADAS

Cicadas are known for one main thing—being loud! They make all kinds of noise early in the day and in the evening. Some species stay underground for 17 years, then all emerge at once in unison. Then things get really exciting!

Some **beetles** have a shiny exterior that looks really neat in the sunlight!

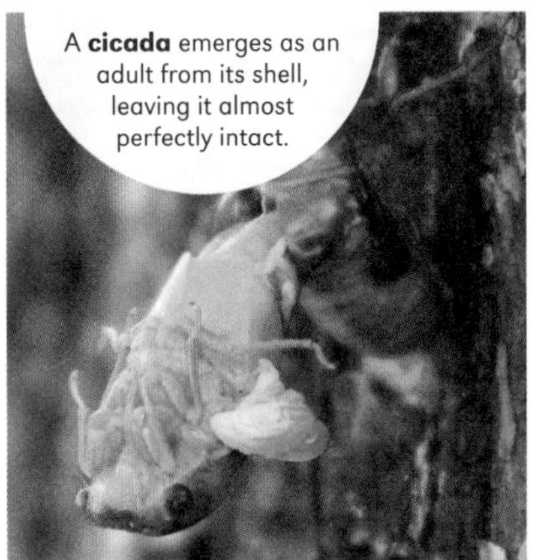

A **cicada** emerges as an adult from its shell, leaving it almost perfectly intact.

GRASSHOPPERS

Did you know that if a human was able to jump as far as a grasshopper can in relation to their body size, a human would be able to jump the length of an entire football field in one bound? Woah!

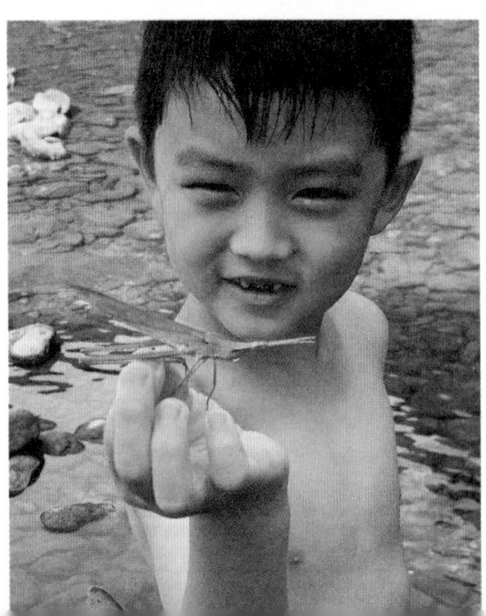

Long-horned **grasshoppers** have ears on their front legs, not their head.

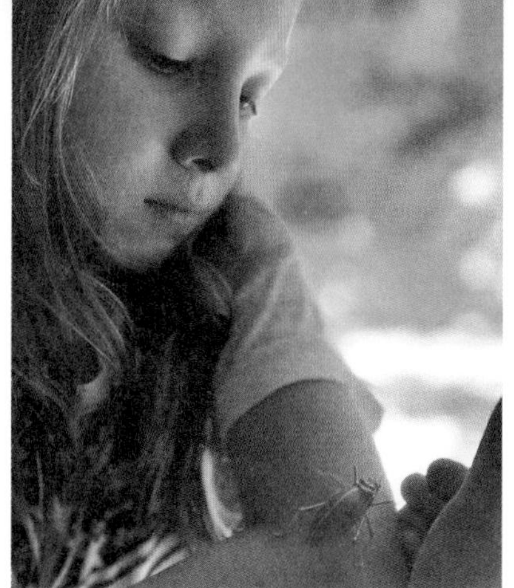

KATYDIDS

Katydids are related to grasshoppers and crickets. They're mostly green so they blend in well with leaves and other foliage—their shape even looks like a leaf at times. Certain katydids make a noise that some say sounds like they are saying "Katy Did, Katy Didn't!"

Katydids are normally nocturnal so they may be hard to find during the day.

LADYBUGS

Also known as a ladybird, this little beauty is helpful because it eats pesky bugs like aphids. It is a type of beetle with spots that comes in pretty colors like yellow, red, orange, or black.

STICK BUGS

There's a good chance that you've walked right past a stick bug without even knowing it! Also known as stick insects, these fascinating creatures are experts at blending in and looking just like sticks!

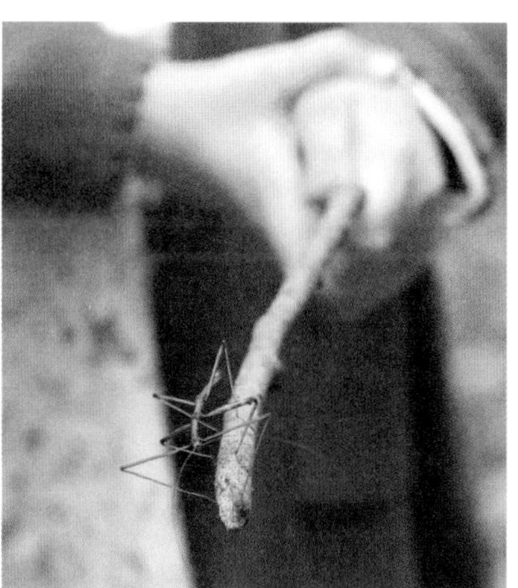

PRAYING MANTIS

A triangular head with big bulging eyes might seem odd, but for the praying mantis, it's perfect! Their strong front legs are good for catching prey, and they also give the praying mantis its name because they make the insect look like it's bent in prayer.

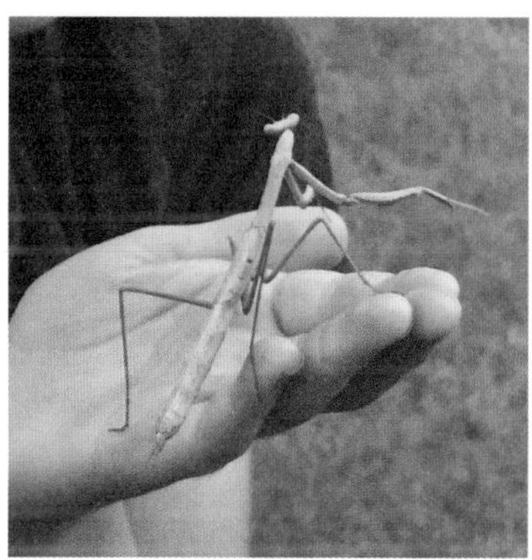

A **praying mantis** is harmless to people, but watch out if you're a grasshopper!

Pay close attention to sticks and branches—one just might be a **stick bug**!

FLOWER FARMING

A flower farm is something you can do right in your own yard. It doesn't have to be big or extravagant. A few flowers turn any space into something magical, and you can even sell small bouquets of fresh cut flowers!

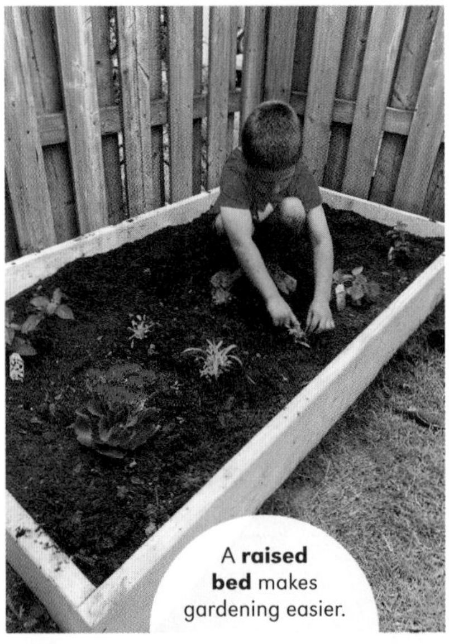

A **raised bed** makes gardening easier.

PLANTING SEEDS

Planting seeds to grow flowers is actually pretty easy. Depending on the type of seed, dig a small hole in the dirt 2 inches (5cm) deep, and continue in a straight line with a hole every 9 to 12 inches (20 to 30cm). Drop a seed (or two) in each hole and cover with dirt. Easy!

HARVESTING FLOWERS

Once your flowers have bloomed, it's time to get them ready for your customers. Depending on the flower, carefully cut the stem right above where another bud is jutting out. This will help the plant continue to grow.

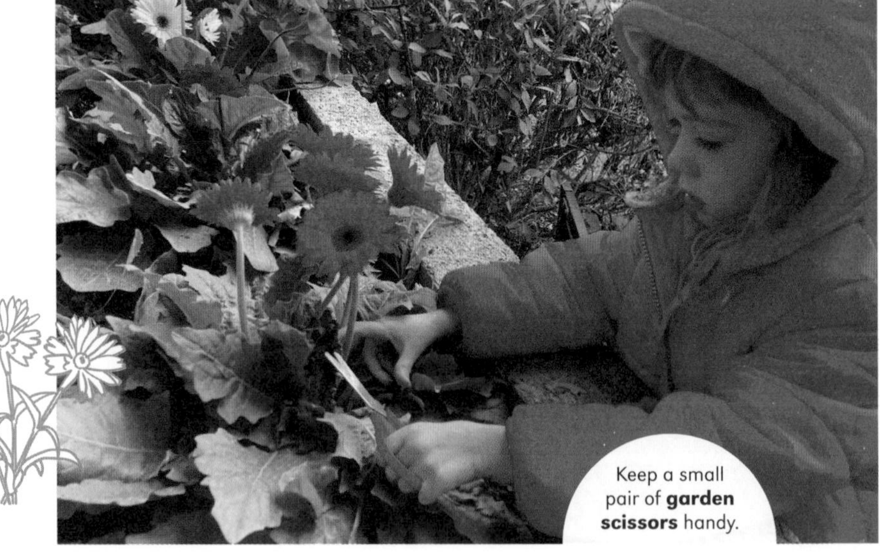

Keep a small pair of **garden scissors** handy.

GATHERING SUPPLIES

Sometimes you can go to farms to pick flowers, where they may have more varieties to choose from. You'll need more than your two hands to carry them all, so take a basket along to hold all the colorful flowers as you pick and choose the very best ones for your customers.

Don't leave flowers **out of water** for too long as they can wilt fairly quickly.

BOUQUET ARRANGING

Sometimes certain flowers look better when paired together with other flowers. There's no right or wrong answer. See which shapes and colors you think look the most appealing bundled together.

MORE IDEAS

- Use **Mason jars** as mini vases to place your flower bouquets in. Just add a little water and a small bunch of flowers to each one for sale.
- Set up a **stall outside** where passing customers can buy your bouquets.

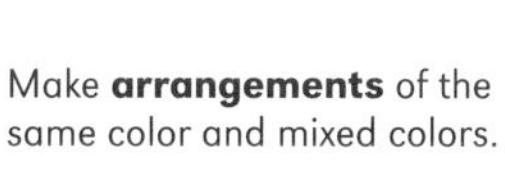

Make **arrangements** of the same color and mixed colors.

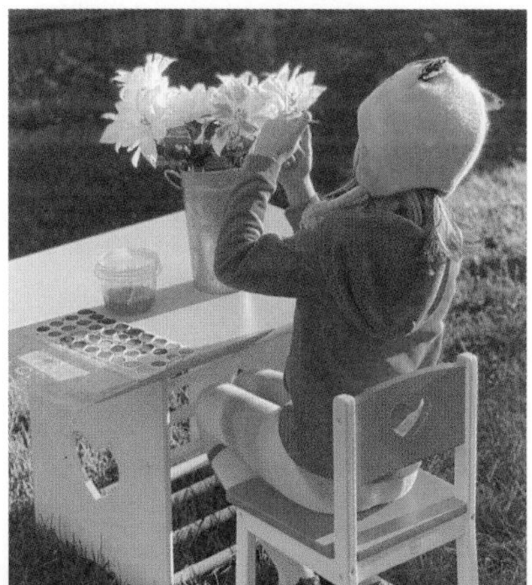

PAINTING FLOWERS

One creative option for getting the exact color of flowers you want is to simply make your own! If you find white flowers like carnations, petunias, or daffodils, you can use watercolor paint to color the petals of the flowers to your liking.

Move a table and chair outside for a **comfortable** workstation.

SIDEWALK ART

30 mins
–2 hrs

All year round, our kids ask to paint. This is a way to indulge their interest without creating a lot of inside mess. Sidewalk chalk drawing has long been a childhood staple, but you can also create pictures and designs with chalk paint. You can make your own chalk paint, and even use up all your old, broken pieces of chalk.

SUPPLIES

- 1 cup (240ml) water
- 1 cup (120g) cornstarch
- Mixing bowl
- Spoon
- Muffin pan or small containers
- Food coloring
- Paintbrushes of various sizes
- Jar of water for rinsing brushes
- Sponge (optional)

INSTRUCTIONS

1. Thoroughly mix together the water and cornstarch in a bowl until there are no clumps left.
2. Divide your mixture into separate containers or the spaces in a muffin pan.
3. Add drops of food coloring to each mixture to create different colors of paint. Be very careful because the food coloring could stain your clothes.
4. Begin painting, allowing some time for your chalk paint to dry.
5. Experiment with using a sponge instead of a paintbrush to create different textures and patterns.
6. The chalk paint may thicken over time, so if you're feeling creative and want to paint all day long, keep some water on hand to thin it out again.

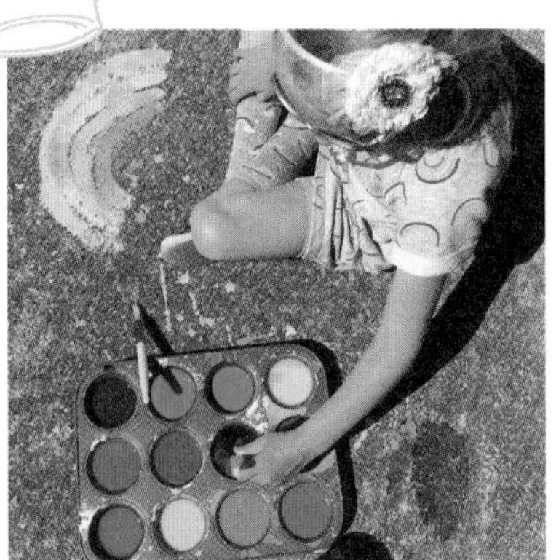

Draw **inspiration** from everything around you—including your clothes!

MORE IDEAS

- You can also make paint with old, **broken chalk pieces** that are too small to write or draw with. Crush them in a bowl and add water, a little bit at a time, to form a thin paste.

TRY THIS!
Draw the classic way with simple sticks of chunky chalk.

TADPOLES TO FROGS

Have you ever looked down near the shoreline and noticed tiny little black circular things swimming all over the place? If so, it's a good chance those were tadpoles—the second stage of a frog's life cycle. Soon, they will become frogs and look like a completely different creature!

LIFE CYCLE

A frog begins life as one of many eggs in jellylike frog spawn, then it hatches as a tadpole. After a few weeks, it grows back legs, then it gets bigger and gets front legs to become a froglet. The tail is absorbed, and then, finally, it's a frog.

HUNTING FOR TADPOLES

Spring is a good time to find frog spawn or tadpoles. Using a net to catch them works well, or you can scoop up water with a bucket and see if you catch any. Use the same bucket to keep the tadpoles in and watch them swimming frantically back and forth.

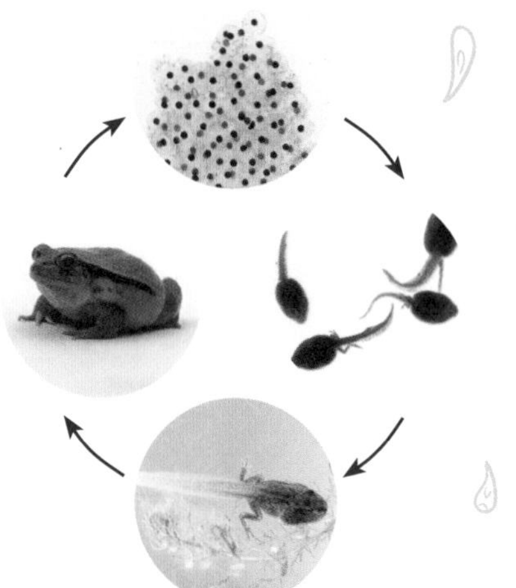

The process of growing into a frog takes about **12 to 14 weeks**.

Frogs will hear you coming, so be **stealthy**.

OBSERVATION STATION

In many places, you can keep tadpoles, but check your local laws. Use a clear container with fresh rain or pond water —not tap water. Acclimatize the tadpoles slowly to the new water, and feed them shreds of broccoli, baby spinach, or lettuce. Always wash your hands after touching frog spawn, tadpoles, or frogs.

Add only a **small amount** of food at once or it will foul the water.

FROG TIME

When the tadpoles grow back legs, start feeding them fish food. Once they have front legs, the froglets need to breathe air, so lower the level of the water and add rocks for them to climb on. While they're froglets, return them to the grass near the water where you found them.

FROGTASTIC

Most species of frogs remain fairly small their whole life, but some can get much, much bigger! Bullfrogs, for example, can be the size of an adult human's hand. Think about how much bigger that is than when the giant frog was just a tiny little tadpole!

If you ever pick up a frog, **wet your hands** first because they are used to being wet.

What's the biggest frog you've ever seen? How **heavy** do you think it was?

TRY THIS!

Make a miniature **tepee** hideout out of sticks in your nature tray.

NATURE TRAY

30 mins

Have you ever heard of portable nature? Well, that's what a nature tray can give you—nature right in the palms of your hands! It's a decorative mini oasis that you can keep in the yard or bring inside your house when you're all done. Either way, a nature tray allows you to transport nature with you, which is always a good idea!

SUPPLIES

- Pie dish, pie pan, or old baking tray with at least 2-inch (5cm) sides
- Dirt or sand for the base layer
- Rocks, twigs, acorns, leaves, and more to create your nature scene

INSTRUCTIONS

1. Creating a nature tray can be as easy or complex as you'd like. Start by filling your pan with enough dirt or sand to fill the bottom of the tray.
2. Decide what sort of nature scene you want to build. Perhaps it's a rocky landscape, a town of twig structures, or a fairy house?
3. Once your creation is complete, enjoy playing with it. You could use sticks and rocks as characters and act out stories about them.

EXTRA TIME

- Press a small bowl into the dirt base layer and fill it with water to make a **little pond** in your nature scene.
- Add **ants or worms** and other bugs to roam around this new world.

A nature tray is a great activity for **smaller spaces** like a balcony or front stoop.

30 mins active time

GROWING TOMATOES

You simply cannot replicate the taste of a homegrown tomato. And what's more, the variety of tomatoes you can grow is astounding. Heirloom tomatoes come in colors from red to pink, to orange, to white, and even black. You can also grow striped tomatoes! Each variety will give your kitchen concoctions a different type of flavor.

SUPPLIES

- Tomato seeds—look for varieties you can't find in a grocery store, such as Amish Paste, Black Cherry, or Green Zebra
- Potting soil
- Water
- 6-inch (15cm) starter pots or paper cups
- Scissors
- Tomato cage (optional)

INSTRUCTIONS

1. Fill your starter pots two-thirds full with potting soil, and water them lightly. Always wash your hands after handling soil.
2. Gently press two seeds into each pot and cover with a thin layer of soil.
3. Set your pots in a warm space with lots of sunlight. Water them every morning so the soil stays moist.
4. Your seeds should sprout in 5 to 10 days. Once they're 2 inches (5cm) tall, cut the smallest sprout, leaving only one plant in each pot.
5. When the sprouts are 3 to 4 inches (7 to 10cm), transplant them outdoors or, if the threat of frost is not over, into a larger pot. Remove them carefully from their pot, with the soil, so you don't break any roots.
6. Depending on your type of tomatoes, you may need to support them with a trellising system.

Tomatoes can grow on a **windowsill** or balcony.

EXTRA TIME

- **Marigolds** are good garden buddies for tomatoes. Plant them nearby and they will save your tomato plants from **slugs and snails**.

TRY THIS!
Save and label a few of your tomato seeds so you can grow more next year.

SHADOW PLAY

Because light waves travel in straight lines, they get blocked when they encounter an obstacle. This absence of light is seen as shadows. On a sunny day, the sun's light makes shadows all around us.

CHANGING SHADOWS

The sun moves across the sky through the day—and its course changes through the year—so it casts shadows at different angles depending on the time and also the season. Watch how your shadow changes shape and direction.

Shadows make **silhouettes**—just the outlines of shapes.

TIP

- To see the **longest shadows**, head outside right near dusk or early in the morning during the winter months. At the longest point, the shadow of an average-size person could be almost 70 feet (more than 20 meters) long!

EXTRA TIME

- Hang a thin **white sheet** from a doorway, turn the lights off, and shine a light behind it. People on the other side can watch your shadow doing silly dances.

MORE IDEAS

- **Shadow puppets** are when you hold your hand in front of a flashlight in a dark room and see what sort of shapes you can make against the wall.

SHADOW ART

It's tricky to trace around a 3-D object, but you can trace its shadow. On a sunny day, place your toys next to a sheet of paper and let the sun cast a shadow onto the paper. Then trace the outline of the shadow with your pencils.

Can you draw an entire scene with only **shadow tracings**?

TELLING THE TIME

Before clocks were invented, people used sundials to tell the time. You can make your own with a paper plate with a stick in its center, or a ring of rocks with a feather in the middle. Every hour, mark where the stick's shadow is and write down the time there. At the end of the day, you will have a clock to tell you the time based on the shadows.

The shadow falls in the **same place** at the same time each day.

STICK ART

25–40 mins

Paint. Yarn. Rubber bands. That's all you need to jazz up boring, plain, brown sticks. What's great is that sticks of all shapes and sizes are plentiful any time you walk out the door. And, even better, if you find sticks that are too big or have too many branches, it's tons of fun to snap and crack them down to the size you want!

SUPPLIES

- Sticks
- Paint (acrylic paint works well)
- Colorful rubber bands
- Colorful twine

INSTRUCTIONS

1. Start your stick hunt. If you want a longer, sturdier stick for hiking or walking, look for one that comes up to about your shoulder.
2. If you want to make a stick scene using clay, find smaller twigs that are a foot (30cm) long or less.
3. Whichever stick you decide to use, lay it on its side and begin painting sections of the stick in different colors. Try some longer sections of one color, mixed in with short bands of contrasting colors to really add variety.
4. Use colorful rubber bands or twine to wrap around the stick—this gives the stick a different look and adds some more texture to it.

Put decorated sticks in a clay base to make a **model tree**.

MORE IDEAS

- Arrange a **painted stick bouquet** in a vase.
- Add **ribbons** and **jingle bells** to the end of a painted stick, turning it into a **fairy wand**.

TRY THIS!
Head out on a hike with decorated walking sticks.

UNIQUE TREE HUNT

There are a whopping 60,000 species of trees, if not more—that's a lot! Each one of them is unique, though some species look quite similar to each other. There are a lot of different things to discover.

TREE HOLLOWS

A large hole in a tree trunk is called a tree hollow. Some are so large that you can walk inside them! Tree hollows oftentimes are the result of a limb that broke off or of bark that was damaged while it was growing.

MORE IDEAS

- Research which trees are **native** to your area. Print out a list of them with pictures and see whether you can find them in your community.

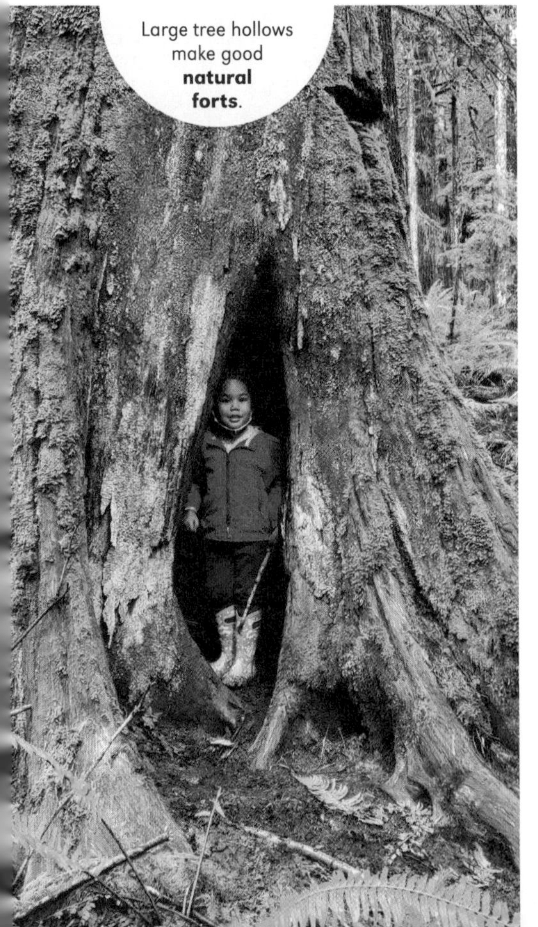

Large tree hollows make good **natural forts**.

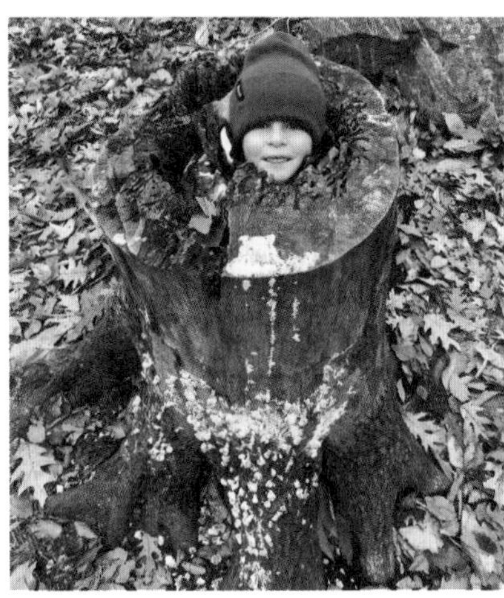

You can tell that this tree was **cut down** because the top is very flat.

TREE STUMPS

You've probably seen tree stumps, either from a tree that broke and fell down or from someone cutting down a tree. Many times those exposed stumps will begin to rot from the inside out, and the spaces they leave are big enough to crawl inside.

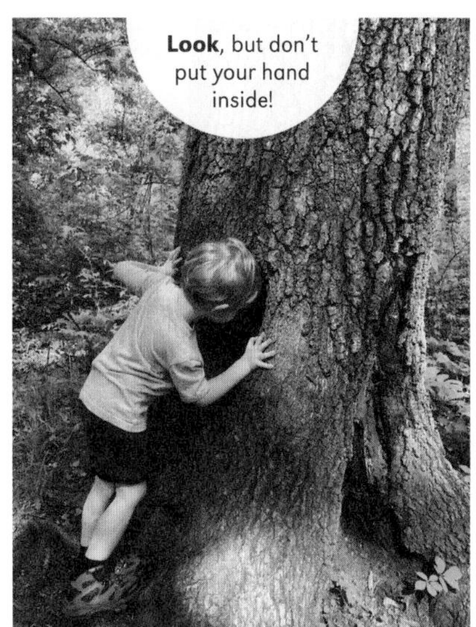
Look, but don't put your hand inside!

TREE CRITTERS

Lots of animals make homes inside trees—squirrels, chipmunks, birds, snakes, and mice are just a few. Peek into any hollows you find to see if you can see any creatures, but don't touch or disturb them.

TREE ART

Loggers and arborists cut down trees to stop them from falling on someone's home, to manage the habitat, or to clear space. You might see that someone has used their chainsaw to create some tree art right in the middle of the forest.

HOW OLD IS A TREE?

For every year of a tree's life, a new ring of wood is formed outward from the center. Scientists can study these rings to learn about the past, including the temperature, climate, and forest fires.

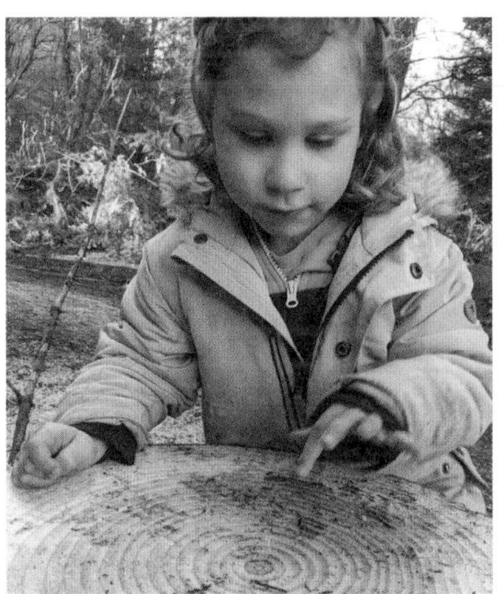

What's the most amount of **tree rings** you've ever been able to count?

This smiley face was carved by someone, but can you find any natural **face shapes** in trees?

TRY THIS!

Set up two ramps and hold some races!

1–2 hrs

PLAY WITH GRAVITY

It's amazing how enticing a simple ramp can be—and there's so much to learn when using them. At different angles, whatever you roll down will go faster or slower. The weight and shape of your objects will also affect their speed. Add in a little water to the setup and you're sure to have hours of fun learning, playing, and exploring.

SUPPLIES

- Thin wood boards, long pieces of cardboard, or plastic pipes
- Chunks of wood or books (optional)
- Objects that roll such as cars or balls
- Plastic tubs (optional)
- Water (optional)

INSTRUCTIONS

1. Set up your materials outside on a flat surface. For the very simplest ramp, you just need supports at two heights and a flat piece of wood or cardboard propped between them.
2. To make your scene more complex, vary the heights and steepness of ramps by stacking pieces of wood or books. Have some ramps that don't go all the way to the ground so your objects will fly off the end.
3. Set up a landing zone such as plastic tubs. You could fill your tubs with water to add a fun splash.
4. Look around for any natural materials that will roll.
5. Make notes of which things roll the fastest and which roll the slowest. How does changing the ramps change the rolling speeds?

An adult could screw a variety of ramps to a fence to make a **play wall**.

MORE IDEAS

- Paint your ramps **black with yellow dashes** down the middle to make them look like roads.
- Use PVC pipes for tunnel-style ramps. These also work great to send **water** through on a **hot day**.

JEWELRY MAKING

STICKY BRACELETS

This is one of the easiest activities to set up, it always turns out beautifully, and it allows you to explore a variety of textures, colors, and smells of nature. Try this activity in different seasons to see what you can find.

BRACELET MAKING

Creating your bracelet is as simple as wrapping tape around your wrist with the sticky side facing out. The wider your tape, the more space you will have. If your tape is too thin, make several loops that connect with each other so that you have a larger surface to decorate.

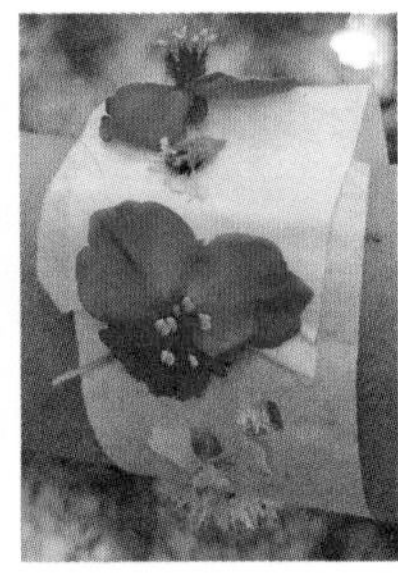

Fill your bracelet with **flat** petals, leaves, seeds, or grasses.

EXTRA TIME

- Make your bracelet **sturdier** by taping a thin piece of cardstock around your wrist. When you've finished, unwrap your cardstock and laminate it to make a **homemade bookmark**.

HIKING BRACELET

Put on a sticky bracelet before you head out on a hike and collect things along the way that will help you retell the story of your adventure. When you return, talk through each thing you found, noting where you were at on the hike when you found it.

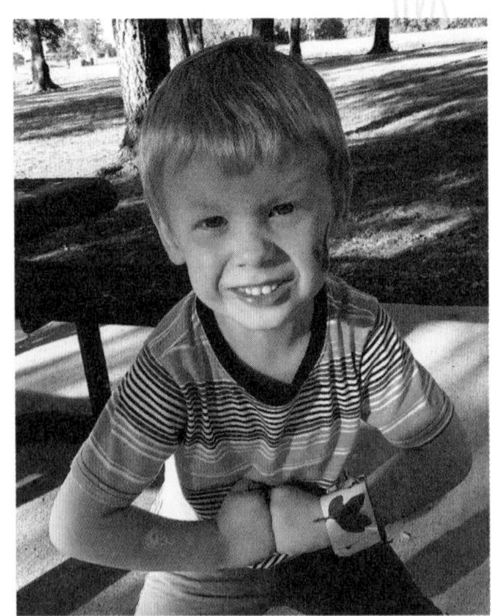

Use **duct tape** or **packaging tape** to get the widest bracelet possible.

NECKLACES AND MORE

DANDELION CHAINS

Choose dandelions with long stems. Pierce a small hole in the stem close to the flower. Pull another dandelion through the hole, stem first, until it stops at the top. Continue adding dandelions until the chain is long enough. To turn it into a circle, put the flower head of your first dandelion through the stem of your last dandelion. You can use the same method with daisies.

Chains of dandelions can make **matching** crowns, necklaces, and bracelets.

EDIBLE HIKING NECKLACE

Instead of carrying food, make snack necklaces before you head out on a trail. Tie a big knot in one end of a piece of string that is long enough to easily fit over your head. Fill it with pieces of round cereal and tie a knot when you're finished.

Make edible **patterns** by alternating colored rings in different quantities.

MORE IDEAS

- Ask an adult to carefully drill small holes through the tops of **acorns**. Then thread a string through them to make a natural necklace.

10–30 mins

SEESAW BALANCE

Of all the playground activities, the seesaw has to be one of the most iconic. It's amazing how such a simple device, leveraging the most basic principles of physics, brings so much joy to people of all ages. But what if you didn't have to go to the local park? What if you could build a seesaw in your own yard, without any tools?

SUPPLIES

- A flat area of ground
- A wooden board that is sturdy, fairly flat, and long and wide enough for a seesaw
- Wood or cinder blocks for the base
- Additional blocks for fulcrum point to rest main board on

INSTRUCTIONS

1. Start by finding the main board that you'll sit on. Check with an adult that everything you use for this activity is solid and sturdy enough.
2. Locate the materials for the base—wooden blocks or cinder blocks will do fine, just make sure they are heavy enough that they don't move. Ask an adult to help you move them and to check everything once it's in place.
3. Set up your base, with an adult's help, so it's even and sturdy.
4. Place the logs or other small boards on top to create your fulcrum point—this is the section that the longer board rests on.
5. Place the long board on top of the fulcrum point and experiment with putting in at different points—how does it affect the structure.
6. Finally, center the long board on top so nobody falls off right away! Once you think it's ready to ride, ask an adult to check that it's sturdy enough. Only climb on once you've got the say-so from an adult.

EXTRA TIME

- Paint your seesaw to make it extra special. Start with just your **name or initials**, or take your paint and **decorate the entire board** and base with bright colors.

MORE IDEAS

- Instead of riding the seesaw, try adding rocks or other heavy items to balance the board out so it's **perfectly parallel** with the ground. Watch out for your hands and feet so you don't drop anything on them.

TRY THIS!

Ride the seesaw by yourself, by spreading your legs out on each end.

TRY THIS!

Do some leaf identification games to learn what kinds of trees grow in your area.

LEAF PRINTING

30–45 mins

The arrangement of a leaf's veins varies depending on what type of leaf it is. For instance, some leaves have a vein that runs up the center of the leaf (called the midrib) with other veins branching off from there, similar to a tree. Leaf printing allows you to clearly see the differences from leaf to leaf.

SUPPLIES

- Leaves of different shapes and sizes—look for ones with thick veins
- Newspaper
- Tempera paint
- Paintbrushes (foam brushes work particularly well)
- Paper
- Rolling pin (optional)

INSTRUCTIONS

1. Set your first leaf onto the newspaper and paint its entire veined side. Make sure you extend the paint all the way to the leaf's edges—it's okay if you go off the leaf because the newspaper will keep your area clean. Work fairly fast so the paint doesn't have time to dry out.
2. Grab the stem of your leaf and place it face down onto your paper.
3. Slightly press every spot of the leaf so the paint transfers to your paper. Be sure not to slide your leaf around or it will smudge your painting.
4. Carefully pull the stem and remove your leaf, revealing a gorgeous print.
5. Repeat these steps for each leaf, but do them one at a time so the paint doesn't dry out.
6. Allow the paint to dry before displaying it.

When you're finished with your leaves, use them to make **leaf potions**.

EXTRA TIME

- Print leaves onto material with **fabric paint** and then make them into shirts, bags, or kitchen towels.

NATURE MATCHING

Matching games are fun and they help with memory recall, pattern recognition, and concentration. But instead of playing a board game, head outside and look for items in nature that you can match by color or shape!

COLOR MATCHING

Paint different-colored blobs on a paper plate, like a painter's palette, and look for items in nature like flowers, leaves, or grasses that match your paint colors. You can then use the paint to try and recreate the things you saw outside!

TIP

- Gather a lot of different items. The more you have, the more fun the matching exercise will be. Look for a lot of different shapes and colors to really make it challenging.

You could cut a **handle** in your plate like a real painter's palette.

EXTRA TIME

- Find six pairs of matching nature items, place them in containers with lids or under paper plates, and play a **matching game**. Each player takes turns to reveal two items. If you find a pair, you keep it. If they don't match, they're covered up again. The winner is whoever has the most pairs at the end.

SWATCH MATCHING

Cut small pieces of colored construction paper into squares or rectangles, then try to find items outside that are nearest to the color of each paper. This really helps you look for and focus in on certain types of natural materials that you may miss otherwise.

Come up with names for the different **shades** of colors you find.

NATURE TRACING

Head outside and collect lots of nature items. Lay them on a piece of paper and trace each one. Then mix up all the pieces and see how fast you can place them back in the right place on the paper. Challenge a friend to do it, too. For an extra-large arrangement, you could use an old bed sheet.

Stop the clock! Everything here is back in **position**.

30–60 mins

FLOWER RAINBOW

Flowers come in every color of the rainbow and also pink, white, and black. Colors can affect our mood, so while you're on the hunt for a rainbow of flower colors, take note of any emotional effects they have on you. Also, pay attention to the shapes and sizes of the flowers you find and work on your classification skills.

SUPPLIES

- A variety of colored flowers (see below for some suggestions)
- Paper (optional)
- Glue (optional)

INSTRUCTIONS

1. Find as many flower colors as you can. If you cut them from your garden, make sure you leave buds for others to grow. Many flowers have several petals so you may need only one per color. Example sources include:
   - **Red**—roses, poppies, marigolds, chrysanthemums, zinnias, tulips
   - **Orange**—begonias, chrysanthemums, marigolds, iris, cosmos, lantana
   - **Yellow**—marigolds, yarrow, sunflowers, goldenrod, coreopsis, roses, lilies, daffodils, gerbera daisies
   - **Green**—day lilies, zinnias, bells of Ireland, hydrangea, cockscomb
   - **Blue**—cornflowers, iris, globe thistle, forget-me-nots, clematis, morning glories, bluebells
   - **Indigo and violet**—lavender, verbena, allium, carnations, china aster, crocus, coneflowers, lupine, pansies, petunias
2. Separate the petals and spread them in arched shapes. If you don't have every color, use different shades—perhaps a light green next to dark green.

If you want to **preserve** your rainbow, glue it onto a sheet of paper.

EXTRA TIME

- Flowers bloom in different seasons. As new colors arrive, **press** your flowers so you can use them for a rainbow later (see page 132).
- Try and **grow** a flower rainbow in your garden or in a large pot.

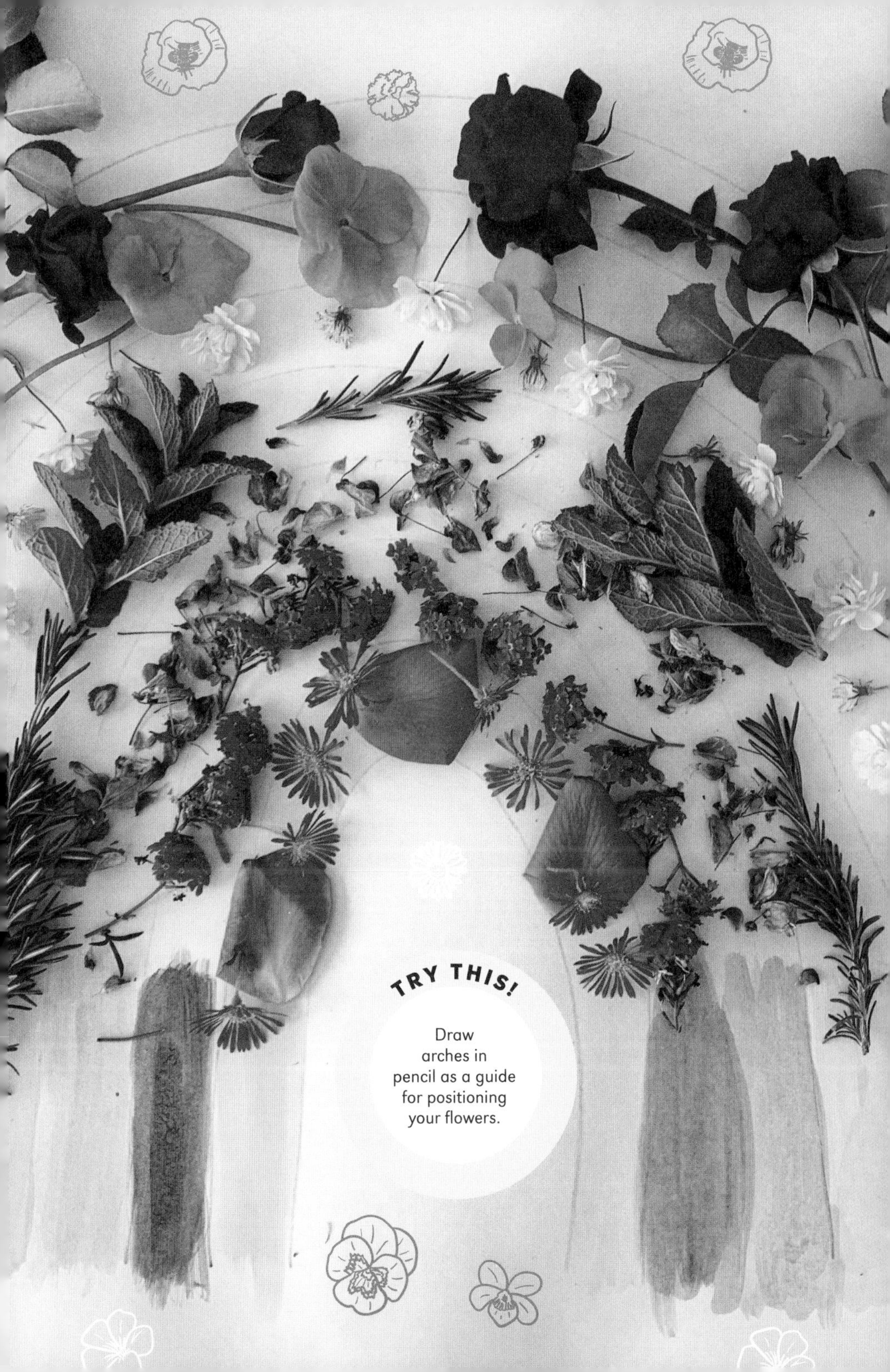

TRY THIS!

Draw arches in pencil as a guide for positioning your flowers.

READING CHALLENGE

When the weather warms up, move your reading nook outdoors and enjoy your books under the natural sunlight. The sounds and smells of nature will enhance your story time. How many different places can you read in?

BEACH READING

A piece of driftwood makes an excellent seat and the sounds of the lapping waves and seagulls give a pleasant surround sound to your book reading experience. Sand brushes off easily from the pages of your book.

TIP

- If you're laying on a towel to read, scour the beach for a **book weight**, like a large shell or small rock, to keep your pages from blowing.

Time seems to **slow down** at the beach.

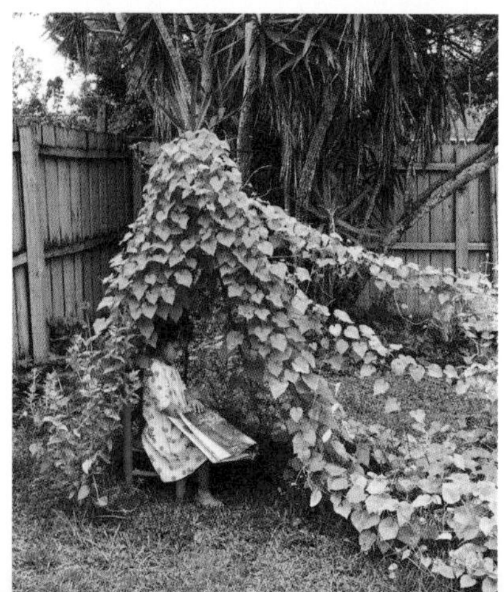

HIDEAWAY READING

Nature makes its own little hideaways among bushes that you can find, but you can always create a garden hideaway using climbing plants or flowers such as snap peas or morning glories. Enjoy your shady, secret spot as you dive into a favorite book.

A hideaway of beans, peas, or tomatoes provides **fresh snacks**.

SPREAD OUT A BLANKET

Take an old blanket and a stack of books and sprawl out for a morning or an afternoon of reading. It's also a great option if you've been playing hard all day and need some down time and rejuvenation in a comfortable location.

A **yoga mat** under a blanket cushions and protects.

TIP

- Being outdoors **relieves stress and anxiety** so take some time during the school day to read outside in nature.

MORE IDEAS

- Make your reading area **extra cozy** by adding throw pillows and blankets.
- Set up a toy **tent** to read inside.
- Host an outdoor **book club** for the kids in your neighborhood.
- String up a tarp to give shade from the sun and **shelter** from rain.

FOREST STORY TIME

Take your classroom, forest school, or friends down a short hiking path and search for a flat place to read together amongst the rustling leaves. Build it into your schedule and host something like a "Wednesday in the Woods."

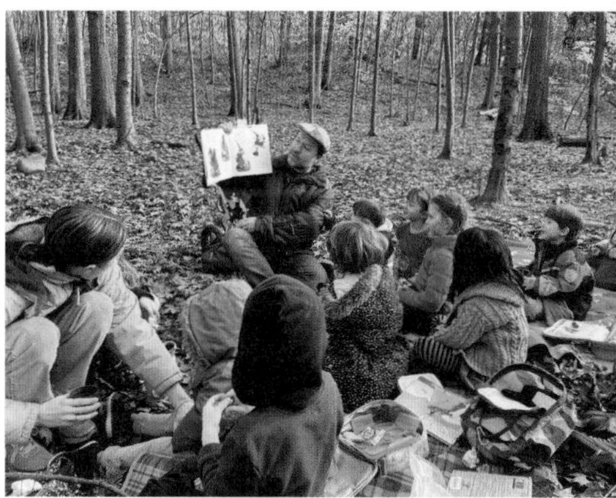

While kids are finishing up their lunch, read them a few favorite **picture books**.

30–60 mins

FRAME IT!

Sticks can be magic wands, tools for excavating, and also fantastic building blocks for crafts. You can make beautiful, rustic frames for presenting your art or for taking quirky photographs. Because sticks are so plentiful, you can experiment with different types of creations and see what you like the best.

SUPPLIES

- Four straight, dry sticks or twigs of similar thickness and length, or Popsicle sticks
- Twine or string
- Scissors
- Camera (optional)

INSTRUCTIONS

1. Overlap the ends of two sticks to make a corner (a right angle) and tie them together using twine or string. Wrap your twine in two different diagonal directions, making an x-shape.
2. Once you've wrapped the twine several times in both directions, make a knot, and carefully cut off the excess string.
3. Repeat steps 1 and 2 for the other three corners of your frame.
4. If you're using Popsicle sticks, overlap them in the corners, glue them together, and give them ample time to dry.
5. Make more frames using twigs of different thickness. You could also make frames in different shapes like triangles or octagons.
6. Use your frame to take creative photos outside and around your home.

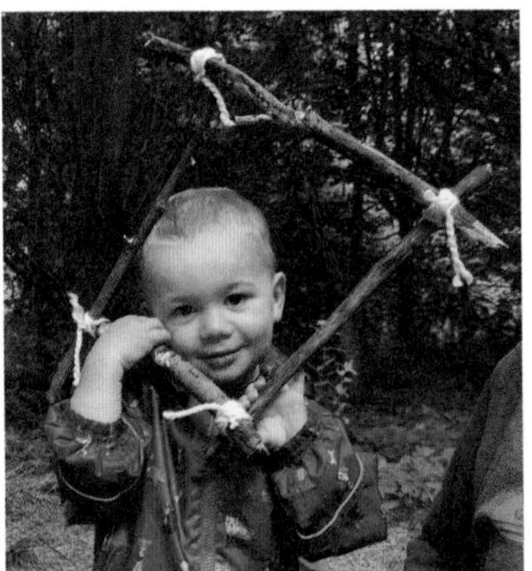

Sticks and twine make good **selfie frames** for photos.

MORE IDEAS

- Affix a few **wildflowers** to the corners of your frame for a more whimsical look.
- **Decorate** your home with these cozy, rustic frames.
- Bundle **several twigs** together on each side of the frame instead of just a single stick.

TRY THIS!
Preserve bright pieces of nature in your frame between two pieces of contact paper.

CLOUD GAZING

Heads up! Gazing at the clouds is a great way to spend time outside. Clouds bring the rain, give us shade, and make some pretty cool shapes. So grab a blanket and head out to lay down and look up!

CLOUD TYPES

Clouds might all seem sort of the same, but there are actually ten different types, including cumulus and cirrus. Some are as high as 20,000 feet (6,000m), which is almost four miles (6km) up in the sky! Others are just over a mile (1.5km) from the Earth's surface.

MORE IDEAS

- Make an art project using **cotton balls** as clouds on pieces of paper. Stretch the cotton balls out to make them look more realistic.

These fluffy clouds are **cumulus** and the wispier ones are **cirrus** clouds.

Tell **stories** about the shapes you see in the clouds.

CLOUD SHAPES

Stretch out on the nearest patch of soft grass and look up. Relax and watch the clouds moving above you. Do you see any with shapes that remind you of anything? Can you see how some clouds are really high up and others are lower?

CLOUD PAINTING

Lay a mirror down on the ground outside. Arrange your painting supplies on the ground as well, and use the mirror to look up in the sky and see the clouds! You can then easily paint what you see without having to stop and look up all the time!

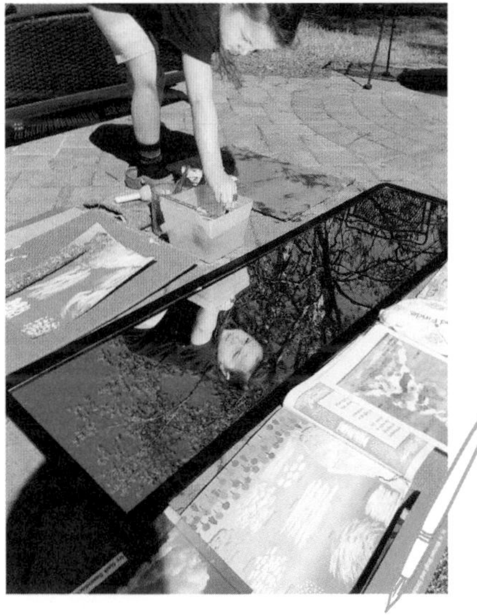

As well as clouds, you could see tree branches from a **new angle**.

HOPSCOTCH

20–30 mins

Did you know that a form of hopscotch has been around for thousands of years? Roman soldiers used to compete with one another, carrying heavy weights in full armor over similar courses of 100 feet (30m)! Today it's a bit more fun than that—all you need is a driveway or sidewalk, some chalk, and lots of energy!

SUPPLIES

- Sidewalk chalk
- Masking tape (optional)
- Stone or rock

INSTRUCTIONS

1. Draw a hopscotch design (see below) in chalk. Make sure the squares are big enough for your feet to fit in.
2. Toss the stone into square one, making sure it doesn't touch the borders. Then hop over that square on one foot. You must land in the next square, without touching the one with the stone.
3. Continue hopping through all the squares (jumping on two feet when two squares are next to each other).
4. At the end, turn around and come back the same way. When you reach the stone, bend over, pick it up, then hop over that square. If you do this without falling outside the squares, then you move on.
5. Next, toss your stone into the second square and repeat the above steps. The first person to complete all numbers wins!

Try using different **color chalk** for the numbers and outline.

MORE IDEAS

- Make the squares different sizes and shapes like **circles**.
- Set a **timer** to see who can do it the fastest without making a mistake.

TRY THIS!
Take turns tackling each number in order.

WILD WEAVING

30–60 mins

Weaving is a great skill to learn, as it assists with dexterity, allows for creativity, and definitely helps with patience! A simple walk around your yard, the local park, or a hiking trail can present lots of great natural materials that you can use. Flowers, grasses, and leaves can truly make this activity "unbe-weave-ably" fun!

SUPPLIES

- Four sturdy twigs of similar size
- Twine or string
- Scissors
- Items to weave in and out of the strings such as leaves, long grasses, and flowers

INSTRUCTIONS

1. Start by finding four twigs. For a square frame, find four roughly the same length. For a rectangle, choose two shorter and two longer ones.
2. Take your string and tie the corners together with a crisscross overlapping motion. Then tie the string off with a good, strong knot.
3. Once the frame is done, wind the string around it, from top to bottom. Each time you wrap it around one side, loop it an extra time around the twig before taking it across to the opposite twig. This will help secure the string.
4. Continue this back and forth until the frame has lines of string across it. Knot the end of the string tightly.
5. Head out on a walk to explore and find natural materials to weave in and out of the strings!

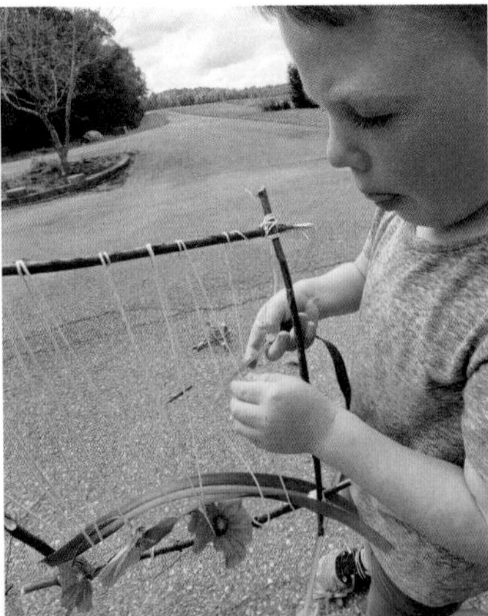

Thread your nature items (the "**weft**") in and out of the strings (the "**warp**").

MORE IDEAS

- Look for **flowers** for colorful patterns.
- Decorate with different **grasses** of various lengths.
- Make several weaves of different sizes and **hang them** as art inside or outside your home.

TRY THIS!

For a year-round loom, put stakes in the ground and change materials seasonally.

TRY THIS!

This fairy home has several stories with windows.

1 hr

FAIRY DOORS

Fairy doors tap into the wonderful fantasy world of our imaginations. They conjure up visions of visiting fairies and other magical woodland creatures, who live side-by-side with us. These doors are gateways to the world of fairies, and some even pretend that only those who believe will be able to find the doors.

SUPPLIES

- Nine Popsicle sticks
- Glue
- Paint pens
- Sticks
- Paint (optional)
- Cardboard (optional)

INSTRUCTIONS

1. While there are many ways to make a fairy door, perhaps one of the easiest is with Popsicle sticks. If you wish, you can paint your sticks ahead of time.
2. Lay seven of the sticks next to each vertically.
3. Put glue on the back of the other two Popsicle sticks.
4. Glue the two sticks diagonally across the seven vertical sticks in order to hold them together. Now you have a door shape.
5. Decorate the front of your door with paint pens.
6. Glue on a few knobbly pieces of stick.
7. You can also make your door by carefully cutting a rectangular shape out of cardboard and decorating it with paint or paint pens. Cardboard allows you to create more varied shapes.
8. Once your door is ready, place it in the crux of some tree roots, resting against the base of a tree, or affixed to a tree in a nonpermanent way—even small nails and screws can damage a tree over time.

EXTRA TIME

- Make some **windows** as well as a door and imagine you're peering into a magical world. What do you see? What would they see if they peered at you from the other side?

MORE IDEAS

- Dream up **the fairy** that visits you. Give your fairy a name and imagine their story. Leave some special decorations around your door.
- Write a **letter** to your fairy. Tell them all about yourself.

FLOWER PRESSING

1 hr

Sometimes flowers are just so beautiful you want to hang onto them forever, or at least longer than they would last in a vase. Flower pressing has been around for thousands of years—even the Greeks and Romans did it. It's a great way to preserve the flowers you grow or pick, or those from a special occasion, for years to come.

SUPPLIES

- Flowers—naturally flatter flowers work better than large blooms. Daisies, pansies, and violets are good picks.
- Scissors
- Pressing kit or book
- Greenery (optional)

INSTRUCTIONS

1. Once you have gathered your flowers, clean them off as much as possible and dry them.
2. If you don't have a flower press, a book with blank pages or book pages lined with newspaper works well. Arrange your flowers and greenery on the page of a book.
3. Once your flowers are in the position you want, slowly close the book to press the flowers flat.
4. Leave something flat and heavy on top of the book for one to two weeks in a dry place that isn't too hot. You could use a stack of hardback books or something else that is similarly heavy.

Make sure none of your flowers will overlap when you close the **book**.

MORE IDEAS

- Adding **greenery** to your flowers will fill in the spaces a little and create a different look.

TRY THIS!
Make a **collage** with your pressed flowers.

MUD PLAY

It's definitely worth the mess to play in the mud! Mud supplies children with endless sensory opportunities, countless ways to be creative, and pure childhood joy. Gather your supplies! All you need is a little (or a lot) of dirt and water.

MUD BUILDING

Mud is an easy medium that can be manipulated and sculpted making it perfect for building structures and so much more! This open-ended activity allows for long-term building or shorter builds with lots of starting over.

FUN FACT

- Exposure to mud boosts your **immune system** and stimulates the feel-good chemical **serotonin**. But you should still wash your hands afterwards.

Use mud like **mortar** to stick wooden bricks together.

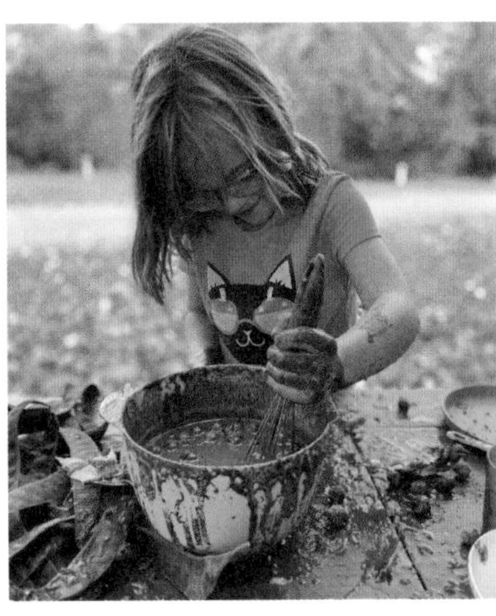

Mix with whisks, spoons, spatulas, tongs, or sticks—or with your hands!

MUD MIXING

Break out the kitchen utensils! All this hands-on mud play helps with large and fine motor development from your fingers to your shoulders. Stir the mud in pots. Add some extra water. Is it harder to stir or easier? There's lots to learn.

EXTRA TIME

- Add extras to your mud like grass, pebbles, leaves, flower petals, or acorns to add to its **texture** and your creativity.
- **Adorn** what you build with nature's extras.

Choose **shoes and clothing** that you don't mind getting muddy.

MUDDY TOYS

Your toys will love the mud! Bring plastic vehicles and animals to your mud pit. Create jungles and forests. Make roads, dig trenches, and drive your trucks through the mud. Then take them to the hose or a bucket of water for a car wash.

Plastic toys are the easiest to wash after their mud adventures.

MUD SWIMMING

There's just something about having mud all over your entire body. It's a sensory experience that cannot be replicated. Go ahead. Lay down, roll around, and pretend to swim. Then rinse it all off and feel how soft your skin feels.

WADING IN MUD

Wading through mud is a form of heavy work that develops your sense of movement and balance. Take off your shoes, move slowly, and feel the pull and the suction every time you step. If the mud is really deep, use a pole to keep your balance.

Play out a **rescue mission** for toys who've gotten stranded in the mud.

1–2 hrs

DISCOVERING SALAMANDERS

Let's go herping! Herping is walking around with the intention of finding herptiles—amphibians or reptiles. Salamanders may look like lizards, but they are actually a type of amphibian. There are more than 700 species, and they can be found in many parts of the northern hemisphere with damp conditions, where land and water meet.

SUPPLIES

- Gloves (optional)
- Flashlight (if out at night)

INSTRUCTIONS

1. Salamanders are more active on land when they're less likely to dry out, so the best time to look for them is on warm, rainy nights, but go out only with an adult. The best places to spot them is along trails, roads, and other openings near streams, wetlands, or ponds.
2. You may need to look under things to find salamanders, but make sure you always leave the habitat as you found them. Tread gently and return everything to how it was. While herping, try these tips:
   - Gently turn over medium to large-size pieces of decaying wood where a salamander might hide and munch on insects.
   - Inspect around rocks. They can create shelter for salamanders and help them maintain high relative humidity.
   - Carefully pull up piles of leaf litter, root balls, and moss mats.

FUN FACTS

- The terms "herping" and "herptile" are related to "herpetology," which is the study of amphibians and reptiles. They come from the Greek word "herpien," meaning to creep.
- Amphibians are a group that includes frogs, toads, salamanders, and newts.
- Amphibians typically live in the water when they're young and then they grow into a new body that can live on land and absorbs water through its skin.

TRY THIS!
Be very gentle if you touch any creature, and then wash your hands.

20 mins active time

PLANT A TREE

In a world of instant technology, planting a tree provides the exact opposite experience—and it's a beautiful thing! There won't be anything noticeable for quite some time, and that's perfectly fine. Planting a tree allows your family to produce something that could last for generations and is vitally important to our environment.

SUPPLIES

- Tree seeds
- Large paper coffee cup
- Pencil
- Soil
- Water

INSTRUCTIONS

1. First of all, go on a hunt for seeds! You don't need to buy any. Maple trees produce seeds in the little "helicopters" that whirl down from the sky; acorns from oak trees are good candidates; and pine cones usually produce two seeds each.
2. Carefully poke a few small drainage holes in the bottom of your cup with a pencil. Fill your cup with soil and place your seed in the soil, about an inch (2–3cm) below the surface. Always wash your hands after touching soil.
3. Once your seedling sprouts, keep it in a warm place with lots of sun and water it every day. Keep your seedling indoors for about a year.
4. When your plant is about 15 to 19 inches (40–50cm) tall, you need to gradually expose it to the outdoors. Start by putting it outside for about two hours a day and then increase this by an hour or two each day for about 10 days. This process is called "hardening off."
5. Find a space with plenty of sunlight, dig a hole, and place your seedling inside. Cover the area with soil and keep your tree watered as it grows.

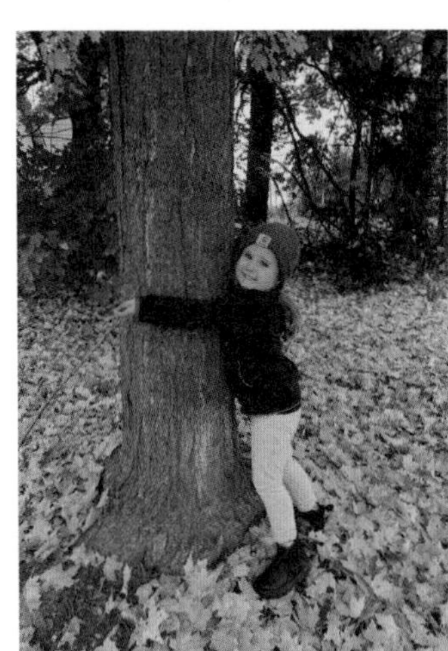

Improve your mood by stopping and **hugging a tree**!

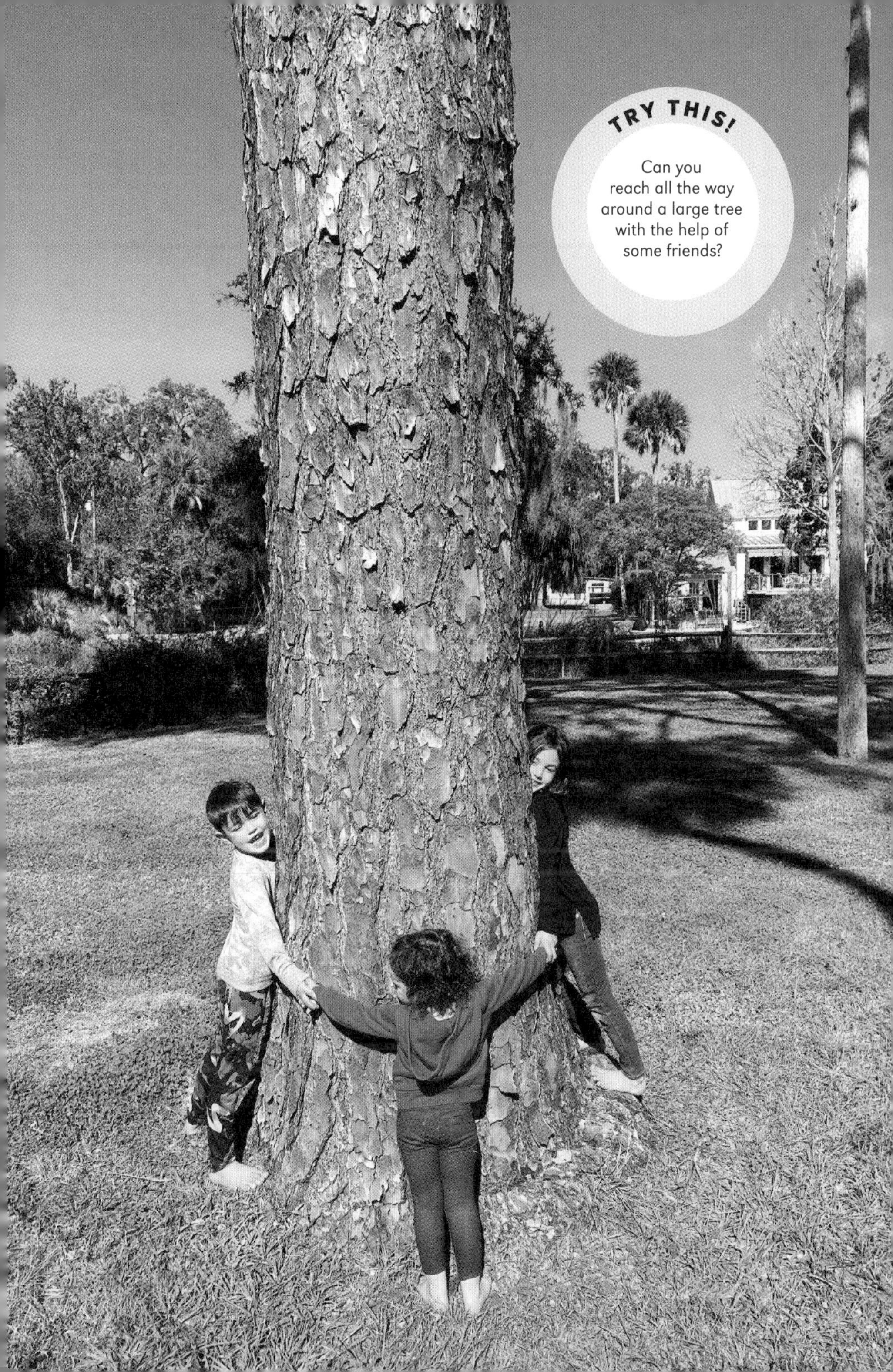
TRY THIS!
Can you reach all the way around a large tree with the help of some friends?

PATTERN SPOTTING

Nature's patterns are stunningly beautiful. Step outside and you'll find symmetries, spirals, branching, tessellations, fractals, stripes, and more. Natural patterns inspire a lot of human art and design as well.

HIDING IN PLAIN SIGHT

You may not notice nature's patterns until you actively search for them, but once you start looking, you'll find that they are all around you. Even simple plants have beautiful, intricate patterns.

EXTRA TIME

- Try **drawing** the patterns you see in nature. Check out the plants or insects at the park or the stripes or spots on animals at the zoo.

Succulents' leaves grow in a beautiful **spiral** pattern that often occurs in nature.

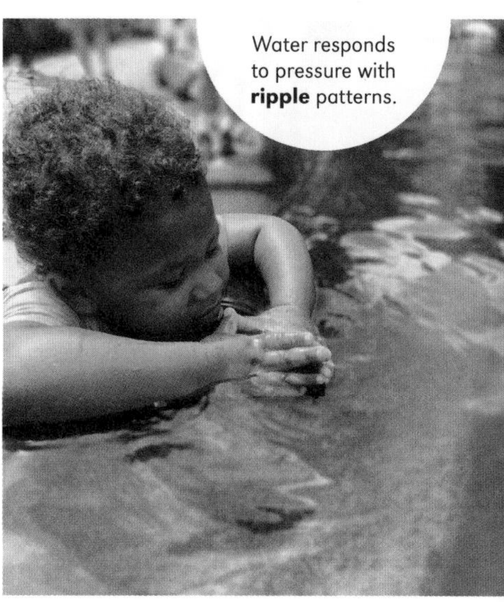

Water responds to pressure with **ripple** patterns.

FRACTALS

Fractals are repeating patterns of a particular shape or shapes that get smaller and smaller (or larger and larger). Fractals can be found in ferns, tree branches, pine cone spirals, snowflakes, and even within the neural pathways of our own brains.

MAKE YOUR OWN PATTERNS

You can use nature's patterns in your artwork, but you can also make real patterns in nature. Explore the patterns and shapes you can make with water. How do the ripples change as you move your hands in different ways?

REAL WORLD MATH

Bees hives are an example of a pattern called a tessellation, where all the shapes fit together without any gaps. In the Fibonacci sequence, each number is the sum of the previous two (0, 1, 1, 2, 3, 5, 8, 13, etc.) and it crops up a lot.

MORE IDEAS

- When you see patterns in nature, think about why they exist. What **benefit** do they give the plant or animal?

The wind often shapes **sand** into a pattern that looks like waves in the ocean.

Sunflowers are math marvels and their seed spirals showcase the Fibonacci sequence.

The spiral pattern of an **artichoke's** leaves also display the Fibonacci sequence.

Spiderwebs show a radial symmetry which is also found in a sliced orange or a starfish.

The pattern on **peacock feathers** is an example of a fractal.

The natural cracking of **wood** adds to the grain pattern that emerges as it grows.

ICE EXCAVATION

1–2 hrs active time

This is an excellent boredom buster that combines fine and large motor skills, determination, patience, and that glorious feeling of touching something cold on a warm day. The possibilities are endless as to what you can freeze, the methods for excavating frozen toys, and also what ice shapes you can create with your freezer.

SUPPLIES

- An assortment of small, plastic toys that won't break easily
- An assortment of plastic containers to freeze water in such as empty yogurt containers
- Kid's hammer or mallet
- Pitcher of warm water
- Spray bottle filled with warm water
- A few towels

INSTRUCTIONS

1. Place one or a few plastic toys in plastic containers and fill them with water. Make sure the water completely covers the object you want to freeze. Be careful not to include anything too small that a young child might try and put in their mouth.
2. Leave your containers in the freezer for a few hours or overnight until they are frozen solid.
3. Remove your blocks of ice and see how you can free the toys. You could try carefully bashing them with a hammer or mallet, spraying them with warm water, or dropping them onto the ground.
4. If this appears to be taking too long and is frustrating, you can always run the ice block under a warm tap. Feel the sensation of the ice melting away.

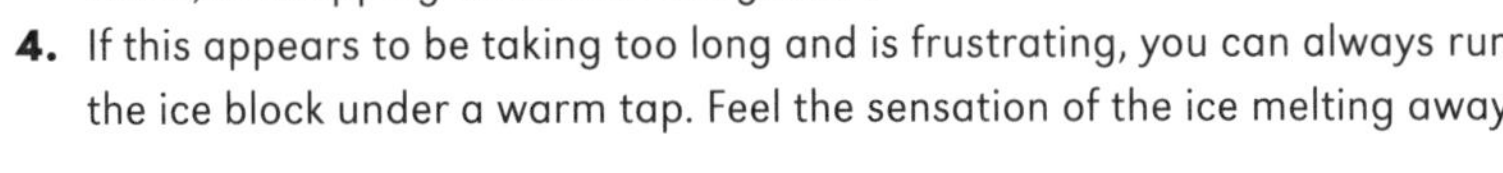

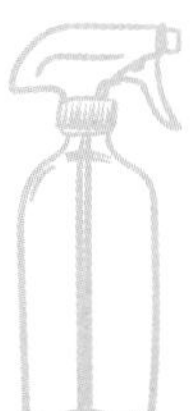

EXTRA TIME

- If you want your toys to be deep in the ice and you have a little extra time to set this activity up, you can **freeze them in layers** so they don't all float up to the top.

MORE IDEAS

- Play **animal rescue** by freezing plastic animals in different containers.
- Add **food coloring** to your ice blocks, but be careful. The colored water could stain things as it melts.

TRY THIS!
Watch what happens to the ice as it melts.

HIKING

One of the best ways to immerse yourself in nature is by hiking. There's something for everyone out on the trail, from the youngest child to grandparent or great-grandparent and all ages in between.

CHILD-LED PACING

When adults hike with children, it allows them to slow down and see the world through a child's eyes and discover with them along the way. Hiking with children generally takes longer than hiking with a group of adults, so be sure to have enough food and water along with you.

GENERATIONS TOGETHER

Hiking is a pleasurable activity at most ages and stages of life. The hike you choose doesn't have to be long or grueling. Slow and easy is the name of the game as you enjoy nature and the company of different generations all together.

Play games like **I Spy** or **Scavenger Hunt** on your hikes.

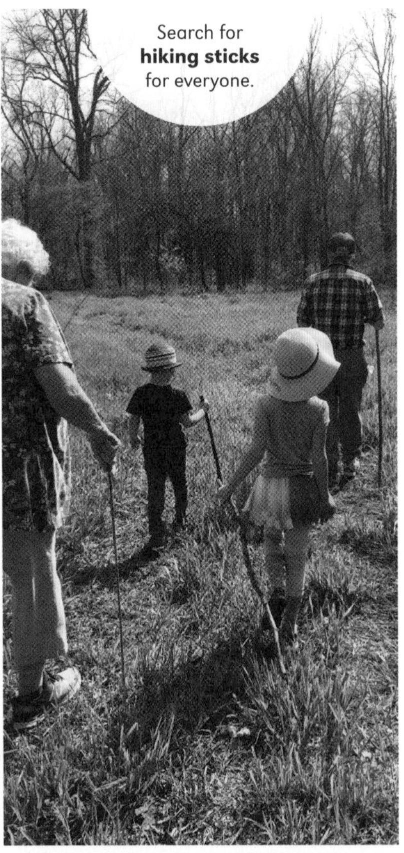

Search for **hiking sticks** for everyone.

MORE IDEAS

- Create **hiking traditions** with your extended family. Hike together on the same day each year or walk certain routes at least once a year.

DRESS-UP

Our kids have always loved to don a cape or a hat and hit the trails. As they run, their capes fly back in the breeze and imagination soars. Play pretend dress-up games in the forest.

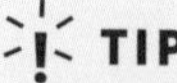 **TIP**

- Match your costume to the **season**. A thick costume is a good top layer in the cold, and capes and crowns are good for a warm spell.

ACTIVITIES EN ROUTE

Along your hike, try geocaching, listen to an audiobook or music, or tell stories. To make a grass whistle, put a long, thick blade of grass between your thumbs, place the backs of your thumbs against your mouth, and blow toward the grass.

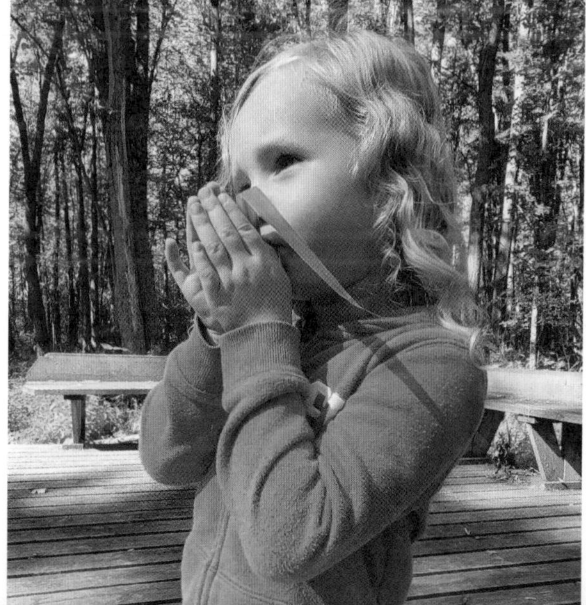

Peter Pan plays in the forest, but so could a robot, a dinosaur, an alien, or anything!

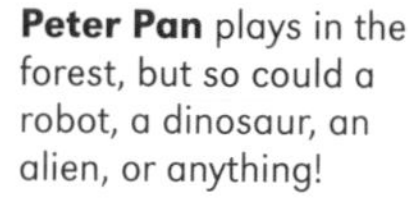

Whistle along with the birdsong.

CHAPTER THREE

SUMMER

45 mins active time

FROZEN FLOWERS

On a hot day, playing with ice is a great way to cool down, as well as being an interesting sensory experience. Why not spruce up your ice play by freezing flowers and plants? This two-part activity starts with an adventure to find goodies to put in the freezer and then, the next day, playing with the mesmerizing ice.

SUPPLIES

- Ice cube trays or muffin pans of different shapes
- Water (ideally distilled)
- Small, colorful flowers
- Freezer

INSTRUCTIONS

1. Fill each section of your ice cube or muffin tray one-quarter full with water and place some flowers or petals in each one.
2. Place your tray in the freezer for about 20 minutes.
3. Take the tray out of the freezer and, if you wish, add in a few more flowers.
4. Fill up the rest of each compartment with water. Freezing the shapes in two stages will ensure that your flowers won't float to the top.
5. Put the tray back in the freezer overnight.
6. Once they are frozen, carefully remove your ice blocks from their trays.
7. Enjoy exploring your frozen flowers as they begin to melt!

These are a great addition to a **mud kitchen** (see page 34).

MORE IDEAS

- If the water isn't as **clear** as you'd like, next time boil your water and let it cool completely before making your frozen flowers.
- Use **edible flowers** such as pansies, geraniums, or miniature roses and add your ice cubes to a drink, but double-check with an adult that your flowers aren't poisonous.

TRY THIS!

Place your ice shapes in a tub of water to play with while they melt.

30–60 mins

SUNCATCHER

Making a suncatcher is a wonderful way to encourage spending time outside on a sunny day. It's also a fantastic way to recycle some of that cardboard that might be piling up at your house from deliveries and put it to good use! What really makes these is the bright cellophane that turns natural sunlight into colorful, novelty shadows.

SUPPLIES

- Recycled cardboard boxes or scraps of cardboard
- Pencil
- Scissors or box cutter
- Cellophane (various colors)
- Glue

INSTRUCTIONS

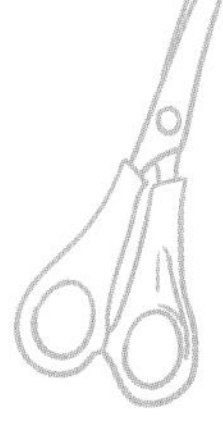

1. Start with choosing whatever pattern you would like to make. Leaves, stars, and umbrellas are great options to begin with.
2. Draw your design on the cardboard. It should be a simple outline shape with smaller shapes within it. You need areas that can be cut out and enough cardboard left to create a sturdy frame around the holes.
3. Using either scissors or a box cutter, very carefully cut out the insides.
4. Cut your cellophane pieces into the same shapes as your holes, but make them at least an inch (2cm) bigger all the way around so they will overlap the cardboard frame.
5. Add glue on the back of the cardboard, all around the edges of the holes.
6. Stick the cellophane over the holes with the glue. Trim off any excess.
7. If you would like, you can cut out a duplicate cardboard shape and glue it to the back of your creation. This will sandwich the "messy" cellophane between cardboard.
8. Take your suncatcher outside to see what kind of shadows it makes!

EXTRA TIME

- Experiment with colors by **layering** two different colors of cellophane together.
- Once it's dark, **point a flashlight** at your suncatcher to see how it looks inside.

MORE IDEAS

- Make cellophane **leaf-shaped** suncatchers and hang them from a tree with string.
- Create patterns for your **bedroom window** to color your room when the sun shines in.

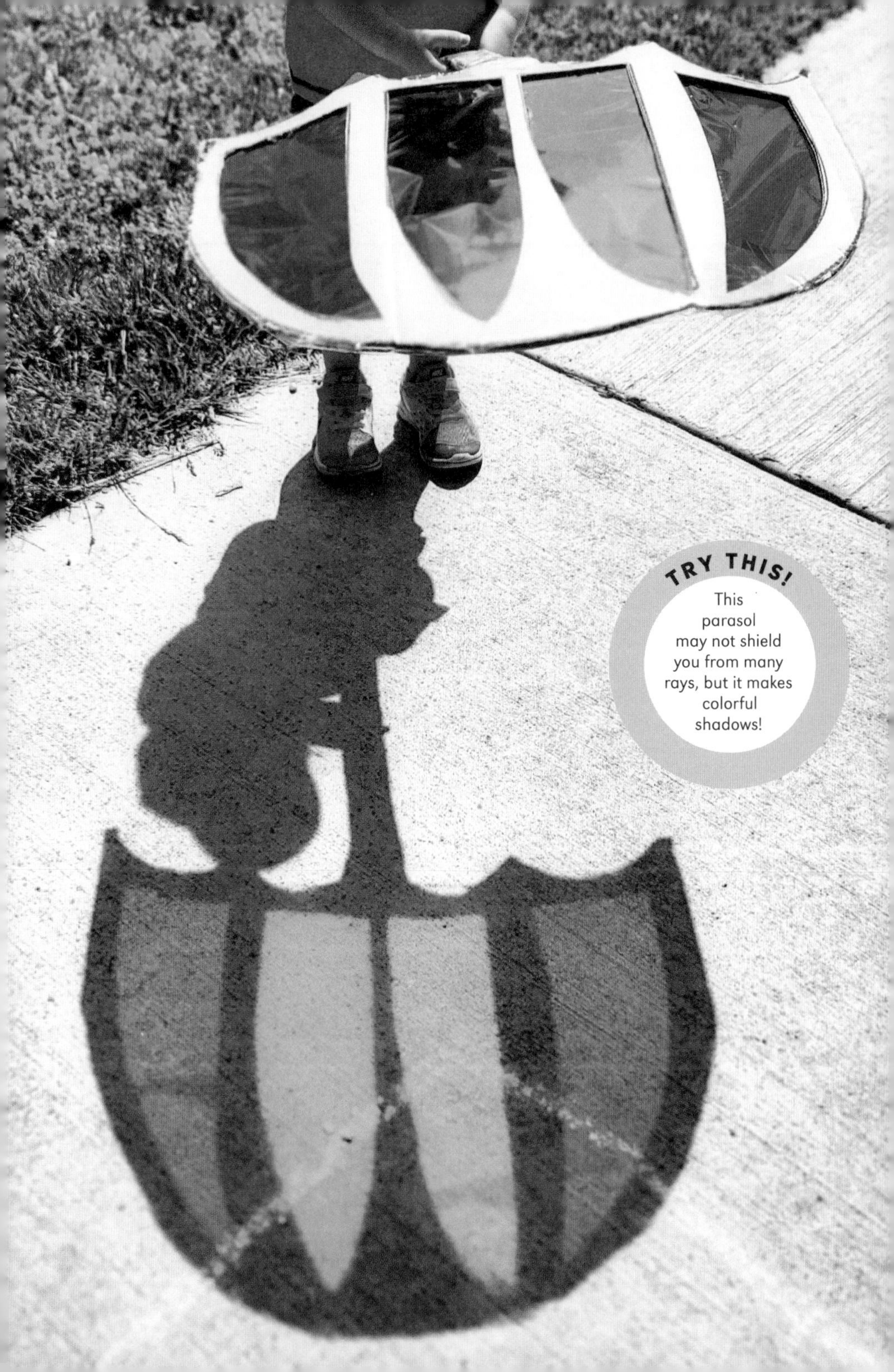
TRY THIS!
This parasol may not shield you from many rays, but it makes colorful shadows!

BUTTERFLY WATCHING

Of all tiny things that fly, the butterfly is possibly the most popular. It begins life as a caterpillar and can transform into a butterfly in as little as 30 days! There are more than 17,000 species of butterflies in the world. Amazingly, butterflies taste with their feet–wow!

CATERPILLAR LEGS

Caterpillars have lots of legs, right? It sure looks that way, but actually they have only six legs, just like butterflies. But they do have fake legs called prolegs that help them hang onto branches and leaves but don't help them walk.

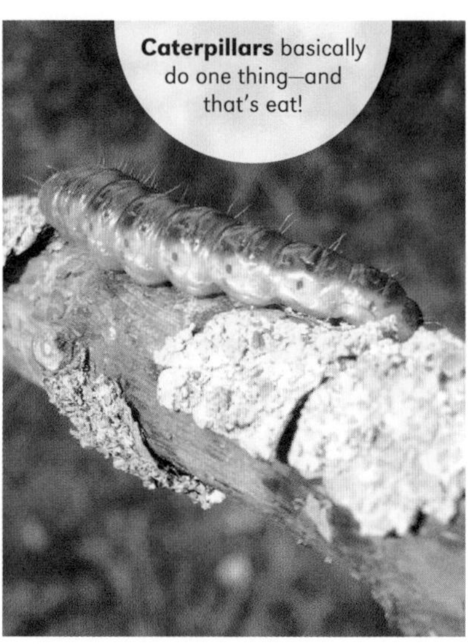

Caterpillars basically do one thing—and that's eat!

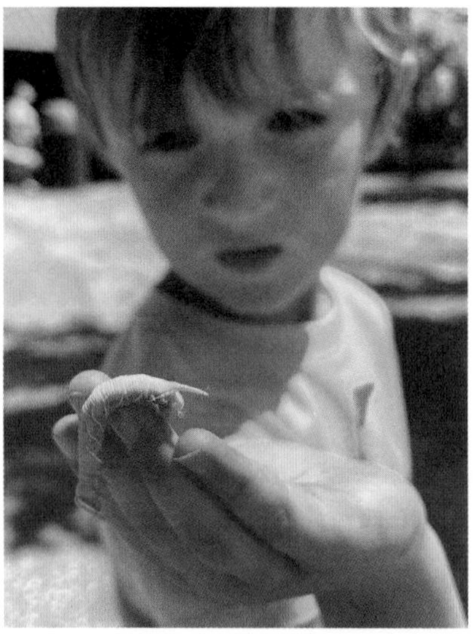

CATERPILLAR COLORS

Caterpillars come in all sorts of colors. Some are very bright in order to warn predators that they are toxic and not to be eaten, while others use color to blend in with their surroundings as a defense mechanism to avoid predators.

There are at least **30 different types** of green caterpillar.

EXTRA TIME

- Take a **walk and see** how many different types of caterpillars or butterflies you can find and what colors they are.

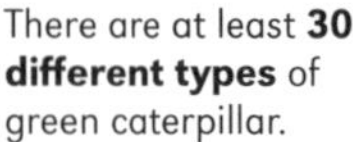

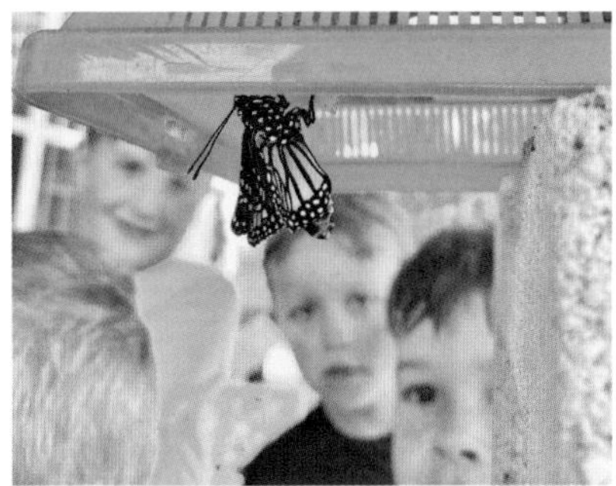

METAMORPHOSIS

Metamorphosis is a big word, but a caterpillar changing into a butterfly is a big deal, so it's fitting! A caterpillar essentially digests itself in a chrysalis, and in an amazing process, transforms into a butterfly!

A **monarch butterfly** takes about 30 days to emerge from its chrysalis.

BUTTERFLY RELEASE

If you keep a caterpillar to watch its transformation, make sure you give it plenty of suitable food. Once the butterfly emerges from its chrysalis, releasing it into the wild is such a rewarding experience.

The best time to **release** a butterfly is about an hour before sunset.

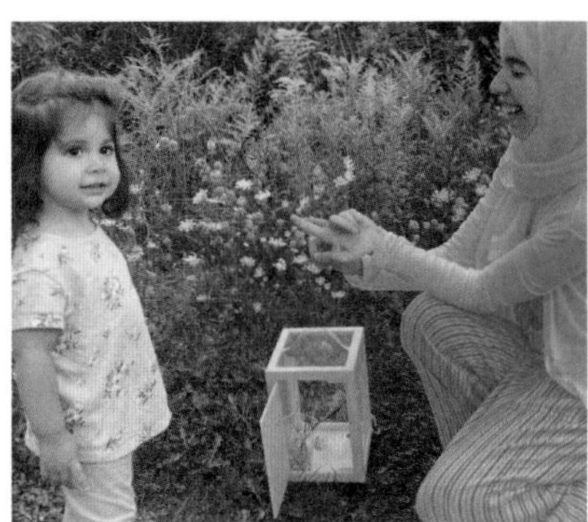

BUTTERFLY CATCHING

If you try to catch a butterfly, be sure to use a special butterfly net. These are made from a soft material suitable for catching these beautiful creatures and won't damage their very delicate wings.

BUTTERFLY DIETS

Butterflies don't eat anything solid—only liquid. They have something called a proboscis, which is curled up until they find nectar to drink. It's like slurping your favorite meal through a straw!

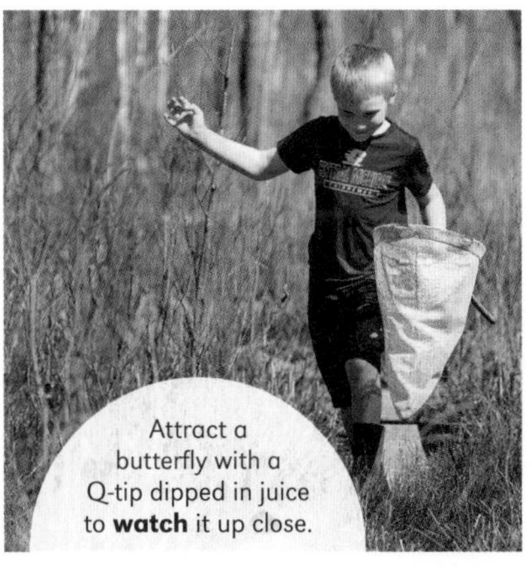

Attract a butterfly with a Q-tip dipped in juice to **watch** it up close.

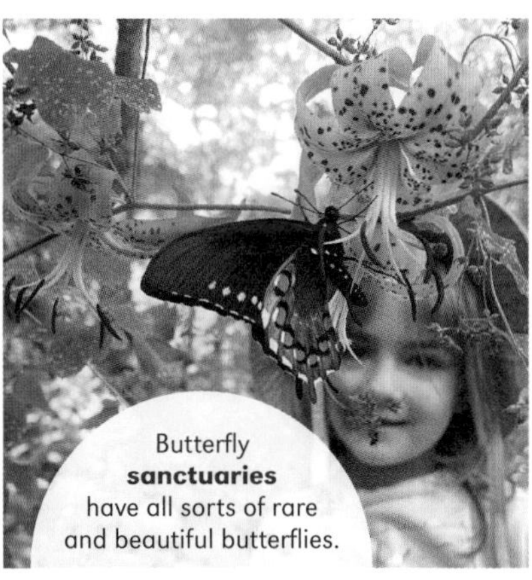

Butterfly **sanctuaries** have all sorts of rare and beautiful butterflies.

2–4 hrs

VINE BASKET WEAVING

Have you ever seen vines growing around trees or hanging from the canopy? Perhaps you've even tripped over them. Why not turn these invasive vines into a basket? Plus you'll work on your finger dexterity as basket weaving is a challenging but rewarding task.

SUPPLIES

- Vines (grape vines work well)
- Clippers to cut the vines
- String or twine

INSTRUCTIONS

1. First, check with an adult that none of your vines are poisonous!
2. Carefully cut the vines with the clippers and an adult's help. Gather more than you'll need because some will break and some simply won't work.
3. Pick three strong but pliable branches, about 2½ to 3 feet (75 to 90cm) long. These spokes will form the structure of your basket.
4. Lay out the three vines so they cross over each other in the middle, with their ends at equal distances like bicycle spokes. Tie them together in the middle with string or twine to make the base.
5. Bend the vines straight up so they meet above the base and tie them about 3 inches (7.5cm) from the ends. Now you have the outer shell of a basket with six spokes that form the base for weaving (the "warp").
6. Starting where the spokes meet, weave a new piece of vine (the "weft"), over and under the spokes. Continue up the sides of the basket as high as you like, weaving tightly. When one vine runs out, simply find a place to tuck it in and start a new vine.

Use your basket for **collecting** eggs, flowers, or vegetables.

MORE IDEAS

- Your woven creation would make an elegant **May Day basket**. The tradition is to fill baskets with flowers and place them on neighbors' doorsteps.

TRY THIS!
Once you've made your basket, why not gift it to someone you love?

POOH STICKS

5 mins

Pooh Sticks is a fun game to play at any age. You can play on your own, with two people, or with a whole crowd. But always make sure that you are very careful around water. If there are enough sticks about, you can play this game over and over again. Watching for the winning stick is definitely part of the fun!

SUPPLIES

- A bridge over moving water such as a river or a creek
- Sticks
- Snacks (optional)

INSTRUCTIONS

1. Find a stick and show your opponents so everyone knows whose stick is whose. If you're playing by yourself, race two sticks against each other.
2. Carefully stand on a pedestrian bridge over the moving water below. Don't climb over any barriers or get too close to the water. Also, play near water only when you have adult supervision.
3. Study which way the river is flowing and then stand facing upstream.
4. Count to three and drop (don't throw) your sticks at the same time. The sticks should float under the bridge, along with the current of the water.
5. Quickly cross the bridge to look for the sticks as they pass underneath you.
6. The person whose stick appears first is the winner!
7. Play over and over again if you can find more sticks. Notice how bigger or smaller or different shapes of sticks perform. Which is best?

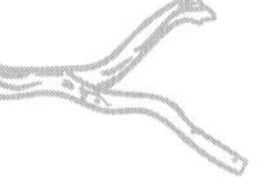

EXTRA TIME

- Have a small Pooh Sticks **tournament**. See whose sticks win most often or play best out of five.
- Bring a blanket and a **Pooh Sticks picnic** so you can stay and play longer.

FUN FACTS

- Pooh Sticks is named after **Winnie-the-Pooh**—the bear from A.A. Milne's books, which were animated by Disney.
- You can read about the **original** game in the book *The House at Pooh Corner.*
- There are annual **World Pooh Sticks Championships**, which have been held in the UK since 1984.

TRY THIS!
Study how your stick behaves in the water. Does it bob or spin or get stuck?

BAREFOOT DAY

Stiff shoes can impair the natural function of our feet, so taking them off for a time can be freeing. When the weather is warm enough for your toes, try a whole day barefoot and see how it feels!

BEAR CRAWL

Pretend you are different animals and walk like they do. You could do a bear crawl, a crab walk, a bunny hop, a frog jump, or waddle through the water like a duck. Try walking just on your heels, your toes, or on the outer edges of your feet. How does it feel?

TIP

- Enjoy the **feeling** of walking barefoot, but watch where you're stepping. The skin on your feet is thicker than on the rest of your body, but it's still delicate.

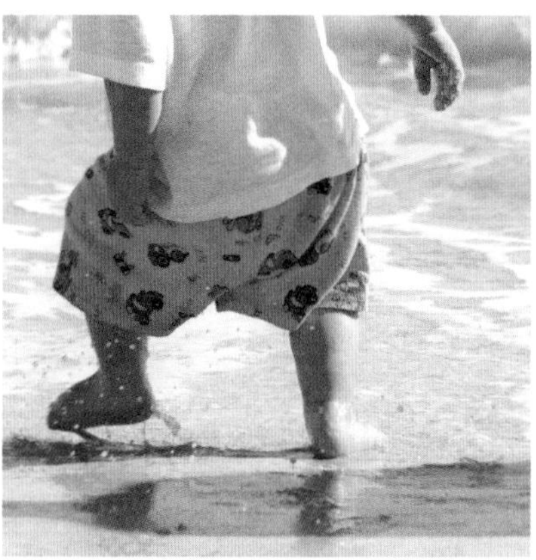

The soles of our feet send a lot of **sensory information** to our brains.

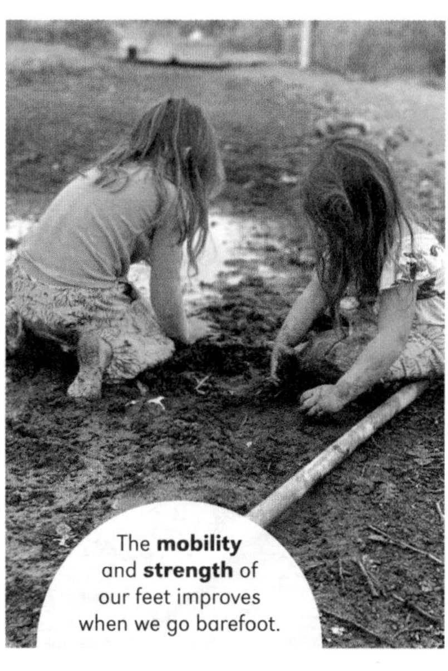

The **mobility** and **strength** of our feet improves when we go barefoot.

MORE IDEAS

- Have a **bean bag** tossing contest—using only your feet! Try tossing the bean bags with your feet and then pick them up using only your toes.

IN THE MUD

Bare feet awaken the senses because your soles have more nerve endings and more sweat glands per square centimeter than any other part of the body. So squelch away, not just with your hands but with your feet as well.

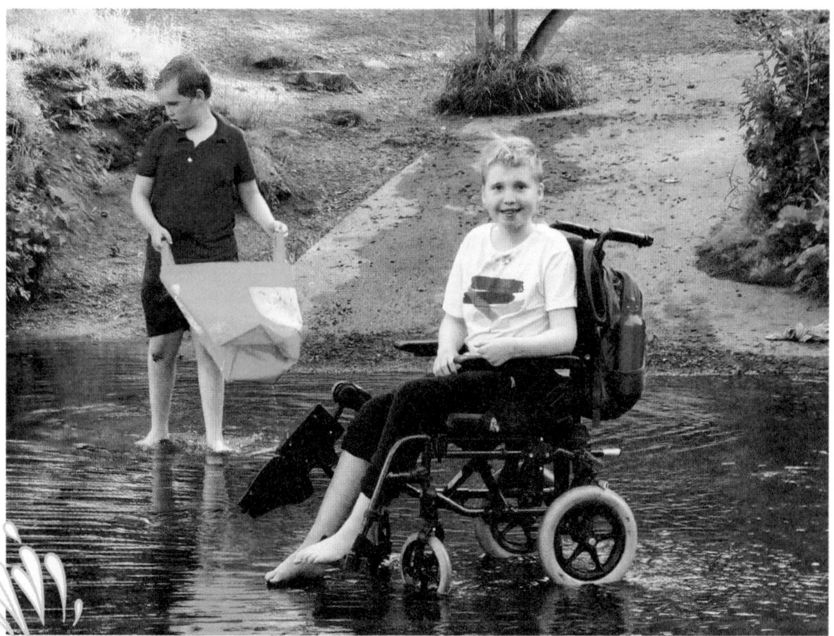

SENSORY EXPLORATION

Check out a shallow creek or a rain puddle to get your feet wet. Put your feet on a variety of outside surfaces such as grass, stones, or the bark of a tree. Notice what differences in temperature and in texture you can feel.

Variances in touch allow us to develop our **proprioceptive sense** which helps us with body awareness.

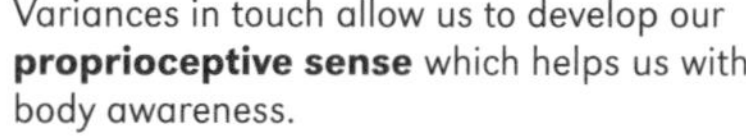

NATURE'S PLAYGROUND

Our feet are meant to be malleable and adapt to different surfaces. Being barefoot helps you climb and scale outdoors because the sensations you feel send information to your brain about the terrain you're in. Use your feet to maneuver through nature's obstacles.

Being barefoot gives you better **control** of your body.

FLOWER SEWING

1–2 hrs

Crowns spark visions of precious jewels embedded in gold, but we much prefer one made of beautiful flowers. Calendula are the perfect flower for sewing into a crown, garland, or other decorations. They are easy to grow at home, but if you don't have a garden, you can often find them relatively cheap at florists or even the grocery store.

SUPPLIES

- Calendula
- Scissors
- Thread (color of your choice)
- Sewing needle

INSTRUCTIONS

1. First, you'll need to collect your calendula, from your garden, a friend or family member's house, or perhaps do a few extra chores around your home so you can go buy some from the store. For a small child's crown, around 20 flowers should be enough.
2. Trim all the stems about an inch (2.5cm) below the flower head.
3. Cut a length of thread big enough to go around your head plus 2 inches (5cm) for tying.
4. Carefully thread the needle and tie a knot in the other end of the thread. Be sure you don't prick yourself or anyone else, and ask for help from an adult for this part if you need to. Gently push the needle through the base of each flower in turn.
5. Once your thread is full of flowers, remove the needle and tie the ends of your thread together. Then you can place the crown on your royal head and head out into your kingdom!

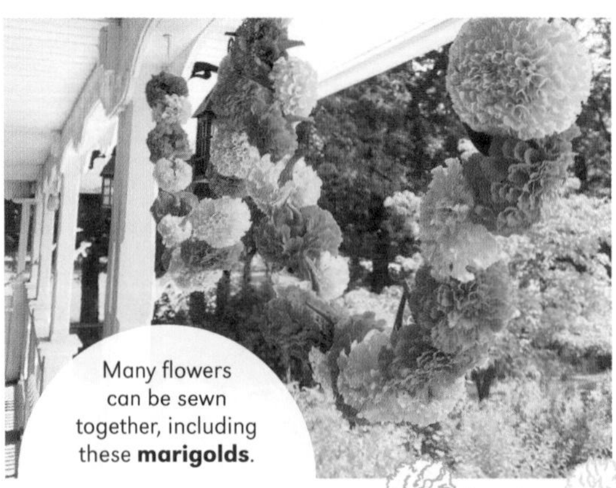

Many flowers can be sewn together, including these **marigolds**.

MORE IDEAS

- You can also use the same sewing technique to make **festive garlands**. Instead of tying your threaded flowers in a circle, hang them from your doorway, porch, or balcony to brighten everyone's day.

TRY THIS!

Make flower crowns for your friends, too, so you can shine together!

30–60 mins

SAND BUILDING

When you think of the beach, the mind wanders to crashing waves, seagulls hovering overhead, and, of course, sandcastles! It's fun to construct sandcastles, but if you don't have castle-shaped buckets, there are plenty of other ways to build. One way to liven up sand is to decorate it with items you find at the beach.

SUPPLIES

- Sand
- Items you can find at the beach—driftwood, shells, pebbles, seaweed, feathers
- Buckets and shovels (optional)

INSTRUCTIONS

1. Choose what type of structure you want to build: big and tall like a mountain? Or low to the ground and spread out like a city?
2. Find a clear, flat spot for your construction site. Think about whether the sea's tide is coming in or going out and choose somewhere where the waves won't soon knock down your build.
3. Hunt for natural materials to use as part of your sand building.
4. Build your sand structure. You may need to get the sand a little wet with sea water to shape it how you want.
5. Decorate it with the items you found.

Why not **sculpt** beach creatures from sand?

MORE IDEAS

- Dig a **moat or a river** that leads down to the water. As the waves roll in, it will **fill with water**.
- How many **shells** can you find that look similar? How much of your build can you cover in the same type?
- Place a seagull or other bird **feather** on top of your building like a **giant flag** for all to see.

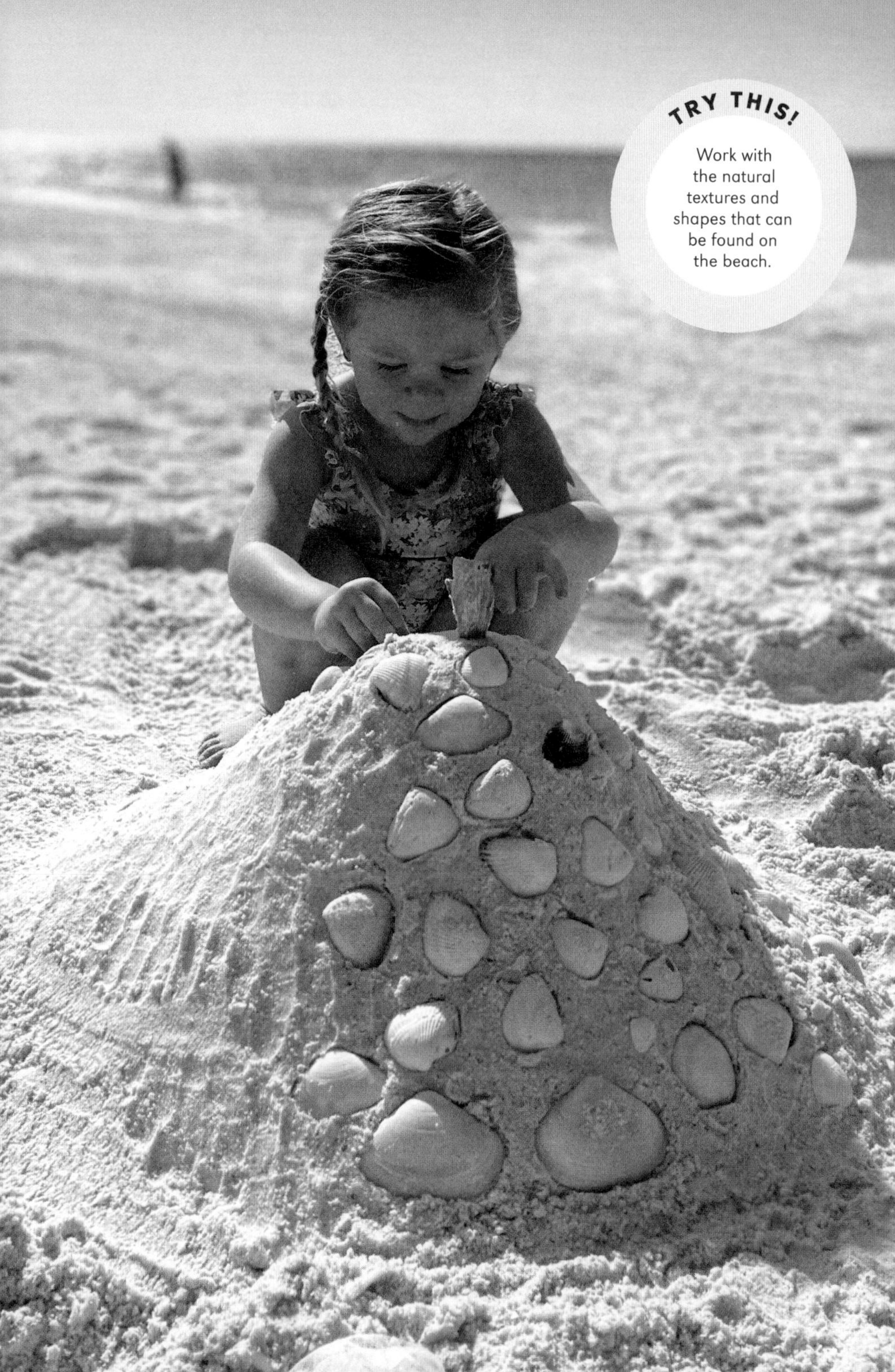

TRY THIS!

Work with the natural textures and shapes that can be found on the beach.

30 mins

GROWING CARROTS

Growing your own food opens your eyes to the incredible variety in our world. There are many types of carrots beyond the standard orange ones at the store. Choose from varieties like Lunar White, Purple Dragon, Atomic Red, Solar Yellow, and Little Fingers. By planting different colored carrots, you could create a rainbow salad.

SUPPLIES

- Soil
- Shovel
- Carrot seeds
- Water

INSTRUCTIONS

1. Carrots are a root vegetable. They grow straight down, so they need loose soil. Loosen up a patch of soil with a shovel and make sure it's free of any rocks or stones. Always wash your hands after touching soil.
2. Make a quarter-inch (0.5cm) deep trench in your soil and drop a few carrots seeds every 3 inches (8cm). Cover the seeds lightly with soil. Keep the area well watered until harvest.
3. Within a few weeks, you'll start to see the tops sprouting. Once they're about 4 inches (10cm) tall, you will need to thin out the plants, which means pulling some out if they are too close together. Grasp the carrot top right at the soil level and pull straight up so as not to disturb the other growing carrots. Removing a few will help the others thrive.
4. When it's time to harvest, moisten the soil first so the carrots are easier to pull out. Carrots will taste best after the first frost because the cold weather sweetens their flavor.

EXTRA TIME

- Some plants help loosen up the soil. Plant **lettuces** by your carrots and they will create an **underground path** for your carrots to grow along.

MORE IDEAS

- Carefully slice your carrots diagonally in 2-inch (5cm) chunks. Mix them with a dollop of **olive oil** and a **sprinkle of salt** and ask an adult to help you bake them at 400°F (200°C) for about 20 minutes or until **lightly browned**.

TRY THIS!

Guess what each carrot will look like as you pull it out of the ground.

WATER PLAY

When the heat of summer sets in, there's nothing quite like playing with water. It can cool you down, but it also provides a beautiful calmness and allows for full sensory exploration.

THE GOOD OLD HOSE

Spray or get sprayed! When it's hot outside, the simple garden hose can provide an immediate cool down, and, depending on how you put your thumb over the nozzle, you can make it spray in all kinds of ways.

Play **water limbo** with a long, high stream of water or play water **freeze tag**.

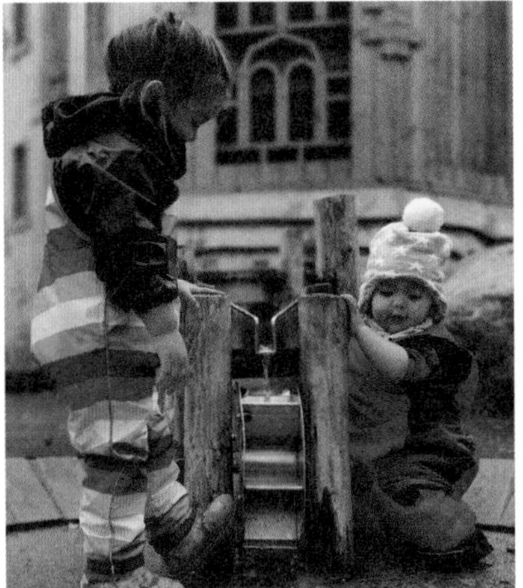

WATER PUMPS

Pumping water and funneling it in different ways is a thrilling pastime for kids and offers endless hours of open-ended entertainment. As kids transport, scoop, pour, and run their hands through the water, they can unwind and relax.

You can make your own water **play equipment** with bits of PVC piping.

WATER SLIDE

Set up a slide with plastic sheeting (and adult supervision), add water and possibly a little soap, and get ready to glide! This whole body movement will cool you off on a scorching day.

Keep the hose on and running for **maximum** slipperiness.

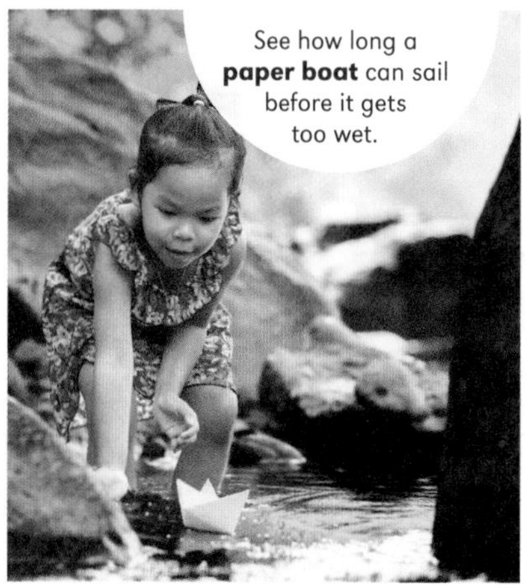

See how long a **paper boat** can sail before it gets too wet.

BOATING

Make your own boat and see whether it floats and stays upright. Play around with which shapes and materials work best. Give your boat sails and try moving it by blowing. Add toy people and race boats with friends.

Use **spray bottles** to clean off the rocks and shells in your nature collection.

SPRAY BOTTLES

Spraying water enables you to see the immediate effects of something getting wet and often you feel the mist, too. Spray bottles help you strengthen your hand muscles. Use them to water plants, wash off sidewalk chalk, or cool off.

MORE IDEAS

- Experiment with a spray bottle of ice water and one with warm water. See which **temperature** is your favorite to play with. Can you explain why?

WAVE JUMPING

Wave jumping is all about anticipation and timing. There's so much delight in jumping over waves and watching them roll over and over again. It's lots of fun, but water can be dangerous so go near the sea only with adult supervision.

Nature is filled with **natural rhythms** such as the tides, the waves, and the seasons.

15–30 mins

SHEET PAINTING

Painting is a timeless activity for both adults and children alike. While painting on a small piece of paper or canvas certainly is fun, you can really let your creativity shine on a large surface such as a sheet of plastic, like an old shower curtain. Get as messy as you like, all while enjoying nature at the same time!

SUPPLIES

- Tape, thumb tacks, or pins
- Old shower curtain or other large sheet of plastic
- Art smock
- Acrylic paint
- Plastic cups or paper plates for paint
- Paintbrushes of varying sizes

INSTRUCTIONS

1. If you want to, you can plan out your painting on paper first. Think about how the backdrop to your clear sheet will show behind your image and incorporate it into your design.
2. Ask an adult to hang up your large sheet of plastic up outside at your painting height. They could use tape, thumb tacks, or pins.
3. Put on clothes that you don't mind getting paint on or cover up with an art smock.
4. Start bringing your artistic vision to life with acrylic paint—it's important to use this sort of paint rather than any other type.
5. Admire your creation from a distance. How does it interact with the background?

Protect any important surface with a **drop cloth**.

MORE IDEAS

- Pick something you see outside—a **bird**, a particular **tree**, a **squirrel**—and incorporate it into your painting.
- Add some **white paint** to all your colors to brighten them up.

TRY THIS!

Tack your sheet between two trees to make a natural easel for your extra large canvas.

3–4 hrs

BEANSTALK HIDEOUT

Throughout history, people have needed hideouts. They give protection from the weather as well as somewhere to sneak off to, like Robin Hood running away from the Sheriff of Nottingham. An especially fun natural hideout is a tepee of intertwining beanstalks.

SUPPLIES

- Beans: any pole bean or runner bean (not bush bean varieties)
- Strong string
- About 5 tomato stakes, ideally 8 feet (2.5 m) tall
- Scissors

INSTRUCTIONS

1. You don't need a big space to grow beans. A small garden or allotment is enough. If you have a balcony, you could plant tall sunflowers in pots.
2. To make your frame, place the stakes in the ground in a circle. Ask an adult (or two) to reach up and gather the tops so they touch in a tepee shape, and then tie string around the stakes so the structure is secure.
3. You can plant your beans directly into the ground, but wait until after the last frost. Plant 10 to 12 near each stake, then water them over time. If you mix varieties, at the end of the season, when you shell the beans, it's thrilling to discover what colors and shapes are inside!
4. As the beans grow, gently wrap the tendrils around the poles so they grow upward. They will take 10 to 12 weeks to grow to maturity.
5. Once they are all filled in, enjoy your amazing secluded hideout!

TIP

- Look online for the average **frost dates** in your area. The growing season for beans runs from the last frost until 10 weeks before the first frost.

Sunflowers also make good hideouts. Can you spot someone?

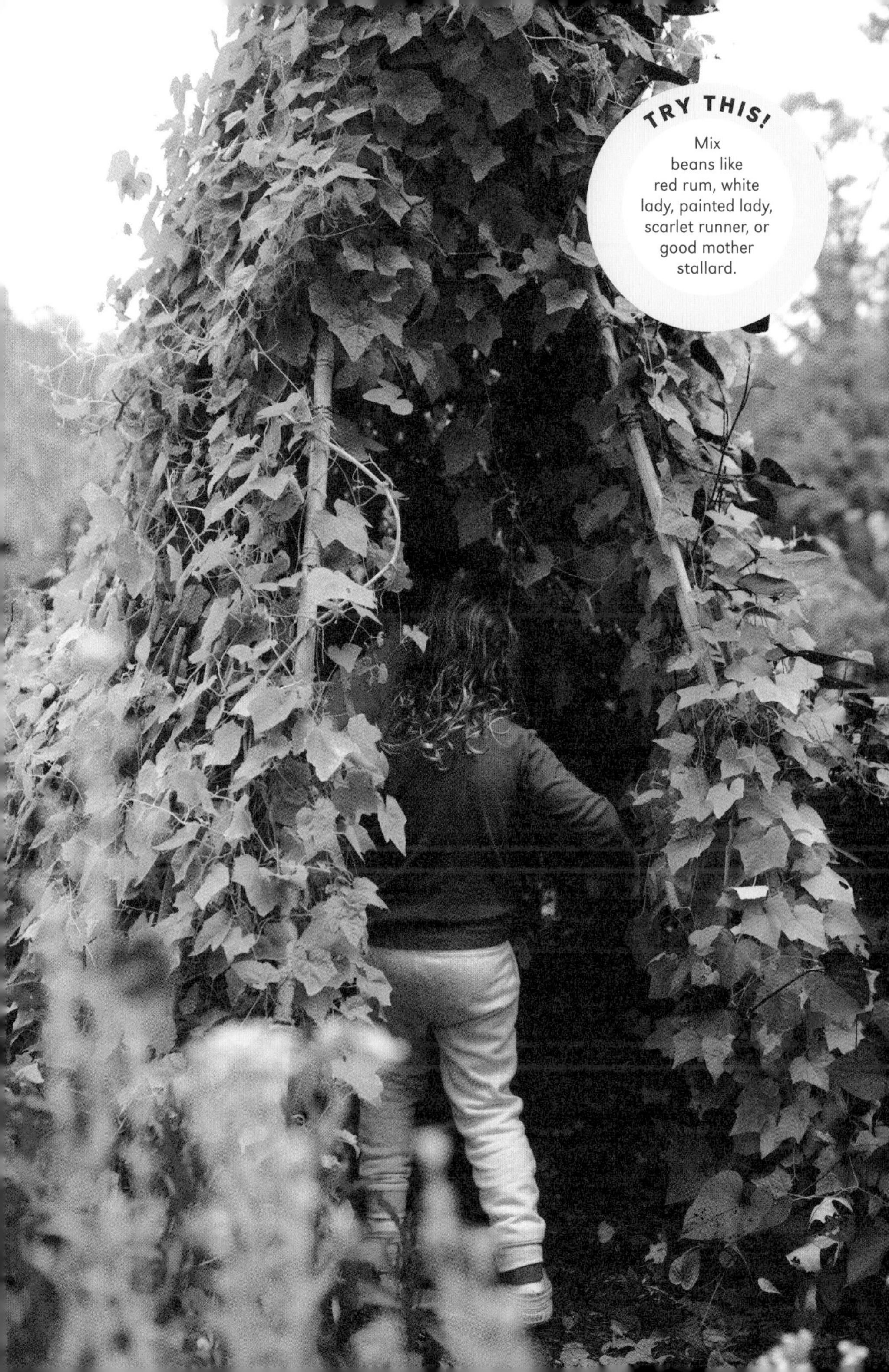

TRY THIS!

Mix beans like red rum, white lady, painted lady, scarlet runner, or good mother stallard.

SUMMER SLEDDING

Summer sledding is becoming an increasingly popular activity. It provides the thrill of sledding without the chill of winter. It can be done in the grass or the sand with only a few objects on hand.

DUNE SLEDDING

This activity is enjoyed by kids and adults alike. Sled only on dry dunes as wet dunes can be more dangerous. The sand can get very hot in the sun, so this is best in the morning or evening. Bring plenty of water for all those long walks back to the top!

⚠ SAFETY FIRST

- Consider a **scarf** to cover your nose and mouth and **goggles**.
- **Knee and elbow pads** protect from hot sand.
- Check for any **debris**.

If you don't have enough momentum, maybe someone will pull you.

SANDBOARDING

Designed specifically for sand, sandboards are made of hardwood and a laminate, and they combine well with special sandboarding wax to create a thrilling ride. Plastic and foam sleds work fine, too, but you can add wax for a smoother ride.

Most **sleds** used on snow should work for sand, but you might need to add wax.

GRASS SLEDDING

A big piece of cardboard and a slope of grass is a good alternative if you don't have sand nearby. Take a seat on your cardboard and move forward slowly until you gain some momentum or have someone give you a gentle push.

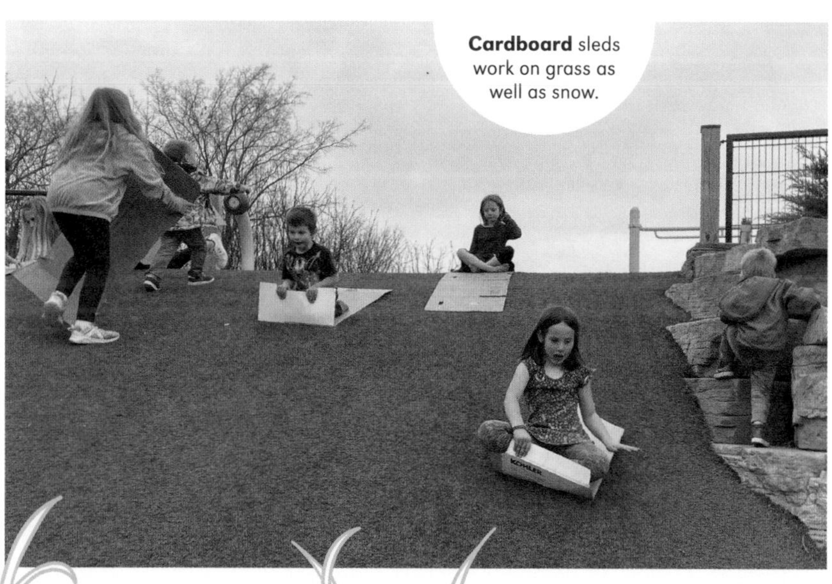

Cardboard sleds work on grass as well as snow.

REPTILES

Nature trails are perfect places to look for reptiles and learn all about their habitats, diets, and daily rhythms. Keep a log of any reptiles you find on your adventures, and always wash your hands after handling any creatures.

TORTOISES

Tortoises live exclusively on land and use water only for drinking and bathing, unlike turtles who spend much of their life in or near water. If you happen upon a group of tortoises, it is called a "creep." These reptiles live a very long time, sometimes even 150 years.

Tortoise **shells** have a more rounded shape than turtles.

TURTLES

Oceans, rivers, lakes, and ponds are what turtles call home. Their feet are webbed (unlike tortoise toes, which are fused together like an elephant's foot). This allows them to easily move through the water. Turtles also have flatter shells than tortoises so can move through the water in a more streamlined way.

Often you can spot the small head of a turtle **bobbing** in the water.

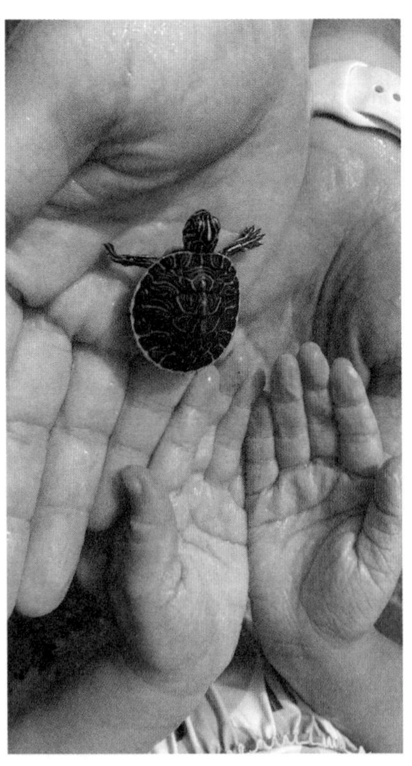

FUN FACT

- In places with warmer climates, tortoises' shells tend to be lighter in color, whereas in colder climates, they tend to be darker.

Garter snakes are harmless to us and they help by eating slugs.

SNAKES

To some people, snakes are fascinating, while to others they are terrifying. Most snake encounters are harmless, but you need to take precautions if you're in an area with venomous snakes. Snakes have no eyelids and they smell with their tongues!

⚠ SAFETY FIRST

- If there are **venomous** snakes in your area, stay out of long grass. Plan ahead and know who to contact in an emergency.
- Never prod snakes with **sticks**.

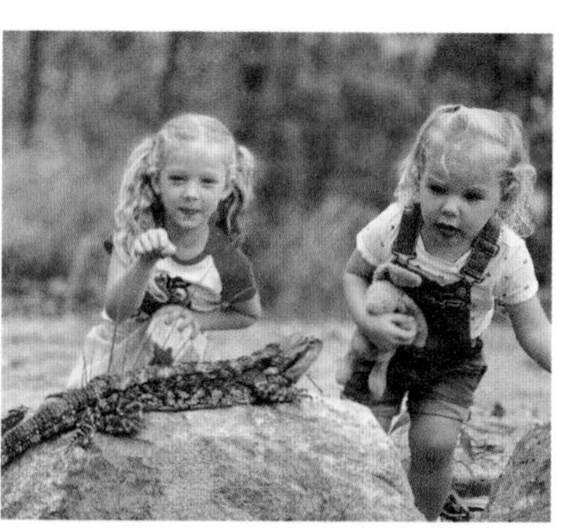

BEARDED DRAGON LIZARD

Bearded dragon lizards are not really dragons, though they do look quite dragonlike. They spend a good deal of their time in bushes and trees, and half of their length is made up of their tail. The lizards bob their heads at each other and sometimes even wave!

This **bearded dragon lizard** lives in Queensland, Australia.

TRY THIS!
Fly away to a distant magical land on a make-believe dragon.

CHALK SCENES

1–3 hrs

Create sidewalk scenes that you can actually be a part of! Dive into the depths of your creativity and spend some time in the fresh air creating elaborate works of art made out of chalk. These pictures will make you the talk of your neighborhood and it will be fun to pose with them and take pictures once you are finished.

SUPPLIES

- Sidewalk chalk, many colors
- Camera

INSTRUCTIONS

1. Grab your chalk and start creating a scene somewhere safe and away from traffic. Draw something you can be a part of by laying down amidst it. Here are some ideas to get you started:
   - **A bunch of brightly colored balloons**—lay underneath them and pretend to be holding the strings as you float away.
   - **A lightsaber**—lay below it and grasp it like you're ready to conquer your enemies.
   - **A rainy day**—lay down below the clouds and raindrops and hold the umbrella with one of your hands.
   - **Birthday cake**—add candles for your age and then lay next to it and pretend to blow them out.
   - **A cityscape**—include cars and trucks for you to drive.
2. Once you're in position, ask someone to take a photo of you in the scene.

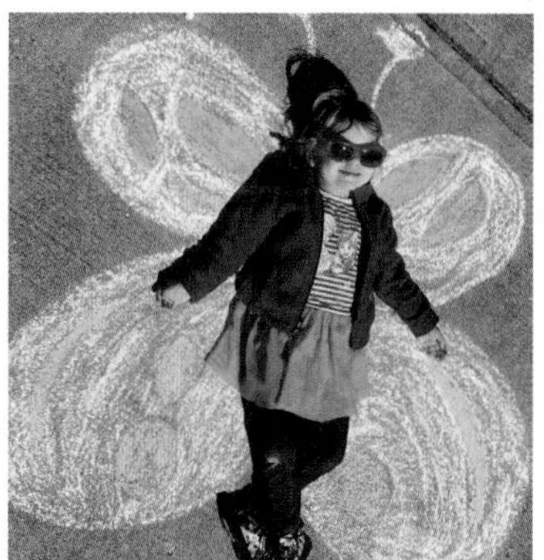

Sprout a pair of your very own **butterfly wings**.

MORE IDEAS

- Invite some friends over and have a sidewalk **chalk contest**! See how realistic you can make photos look.
- Make a scene for several people at once—like three people on **a row of swings**.
- Create a scene for **someone else** to step inside of.

SAND BURYING

30 mins

There's something very compelling and satisfying about covering part of your body in warm sand. When any of your limbs are buried, it helps develop your proprioceptive sense—the sense that tells you where your body is in space. But go carefully because not everybody likes the sensation of sand on top of them.

SUPPLIES

- Sand
- Shovels

INSTRUCTIONS

1. Start small! Bury just one part of your body like a hand or a foot and see how it feels. Is it easy to free yourself? Scoop sand onto your arms or legs and then watch as you escape the blanket of sand.
2. If you like the feeling of being covered in sand then bury a little bit more. See how it feels to have both legs buried. Is it warm? Cold?
3. Have a friend or family member cover your entire body with sand up to your neck. Put your arms straight out to the side or down at your sides. Consider keeping your eyes closed so that no sand flings into your eyes. If your neck's uncomfortable, ask someone to build you a sand pillow to rest your head on while you're buried.
4. If you're not keen on being buried under sand, that's okay. Instead, ask someone to draw around you with a stick and then make the outline 3-D by piling on sand. Add natural materials to make facial features.

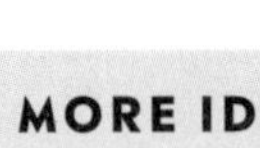

SAFETY FIRST

- Don't bury yourself or anyone else too deep or the **weight** of the sand could be too heavy.
- Instead of digging a hole, it's **safer** to cover yourself in sand.
- Be careful to keep sand out of **eyes**.

MORE IDEAS

- Make a **sand family** by tracing the outlines of your friends and family members at the beach.
- Sculpt the sand covering someone into a shape like a mermaid's tail, a **whale's tail**, or robotic parts for a **cyborg** body.

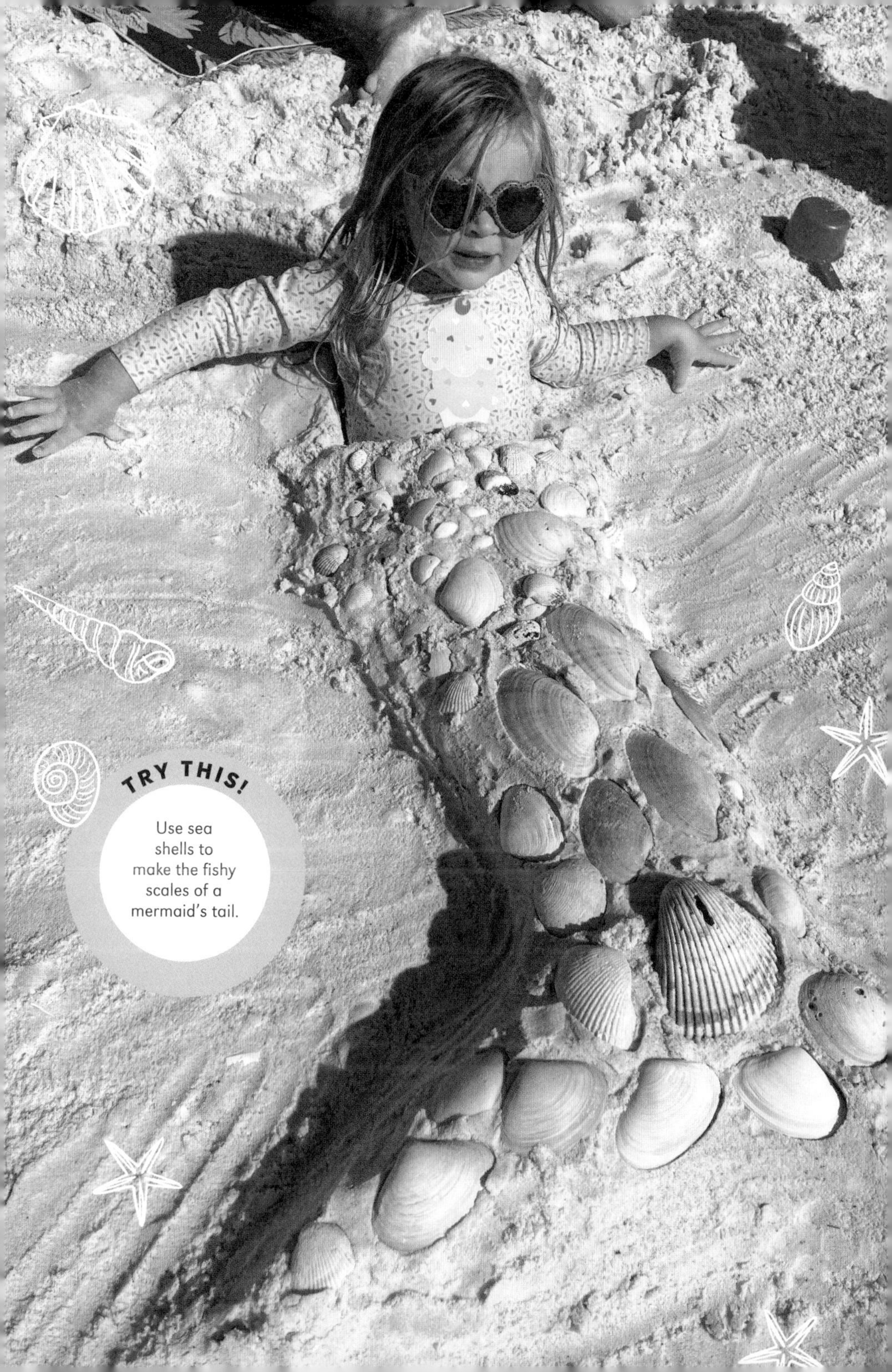
TRY THIS!
Use sea shells to make the fishy scales of a mermaid's tail.

CREEKING

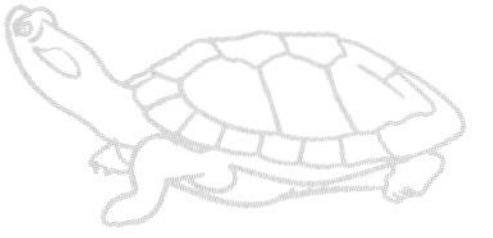

Creeking is exploring, wading through, or playing in shallow creek beds and streams. There are so many things to do and see in and around a creek, but go near water, even shallow water, only with adult supervision.

WADING

Wading is walking through water instead of swimming, and sometimes it's a necessity as you navigate a creek. Go carefully as you're bound to come across deeper sections that you'll be forced to wade through, but that's part of the fun!

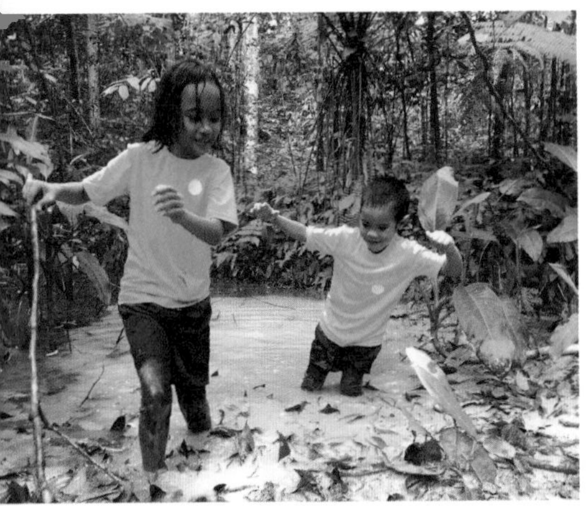

Using a long stick to **test the depth** of the water is a good idea.

NETS

Bringing a net to a creek is always a good idea. You could see all sort of critters—frogs, snails, salamanders, and fish. Catching them helps you study them more closely—just make sure you're gentle with them and you put them back.

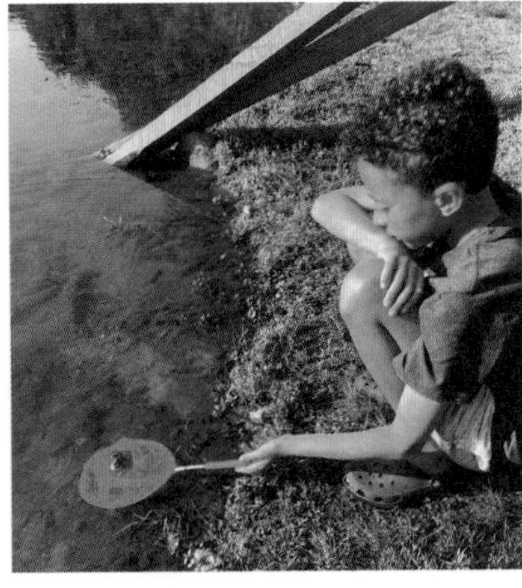

Use nets very **gently** so as not to injure delicate creatures like frogs.

CLOSE ANALYSIS

Documenting the treasures and creatures you find while creeking adds to the fun. Did you find a turtle? Write down what kind it was, its colors, and how big it was. See a snail? Look at it through a microscope to study its shell.

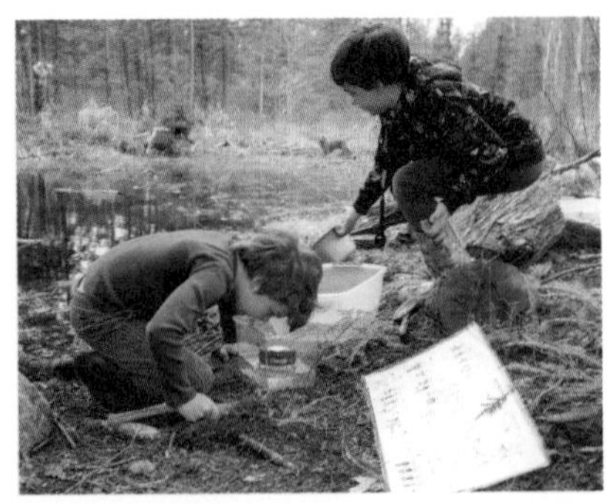

Keep the critters **in water** while you study them under a microscope.

TIP

- Depending on how deep and cold the creek is, a good pair of **rubber rain boots** can help extend your time in the creek by keeping feet dry.

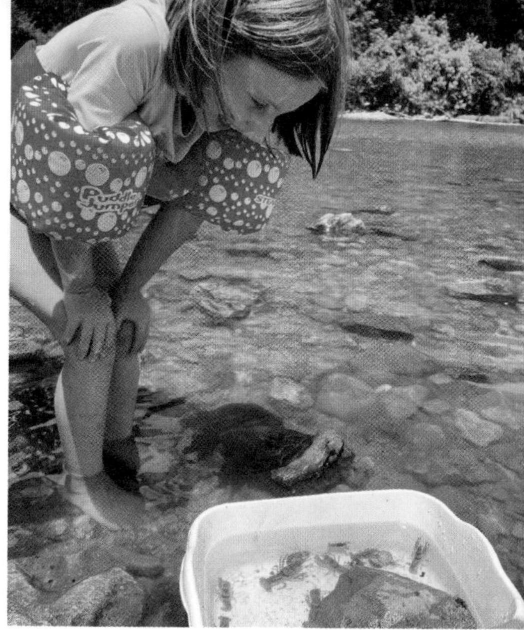

Bring along old plastic bins to place your **fresh catches** in.

TIDE POOLING

If you live near the ocean, you might know about the tides that come in and out every single day. Find an area of the shore with rock outcroppings and look for creatures that have been stuck in the pools that form as the tide goes out.

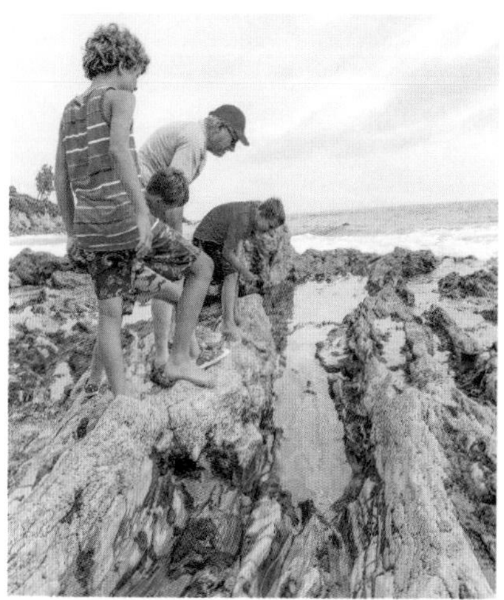

Make sure you know when the **tide is coming in** so you don't get stuck!

CRABBING

Crabs and crayfish can pinch you, if you're not careful! But that shouldn't stop you from trying to catch them. A special crab net with some bait makes it easier. Collect crabs in a bucket of water and then transfer them back in the net.

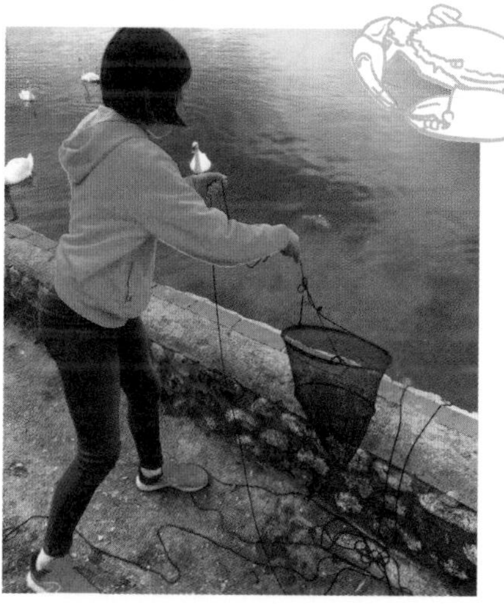

Clip **bait** to the bottom of a crab net—bits of meat or fish work well.

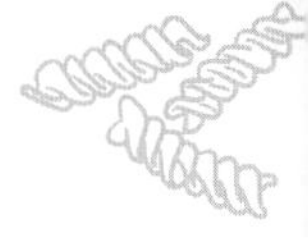

30–60 mins

SENSORY BIN

A sensory bin might just seem like a container filled with stuff, but it's so much more than that! It's an opportunity to learn through hands-on play. You can learn how to pour, how to measure, what different materials feel like, and how to patiently look for certain objects hidden within. They also help develop fine motor skills.

SUPPLIES

- Towel
- Container
- Dry rice, pasta, or even aquarium rocks
- Measuring cups (optional)
- Items of your choosing—alphabet letters, miniature toys, natural items you find, etc.
- Chopsticks or tweezers (optional)

INSTRUCTIONS

1. Place a towel under the container to easily collect the inevitable mess.
2. Add your base filler to the container—colorful aquarium rocks are a great choice, but so is dry rice or pasta.
3. Select which items you want to place on and in the base layer.
4. Dig into the sensory bin. Enjoy the freedom and exploration.
5. Play games; for example, see who can find the most mini dinosaurs or count the most pieces of wagon wheel pasta.
6. Over time, change out the contents once the newness fades.

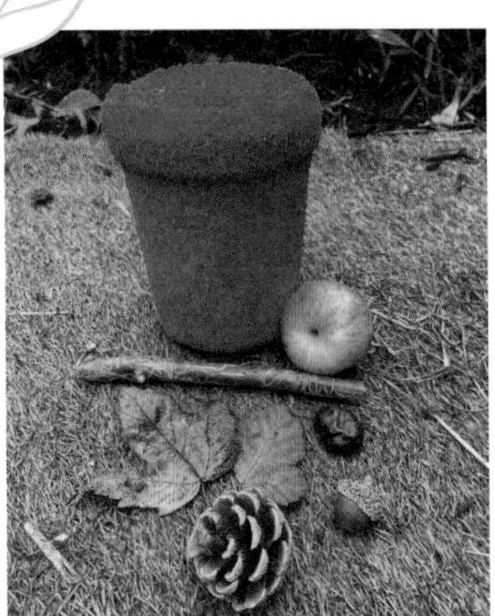

Nature provides a whole variety of items that **feel** very different to the touch.

MORE IDEAS

- A **feely tub** is an alternative sensory experiment, only this time you use a small container with a lid or bag with a variety of items inside. Slowly slide the lid over and allow someone to place their hand inside the feely tub and guess what they are touching.

TRY THIS!
Use tweezers to build hand strength for writing.

HAMMOCKS

Did you know that hammocks have been around for more than 1,000 years? These days, they're generally used for leisure and just relaxing, though some people still use them to sleep up off the ground when camping.

OUTDOOR BUNK BEDS

Instead of hanging just one hammock between two trees, hang two or more, stacked on top of each other for outdoor bunk beds. Leave enough space between them so you're not hitting the ones below. Once you're set up, invite friends to hang and relax with you!

Always make sure hammocks are **very secure**, but especially if there's another one underneath.

READING

Bringing nature inside is always fun, but taking inside things, like reading, outside is another option. Grab your favorite book, head on out to the hammock, and lay back and enjoy your story under the open sky, swaying in ultimate comfort.

There isn't much better than **being read to** while swinging in a hammock.

EXTRA TIME

- If you have a **tarp**, string it in the trees above your hammock to keep off any possible rain.
- You could even **sleep outside** overnight in your hammock!

SNUGGLING UP

Hammocks aren't just for the summer. Even when it's cold, you can still bundle up in warm clothes, snag a blanket, and head outside with a sibling or friend to snuggle up with. Hammocks keep you warmer than lying on the ground.

Double hammocks are better for sharing with a friend!

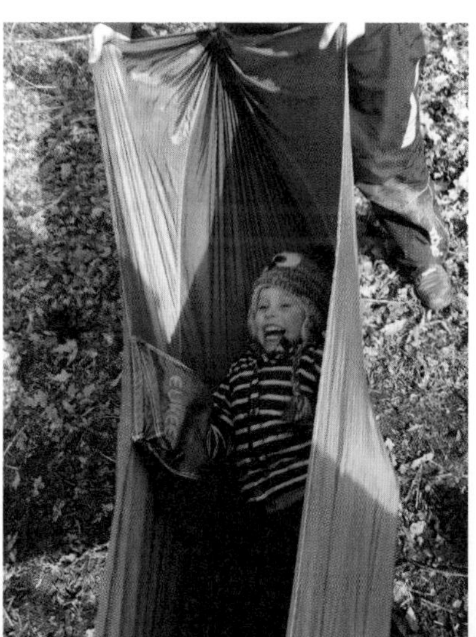

SWINGING

Hammocks are versatile! If they have high sides, they can be used as a giant swing. Lay down inside a hammock that is attached to trees or something secure, and have an adult pull up the sides of one end and swing the whole thing back and forth. Careful not to fall out!

Hammock swinging is safe only when it's really **securely** attached.

FLOWER ART

30–60 mins

Art comes in all shapes, sizes, and forms—oil paintings, sculptures, or wonderful symphonies. The common thread between artists is a desire to be creative, and you can do that with flower art. Flowers are already beautiful, but you can rearrange them in ways nobody has ever seen before so your flower art will be one of a kind!

SUPPLIES

- Fresh or dried flowers and leaves
- Cardboard or paper (optional)
- Glue (optional)
- Paint, pens, or crayons (optional)

INSTRUCTIONS

1. Lay the flowers, petals, and leaves out in a way that is pleasing and beautiful to you. Your display could be very symmetrical or wild and messy. It could be something temporary on the ground, in your driveway, or in your home, or you could stick it onto a base.
2. Once you're happy with the placement, glue your flowers in place if you're using a base. Or you could poke holes in thick cardboard and thread the flower stems through so they're secure.
3. Enhance your flowers by drawing your own colorful details around them.
4. If your art has fresh flowers, take a photo before it wilts.
5. If you used dried or pressed flowers, your creation will be more permanent so you can hang it up or give it away as a gift to a loved one.

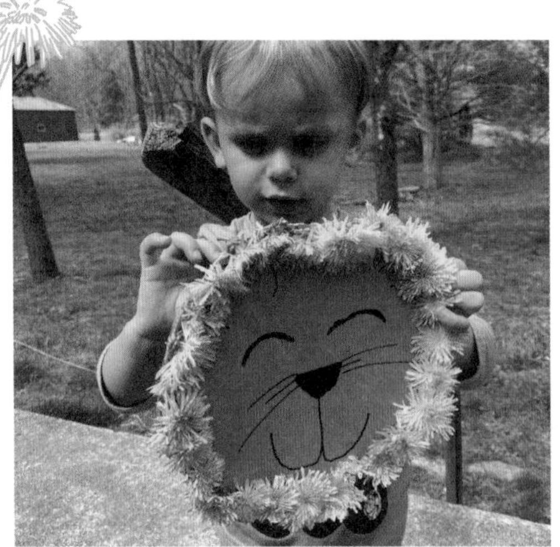

Think about what else the flowers **look like**—for example, the furry mane of a lion.

MORE IDEAS

- Use single petals or **whole sprigs**, leaves and all, for your pictures.
- Make the most of nature's stunning **color palette** to create vibrant displays.

TRY THIS!

Use flowers as flowers like these dandelions—or use flowers to be something else!

TEA PARTY TIME

Tea parties can be fun indoors or out, but if you take yours outside, underneath the sky, you can add bits of nature and feel free to make a little bit more of a mess as you stretch your imagination.

FURRY FRIENDS

Dolls and stuffed animals love to join in with outdoor tea parties. Set the table for them with place settings and have a spot for them to sit. Have a small pitcher so you can pour them a favorite drink like water, juice, lemonade, or milk.

EXTRA TIME

- Have a **basket** ready to collect sticks, pine cones, pretty stones, shells, and flower petals for natural table decor.

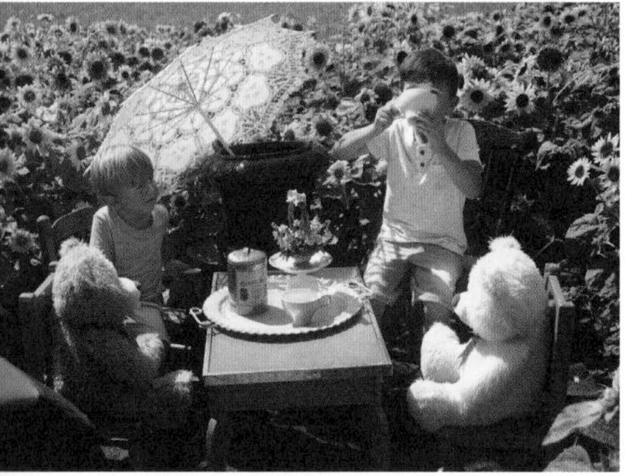

A **flower patch** makes a beautiful backdrop for a tea party

MORE IDEAS

- Make each of your visitors a unique **place setting**.
- Add nonedibles to your pretend guests' dishes, such as **sand seasoning** or **shell sprinkles**.

CELEBRATE!

Set up your tea party as a celebration for a birthday, graduation, or perhaps a milestone in your 1000 Hours Outside journey! A pretty tablecloth and a few festive hats are all you need to make it feel like a special occasion.

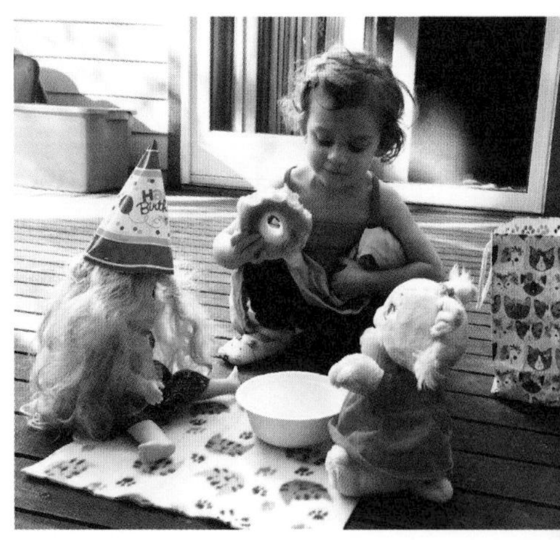

Chairs are optional—why not spread your tea party out on a **blanket** on the ground?

FOREST FURNITURE

Tree stumps make practical and natural outdoor furniture. These characterful tables and chairs are perfect for a tea party. You could add cushions to the chairs, and use smaller wood slices as pretend plates or place settings.

Serve either **pretend or real food** on your forest furniture.

AFTERNOON TEA

All you need is a teapot, a few teacups, and a friend to get started! If you set your cups on a pretty piece of fabric as a tablecloth, you will feel like royalty! Add a small tray of snacks and you'll have a delightful time together.

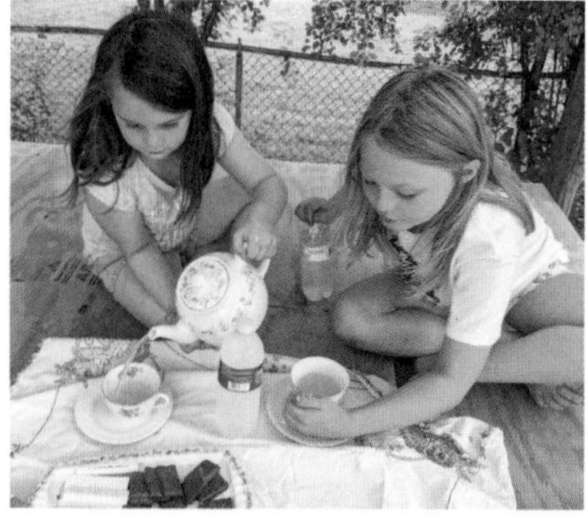

If you don't like tea, fill your **teapot** with something else like milk or juice.

TEA PARTY PICNIC

If you're looking to serve a larger meal outdoors, you can set out a tea party picnic. Include lots of colorful fruits and vegetables as well as dainty tea-party sandwiches, and a decadent dessert or two like cookies or cake.

Nature provides a **colorful** and healthy snack table.

SPLATTER PAINTING

15–45 mins

Rembrandt, Matisse, da Vinci are all artists who meticulously and painstakingly painted their subjects and scenes with great care. But that's not what this activity is all about! Splatter painting is not about precision or accuracy, but about being wild and free and having no limitations on what you do with paint.

SUPPLIES

- Paper, canvas, or plastic sheeting
- Runny paint—liquid watercolor or watered-down tempera or acrylic paint
- Cups for paint
- Paintbrushes or spoons
- Sticks (optional)
- Art smock
- Drop cloth (optional)

INSTRUCTIONS

1. It's highly recommended to do this outside. If you're using a surface that needs protecting from paint, lay a drop cloth under your paper. It's also a good idea to protect your clothes with an art smock.
2. Fill cups with different paint colors.
3. Dip a paintbrush or spoon into the paint and then fling it at your paper.
4. Try splattering paint super close to the canvas and also far away. What difference does it make to the paint drop size?
5. Experiment with wrist flicks, full arm motions, circular, and up and down motions.

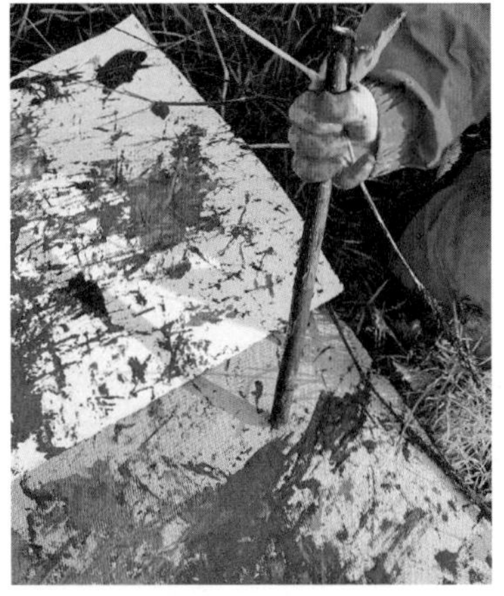

Splatter painting is about making a mess that is **fun**, **colorful**, and **unique**!

EXTRA TIME

- Once your splattered paint is dry, use the colorful paper to make **garlands** or a **pennant** by cutting triangles or flag shapes, stringing them together, and then hanging them on your wall.
- If you use a drop cloth, use the **colorful fabric** to drape over your stick fort.

TRY THIS!
Use sticks to scratch decorations in the paint.

BEACH TOURNAMENT

There are so many fun activities to do at the beach. Why not hold a tournament of beach games and sports? The winner of each event gets a point, and the player with the most points at the end wins!

LONG JUMP

Draw a line in the sand and take turns to see who can jump the furthest. Mark each contestant's landing spot with another line in the sand so you can compare all the distances. Try taking a long run up and then compare it with a standing long jump.

Sand is perfect for **landing**—just like at a real athletics track.

HANGMAN

To play Hangman, one person thinks of a word and draws a line for each of its letters. Everyone guesses letters, and every time they're wrong, a line is added to the picture of a hangman. The race is on to guess what the word is before the hangman picture is complete.

Draw in the sand with your fingers, stones, sticks—or whatever you find on the beach.

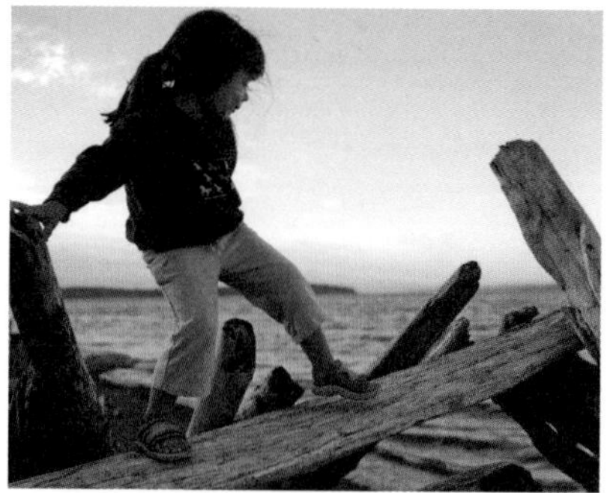

OBSTACLE COURSE

Look around the beach for driftwood to be part of your obstacle course. Also lay out beach toys and beach chairs, etc. Include things to jump over and to run around, and add mini-challenges to complete around the course.

Use what's **already** on the beach, but add new rules about what to do with it.

PEBBLE DARTS

Draw a circular bullseye target in the sand, with two or three bigger rings around it. Draw a straight line for everyone to stand behind, an agreed distance away. Gather three pebbles or shells each, and see who can toss their "dart" closest to the bullseye.

Use a different type of **"dart"** for each player so you remember whose is whose.

MORE IDEAS

- Play a best of 7 **Tic-Tac-Toe** match (see page 210).
- Play **Hopscotch** (see page 126). Hot sand makes this game extra challenging!

WATER CARRYING

Create a challenge where each player or team must fill buckets of water and carry them up the beach without spilling them to fill another container. It's a game of both going quickly and going carefully!

The more water you **spill**, the more trips you'll have to make!

MUD POOL

1–2 hrs

There are many things you can do with a small kiddie pool besides just filling it with water. You can turn one into a small garden box; you can fill it with plastic balls to play in; or you can make it into a mud pool. This avoids having a permanent mud pit in your yard, while still creating a fantastic sensory play experience.

SUPPLIES

- Small kiddie pool (or other large container you can fit in)
- Dirt
- Water
- Shovels
- Toys
- Goggles (optional)
- Hose (optional)
- Towels

INSTRUCTIONS

1. Fill your kiddie pool or other container with several shovelfuls of dirt. It's a good idea to have a hose and towels on hand for cleaning off afterward.
2. Add water and mix it with the dirt until you have the consistency of mud that you will enjoy the most. The more water, the more thin and slippery the mud will be.
3. Wearing a bathing suit or clothes you don't mind getting dirty, climb into the mud pool.
4. Enjoy the mud much as you would sand—dig in it, build with it, bury things in it. Feel the textures with your hands and your feet.

FUN FACT

- Beyond just being fun, playing in the mud has been shown by researchers to help children build **stronger immune systems**.

MORE IDEAS

- Bury things in the mud such as small gemstones or coins for your friends to find like **hidden treasure**. Make sure the items aren't choking hazards for the age of the kids who are digging.
- Put on some **goggles** and add to the mud with lots of extra dirt and water to make a **mud paddling pool**.

TRY THIS!

Keep the mud in one area of the pool so it's a little cleaner to play in.

EPHEMERAL ART

30 mins
–2 hrs

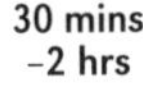

Ephemeral art is any type of creative project you make that is temporary. Art using natural materials is often made for the joy of creativity alone because we don't often have ways to preserve the artwork we make outside. Making ephemeral art is a great way to explore the different textures of our natural world.

SUPPLIES

- A large collection of natural materials such as twigs, reeds, leaves, flower petals, seed pods, stones, grasses, or branches

INSTRUCTIONS

1. Think about what to create with the materials you've collected. You could make a picture, a sculpture, or anything—even mud kitchen creations are a type of ephemeral art. Draw inspiration from different types of animals, patterns, and fun scenes you enjoy.
2. Consider where to construct your ephemeral art. You could build it around a part of nature that is permanent, such as tree roots or a large stone, or it could stand on its own on a natural background like green grass, a wooden table, or a stony path.
3. When you're about finished, look around you to see if there are any extra colors or textures that you can add as a final touch.
4. Remember that your artwork won't last forever, but it brings enjoyment during the process, and you can always take a picture when you're finished to remember what you have made.

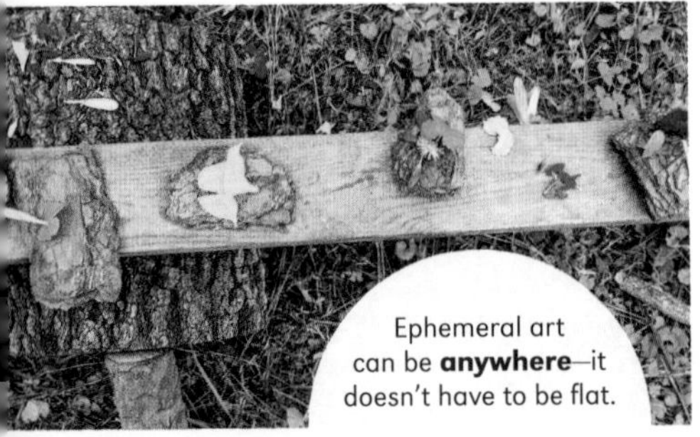

Ephemeral art can be **anywhere**—it doesn't have to be flat.

MORE IDEAS

- Make a list of **all the different types** of ephemeral art you have seen. Add to it as you come across more examples.
- Leave a work of ephemeral art for **someone else** to see and enjoy.

TRY THIS!
See how many different textures, colors, and shapes you can find.

BERRY PICKING

Have you ever eaten fresh berries that you picked, or even grew, yourself? Picking strawberries, raspberries, blueberries, blackberries, mulberries, or others, is so much fun. And the best part is you get to snack on tasty berries along the way. Take water with you to wash them in the field.

LOCAL BERRY PATCHES

Do you know where your local berry patches are? If not, start there! Then research when each berry's harvest season is. Once you know the where and the when, then it's time to gather up your favorite sun hat, a bottle of cold water, and head to the patch!

BERRY CARRIER

You'll need something to collect all your berries in. A bucket is a good choice, but if you're looking for a hands-free option, you can cut the top off of a plastic milk jug and then loop the jug handle through your belt loop. You won't have to keep picking it up to move, either.

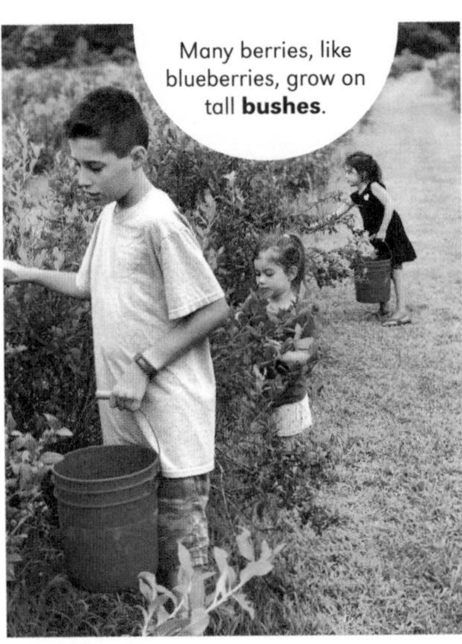

Many berries, like blueberries, grow on tall **bushes**.

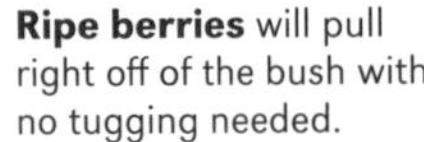

Ripe berries will pull right off of the bush with no tugging needed.

EXTRA TIME

- You can **freeze** any glut of berries. Wash them and make sure they're completely dry. To prevent them from sticking together, freeze them in a single layer on a baking sheet lined with parchment paper.

SUMMER SWEETHEARTS

You'll find strawberries low to the ground as the original plant creates "runners," which eventually root and become "daughter plants." Those daughter plants then create more runners so strawberry plants are not tall but often cover a lot of ground.

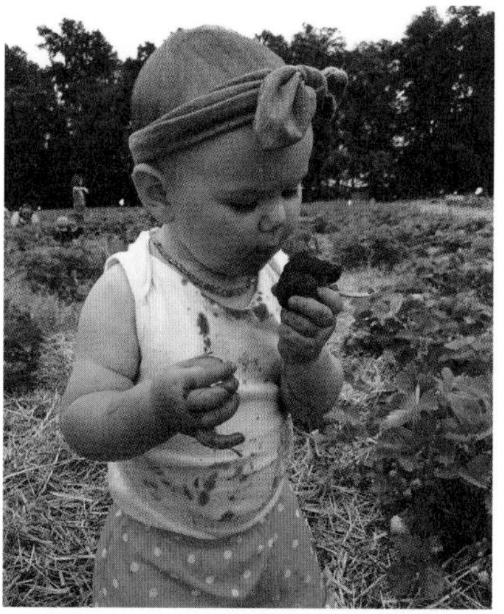

Conduct your own **taste tests** in the field.

RIPEN ON THE VINE

Strawberries stop ripening when they're removed from the vine, unlike tomatoes, which continue. Look for strawberries that are fully red with no green spots on them, but don't wait too long or they will overripen.

TIP

- Berry pick **earlier in the day** before the heat of the afternoon sets in and before the berry crop has been picked over by others.

MORE IDEAS

- Use your fresh strawberries to **bake** pies, tarts, and shortcakes.
- Mush up berries to create "**paint**" for making art.

Combine all your berries into a summer **fruit salad**.

TRY THIS!
Jars of jam make beautiful gifts.

JAM MAKING

45 mins

There are many ways to make jam and preserve the tastes and smells of summer, but this recipe has only a few ingredients and doesn't need any canning equipment. Most jam recipes use an ingredient called pectin to thicken up the jam, but you can create a tasty jam using a little extra time instead.

SUPPLIES

- 5 cups (1kg) of fresh or frozen berries
- 2½ cups (500g) of sugar
- 1½ tablespoons of lemon juice
- Medium saucepan
- Potato masher or fork
- 2 clean 16-ounce (500ml) glass jars with lids

INSTRUCTIONS

1. First of all, you need to sterilize your glass jars. You can either run them through the dishwasher or an adult can pour boiling water into them.
2. Wash your berries and remove any stems.
3. In a medium saucepan, combine the fruit, sugar, and lemon juice.
4. Ask an adult to help you cook the mixture on medium heat, stirring frequently until it comes to a rolling boil. Be careful because it will be hot.
5. Reduce the heat to a simmer. Smash up your berries with a potato masher or fork, being careful not to splash the hot mixture.
6. The fruit and sugar will take time to thicken. Start checking the jam for your desired thickness after 20 minutes. If it's still too thin, keep it simmering.
7. Remove the jam from the heat and pour it into jars. You can store them in the refrigerator for up to two weeks or in the freezer for up to three months.

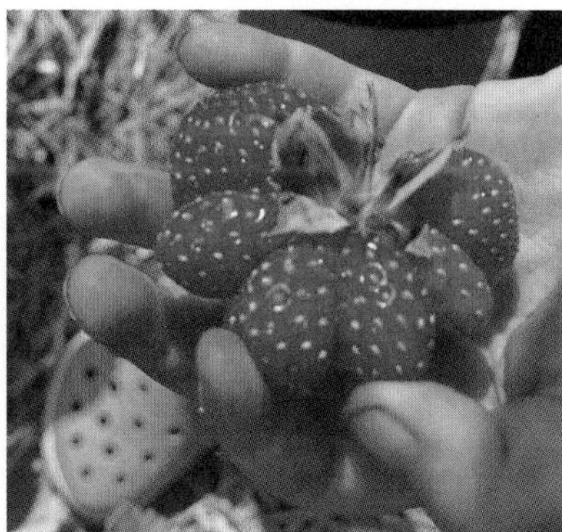

Freshly picked berries make the best jam!

MORE IDEAS

- How will you **eat your jam**? On toast or French toast? Mixed in with oatmeal or swirled with plain yogurt? On a PB & J sandwich or muffins? As an ice-cream topper? The list is endless!

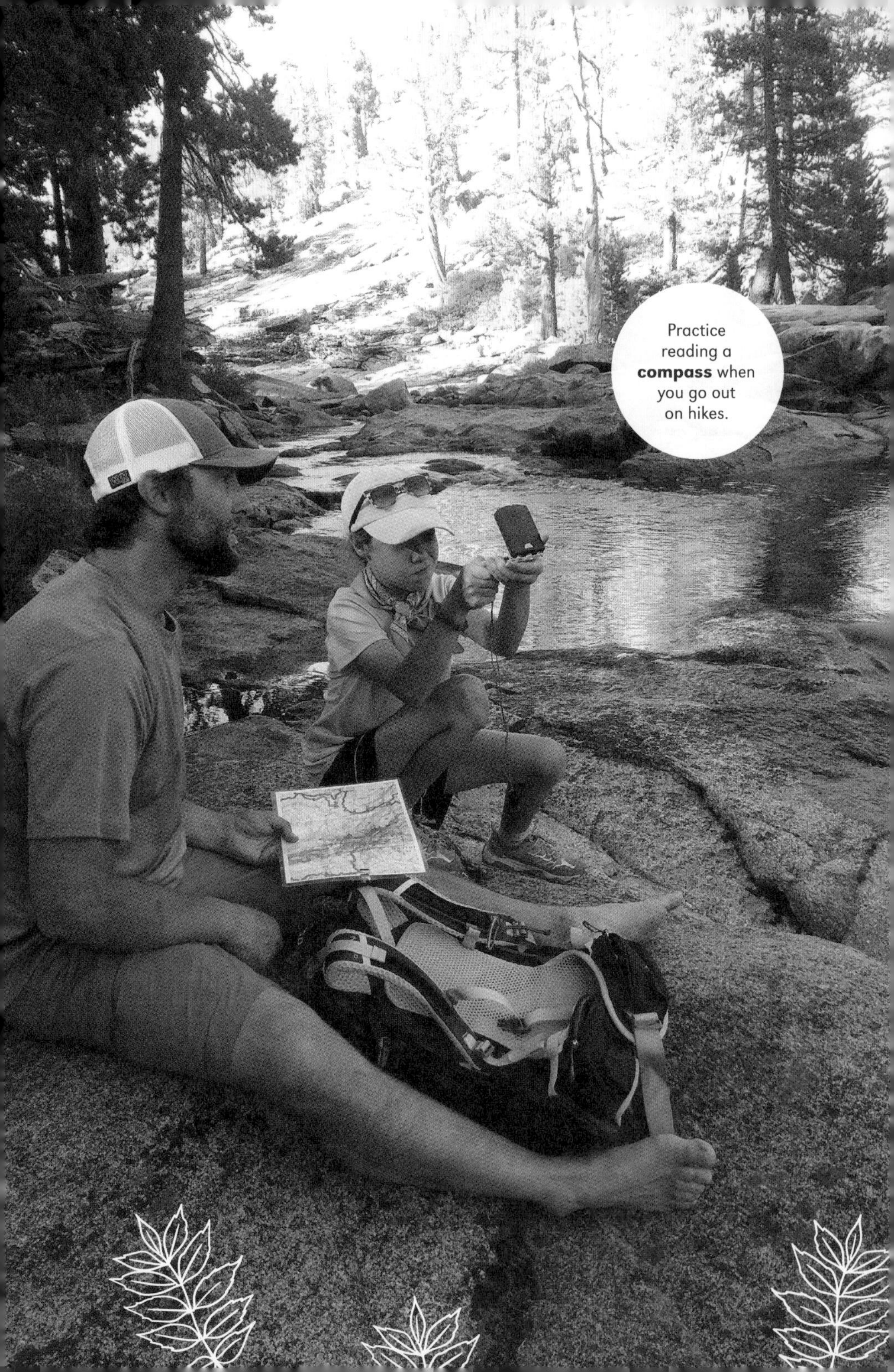

Practice reading a **compass** when you go out on hikes.

COMPASS TIME

Spending time around compasses and maps helps you learn about spatial reasoning and develop a good sense of direction, both of which are valuable for all outdoor enthusiasts.

COMPASS BASICS

The needle of a compass always points north because it lines up with the Earth's natural magnetic fields. Use a compass by holding it completely flat. If you want to go in a direction other than north, set a bearing on your compass and follow its lead, even when the terrain dips.

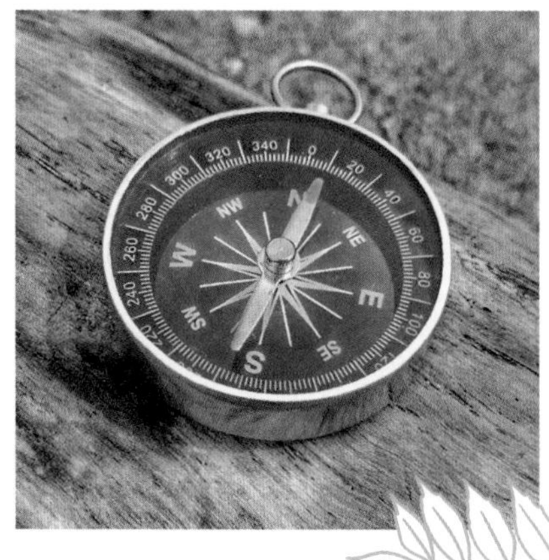

The four main points of a compass are north (N), east (E), south (S), and west (W).

MORE IDEAS

- Try **orienting** your location using other methods like GPS or the sun. You may conclude that a compass is more **reliable** as it doesn't depend on being in range of technology or the weather.

COMPASS GAME

Using a compass, play a game where one person gives instructions like, "Take five steps east" or "Go eight steps north," and the other person follows the directions to see if they can end up in a designated location.

Compare two compass readings.

60 mins

BEACH ART

Refreshing water ... sand between your toes ... the sun setting over the horizon ... nothing can make a day at the beach better. Or can it? Have you ever made beach art? Scour the shore for interesting items that have washed ashore—sea shells, driftwood, rocks, or even a crab claw or two—and use the sand as your vast canvas.

SUPPLIES

- Towel (or bucket)
- Sea shells
- Driftwood
- Colorful rocks
- Sea glass

INSTRUCTIONS

1. Grab a towel to use as a mini basket as you go off down the beach to hunt for treasures to create your art with! Look closely along the edges of the water or in the shallow water for anything that you might be able to use to create something beautiful in the sand.
2. Use your riches to make your art. It could be a rainbow, a self-portrait, a scene with a house and tree, or even a decorated magical sand castle, complete with seashell windows and a driftwood drawbridge.
3. You can't take your beach display home with you, so take a photo to remember your brilliant creation.

Even similar objects like flat shells can bring a wide array of **colors** and **details** to your art.

TIP

- When you leave, be sure to not leave anything unnatural in the sand. If you can, **collect any beach trash** you find so you can throw it away—every bit helps! But ask an adult before you pick up anything sharp or unusual.

TRY THIS!
If your items aren't secure in the sand, just add some water—no glue needed!

HEART HUNT

In many cultures, the shape of a heart holds deep meaning. Looking for shapes is a great way to train the eye to really see your environment, and having something to search boosts enthusiasm for getting outside.

HEART LEAVES

Look for Bermuda buttercup, wood sorrel, clover, or other weeds with single or double heart-shaped leaves. Morning glories have heart-shaped leaves as well as radishes, both of which can be grown in pots or in gardens.

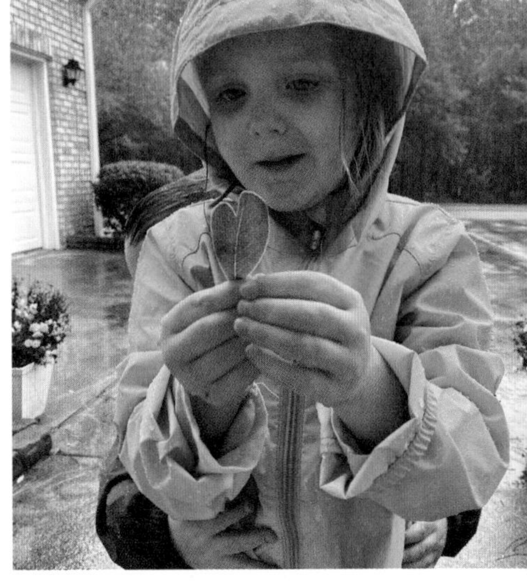

Paying close attention to **leaf shapes** helps you distinguish between plants and weeds.

HEART ROCKS

Heart-shaped rocks are often perfectly imperfect and are a treasured find. Look for tiny ones or huge ones. Keep a collection of your smaller finds in a small jar or displayed on a shelf to remind yourself of your nature adventures.

Rockhounding is the term for hunting out interesting rocks.

EXTRA TIME

- Turn your heart finds into **Valentines** for friends. Paint rocks or make leaf rubbings (see page 156).
- Give a package of **radish seeds** with a message like "Let love grow" or "Love is sprouting."

NATURE'S HEARTS

Hearts can show up anywhere in nature—the bark of a tree, the insides of a black walnut, the limbs of a cactus, or high up, in the clouds above us. Go on a heart-shaped scavenger hunt and see how many kinds of heart shapes you can find in one outing.

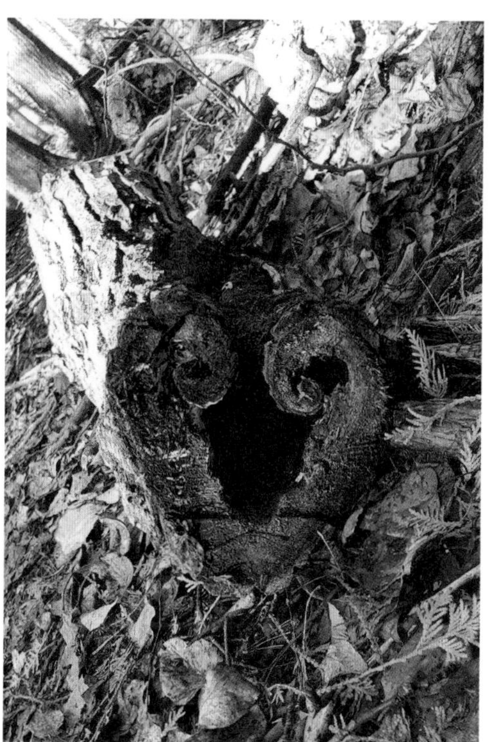

The edges of this tree have both **curled** over, making a heart shape.

MORE IDEAS

- If you see something in the shape of a heart, don't point it out right away. Play a game of **I-spy** and see whether others can find what you've spotted.

MAKE A HEART

If you went searching but didn't find any hearts, you can make your own. Using flower petals, pine needles, small pebbles or rocks, or bits of grass, form what you've found into the shape of a heart. Or use your own bodies!

TIP

- Even if a heart isn't a perfect **symmetrical** shape, it's still a fun find. Look above you, beside you, and along the ground.

Grab a **friend** and make a heart shape outdoors.

SUNFLOWER DISSECTION

Due to its sheer size, a sunflower head is a fabulous natural item to investigate. Covered with hundreds of smaller flowers, sunflowers can be taken apart, and each part can be examined and understood.

COMPOSITE FLOWERS

Sunflowers are an example of composite flowers, meaning that one is actually made up of many tiny flowers. Its center is filled with disc flowers, which produce seeds. The ray flowers look like petals around the edge and they attract pollinating insects.

As well as **golden yellow**, sunflowers come in orange, red, and even white.

LIFE CYCLE

If possible, gather sunflowers at different stages—the bud stage, when they form seeds, and fully mature. See whether you can even find a sunflower where the pollen is still covering the stigma. These different flowers will help you understand how they develop.

MORE IDEAS

- Use **tweezers** to remove seeds and develop fine motor skills.
- Add in a little math by **counting** how many seeds you are able to remove.

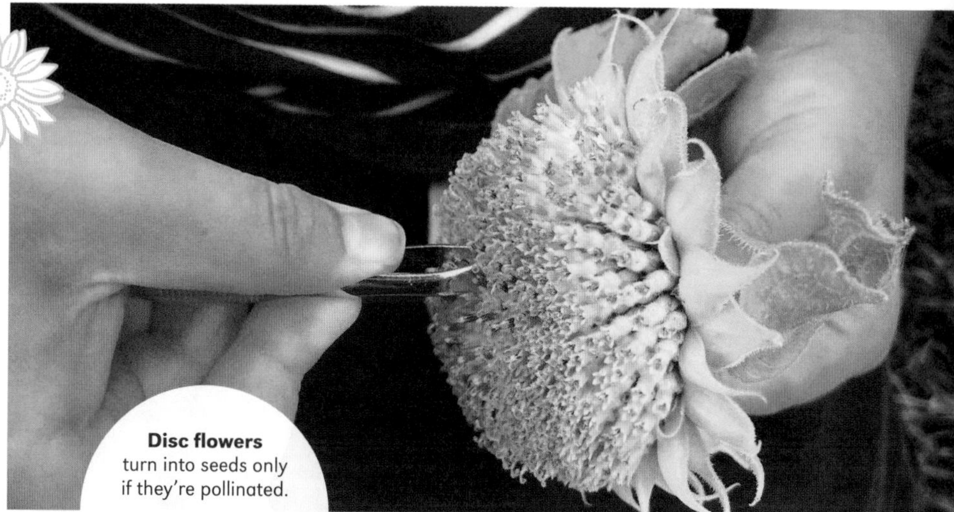

Disc flowers turn into seeds only if they're pollinated.

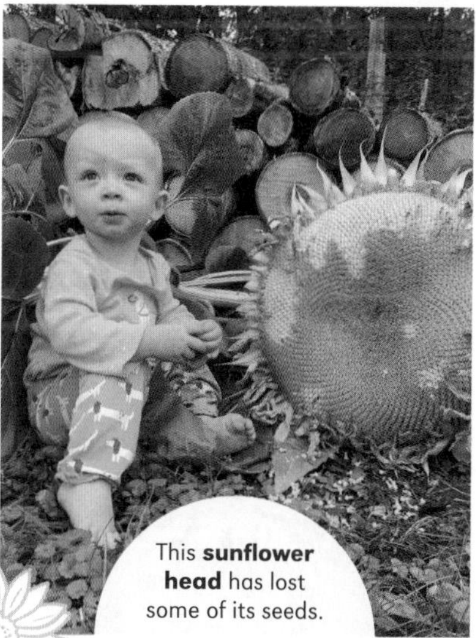

This **sunflower head** has lost some of its seeds.

FUN FACT

- Sunflowers are **heliotropic**, meaning they face east at sunrise and follow the sun. But once they've bloomed, they face only east.

MEASUREMENTS

Measure the different parts of your sunflower: its height, the diameter of the head, the length of the ray flowers, and the seeds. The largest sunflower head ever recorded was 32 inches (80cm).

TIC-TAC-TOE

20–60 mins

The classic childhood game Tic-Tac-Toe is usually played indoors with paper and a pencil, but why not add a twist by playing outdoors? There are more than 350,000 unique ways to place the pieces onto a Tic-Tac-Toe board, and there are also many ways you can construct your own outdoor board and playing pieces.

SUPPLIES

- 4 sticks approximately the same length or chalk
- 5 pieces of a natural object, say white pebbles or flowers
- 5 pieces of another natural object, say pine cones or black walnuts

INSTRUCTIONS

1. First of all, create a Tic-Tac-Toe board on the ground. It's a grid divided into three rows and three columns. You can use four sticks, draw in gravel or sand with a stick, or chalk directly onto the ground. If it's snowy, play Tic-Tac-Snow by writing in the snow.
2. One player has the first set of objects, the "Xs," and their opponent has the "Os." The Xs go first, then players take turns placing one of their pieces on one of the squares on the board.
3. The first player to get three of their pieces in a row is the winner!
4. If that seems too easy, make two or even three Tic-Tac-Toe boards and play them all at the same time!

FUN FACTS

- Tic-Tac-Toe is also known as "Xs and Os" and "**Naughts and Crosses**."
- The game dates back more than a thousand years. In **ancient Rome**, it was called "Terni Lapilli," which means "three pebbles at a time."

Paint your pieces and use them for story stones (see page 38).

TRY THIS!

Play on grass for a comfortable, cushioned playing surface.

BEACH CLEANUP

Helping to collect up bits of trash you see on your outings is helpful, but purposefully engaging in a beach cleanup is both fun and rewarding. If you come across anything sharp or unfamiliar, ask an adult to pick it up.

TIP

- Keep a **trash bag** along with your beach toys, boogie boards, and towels for whenever you see trash. Dispose of it at the end of your outing.

PICK YOUR SITE

Choose a beach that could use some tender loving care and set aside some time to do a cleanup. Invite friends or family members to join you and watch how, with just a little bit of effort, you can transform a natural space.

RAKES AND SHOVELS

Special grabber tools are good for collecting garbage, but regular rakes and shovels are useful as well. They help you find and remove any items that might be lodged or buried in the sand—and they're fun to use, too!

Separate out what can be **recycled** from the other garbage that you've found.

HIKING CLEANUP

You can also clean up along a hiking trail. The best way to do this is to collect the trash you find on the return leg of your hike so you don't have to carry the trash so far.

Always wear protective **gloves** when dealing with any garbage and unknown items.

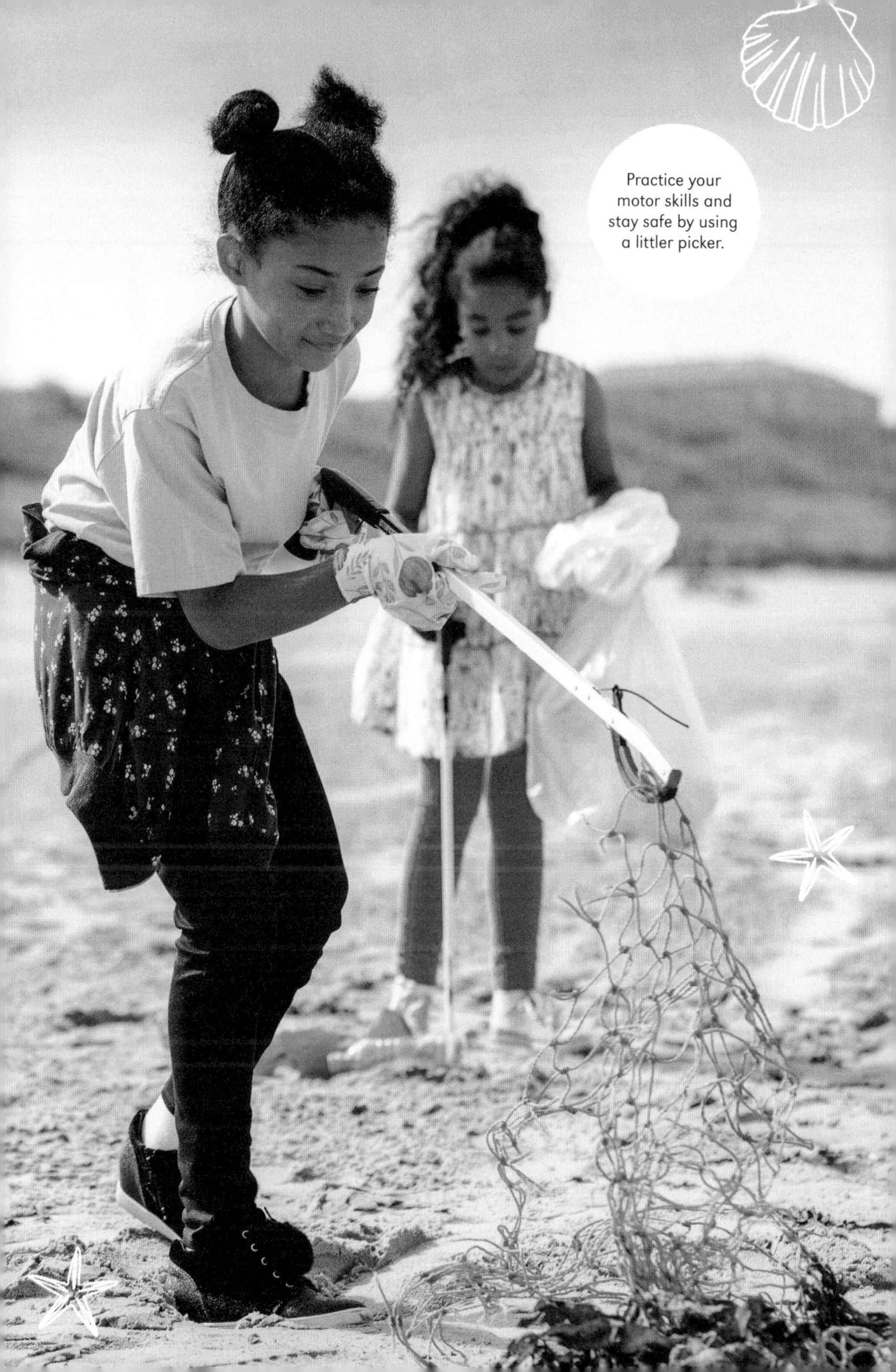

Practice your motor skills and stay safe by using a littler picker.

TRY THIS!
Make crisp footprint shapes or smear the paint with your feet.

20–30 mins

FEET PAINTING

Painting with feet is a gloriously messy and colorful sensory experience. Get ready for lots of giggles and an explosion of color. Each of your feet has more than 7,000 nerve endings so your brain will thank you for this low-prep, messy activity that explores the sense of touch and helps you work on your balance.

SUPPLIES

- A long piece of white butcher paper or a large canvas or board
- Four rocks to weigh down the corners of your paper
- Washable tempera paints
- A hose or bowl of warm water for cleaning your feet
- Towels

INSTRUCTIONS

1. First of all, make sure you're wearing clothes that are OK to get paint on.
2. Spread your paper out on flat ground.
3. Weigh down each corner with a rock so your paper won't blow away.
4. Drizzle a small amount of paint along the paper in long thin lines or in circular dots.
5. Walk carefully across the paper with bare feet.

Instead of your feet, you could use your **hands** for painting.

MORE IDEAS

- Carefully roll up your dry art and use it as **one-of-a-kind** wrapping paper.
- Put only **primary colors** (red, yellow, blue) on your paper and watch new colors emerge as you walk through them all.

CHAPTER THREE

FALL

1–2 hrs

PETAL-STAINED GLASS

As we move from one season to the next, we can commemorate this change with activities combining elements of both seasons. Petal-stained glass combines the brilliance of summer while preserving the beautiful tones of fall. The sun will highlight the shapes, veins, and hues of the materials you use.

SUPPLIES

- White paper
- Thick black pen
- Scissors
- Contact paper
- Natural materials that are flat such as leaves, petals, or grass
- Tissue paper

INSTRUCTIONS

1. Choose a shape and draw it on white paper using thick black lines. It could be a butterfly, a geometric swirl, a pumpkin—anything you can think up.
2. Carefully cut out your shape, including the in-between white spaces.
3. Place your cut-out shape, with the black lines facing down, onto the sticky side of a piece of contact paper.
4. Fill the spaces between the black lines with leaves, petals, grasses, or tissue paper. This is great for fine motor skills and creativity! Make sure the more colorful sides of your items face the sticky side of the contact paper.
5. Once the transparent areas are completely filled, place a second piece of contact paper sticky-side down on top of your creation and cut the whole shape out. Your stained-glass picture is like a sandwich: contact paper, cut-out picture and natural items, contact paper.
6. Hang your artwork where natural light can shine through it.

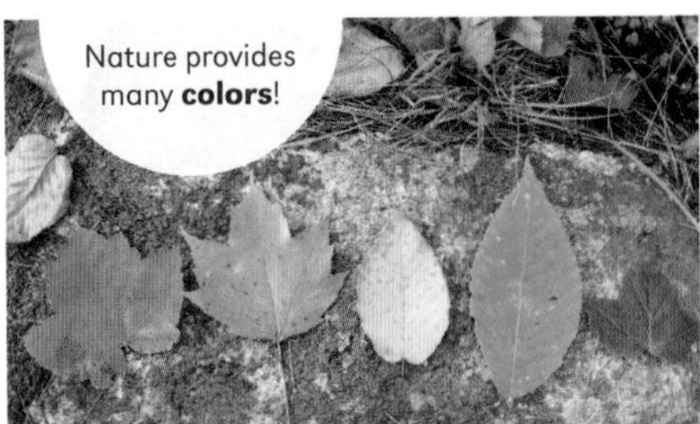

EXTRA TIME

- Experiment with a variety of natural elements in different **shapes** and **colors**.
- If you don't have varied, colored leaves, you can **paint** them.

TRY THIS!

Hang your art so people outside can admire it, too.

BLOWING BUBBLES

If there's one thing that seems to capture the attention of kids young and old, it's bubbles! Playing with bubbles is a valuable sensory experience, but don't ever be tempted to drink bubble solution.

Playing with bubbles is a good activity you can do **by yourself**.

Play a **game** like who can pop the most bubbles?

THE CHASE IS ON

Chasing bubbles is always fun, but chasing the biggest ones is where the real action is! Letting a bubble float away and seeing how far it can go before you pop it is a test of patience and timing. Try popping it with parts of your body other than your hands.

BRING IN THE MACHINES

Bubble machines are a great way to make lots and lots of bubbles—way more than you could ever do on your own. These handy little machines are great for large groups of kids who all want to get involved in games of chasing and popping bubbles together.

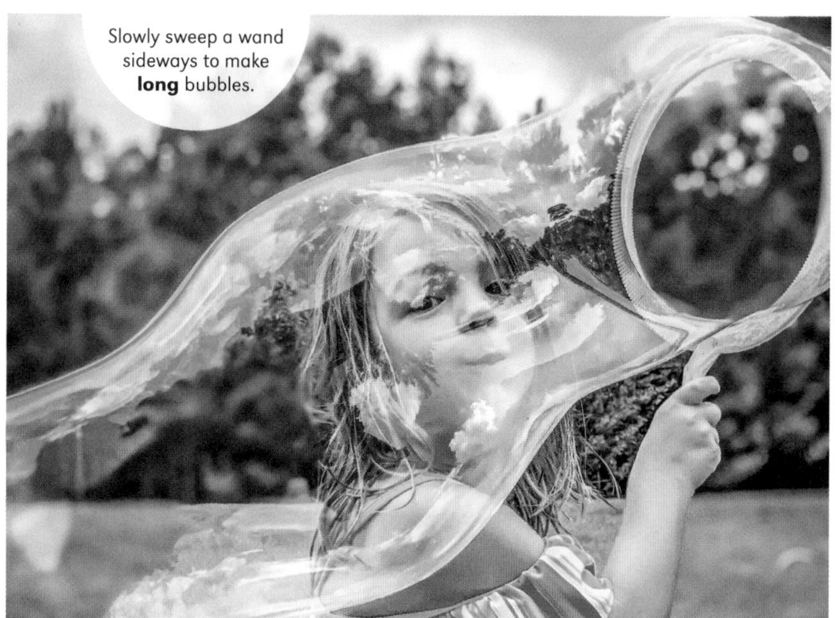

Slowly sweep a wand sideways to make **long** bubbles.

BIGGER AND BETTER

Giant bubbles can be harder to make because they need to be stronger. A great recipe for bigger bubbles is:

- 6 cups (1.4l) of distilled water
- ½ cup (120ml) of blue dish soap
- ½ cup (100g) of cornstarch
- 1 tbsp baking powder
- 1 tbsp glycerin

FUN FACTS

- The Guinness World Record for the **biggest bubble** made with a bottle wand is 4½ feet (1.38m).
- The Guinness World Record for the most **bounces** of a single soap bubble is 424.

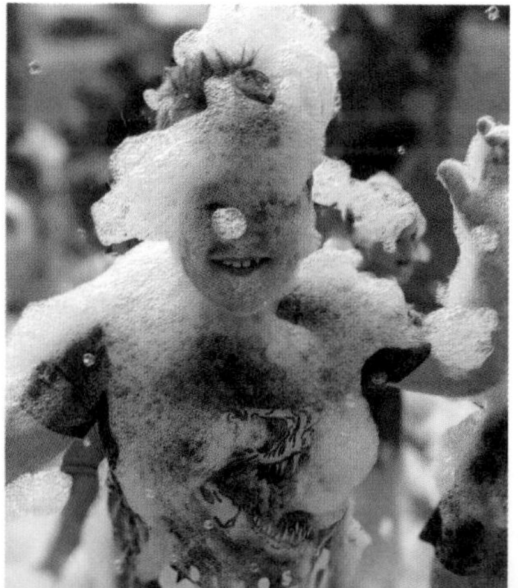

SUDS AND BUDS

Have a bubble party with friends! If you want sudsy bubbles, you can buy a special formulation for foam that is safe for spreading everywhere. Try to cover your whole body in it—you might look like a mummy! Play some music and dance in the foam.

Can you transform into a **bubble monster**?

LEAF RAINBOW ART

30–60 mins

Once a year, leaves change color because they lose their chlorophyll. Leaves with anthocyanin turn red, while those with carotenoid produce yellow and orange leaves. Once you've begun to look for leaves in a rainbow of colors, see what other things in nature you can find that come in a beautiful range of hues.

SUPPLIES

- Small basket for collecting leaves
- A variety of leaves
- Scissors (optional)

INSTRUCTIONS

1. Hunt for as many colors of leaves as you can and identify them:
   - Find red leaves by looking for the following types of trees: maples, oaks, dogwoods, and some sassafras trees.
   - Find orange and yellow leaves from hickory, ash, maples, white oaks, birch, and yellow poplar trees.
   - Sweet gums have leaves that turn a purple shade.
   - The green leaves you find have not lost all of their chlorophyll yet.
   - Leaves with several colors within one leaf are a rare and exciting find!
2. Make a design or collage with your haul. If you carefully cut off the stems, then the leaves will be easier to lay flat or on top of each other.

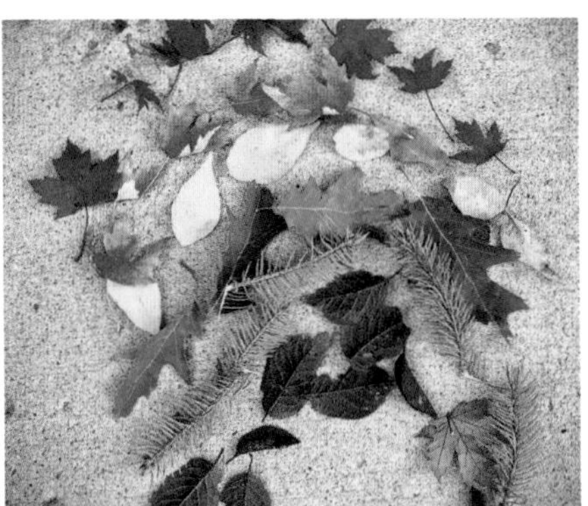

Set up your **rainbow leaves** to look like an actual rainbow!

MORE IDEAS

- What other **shapes** can you make with your rainbow leaves? A heart, a triangle, an arrow?
- Talk about which colors of your rainbow were **hardest** to find? Which ones were the **easiest**?

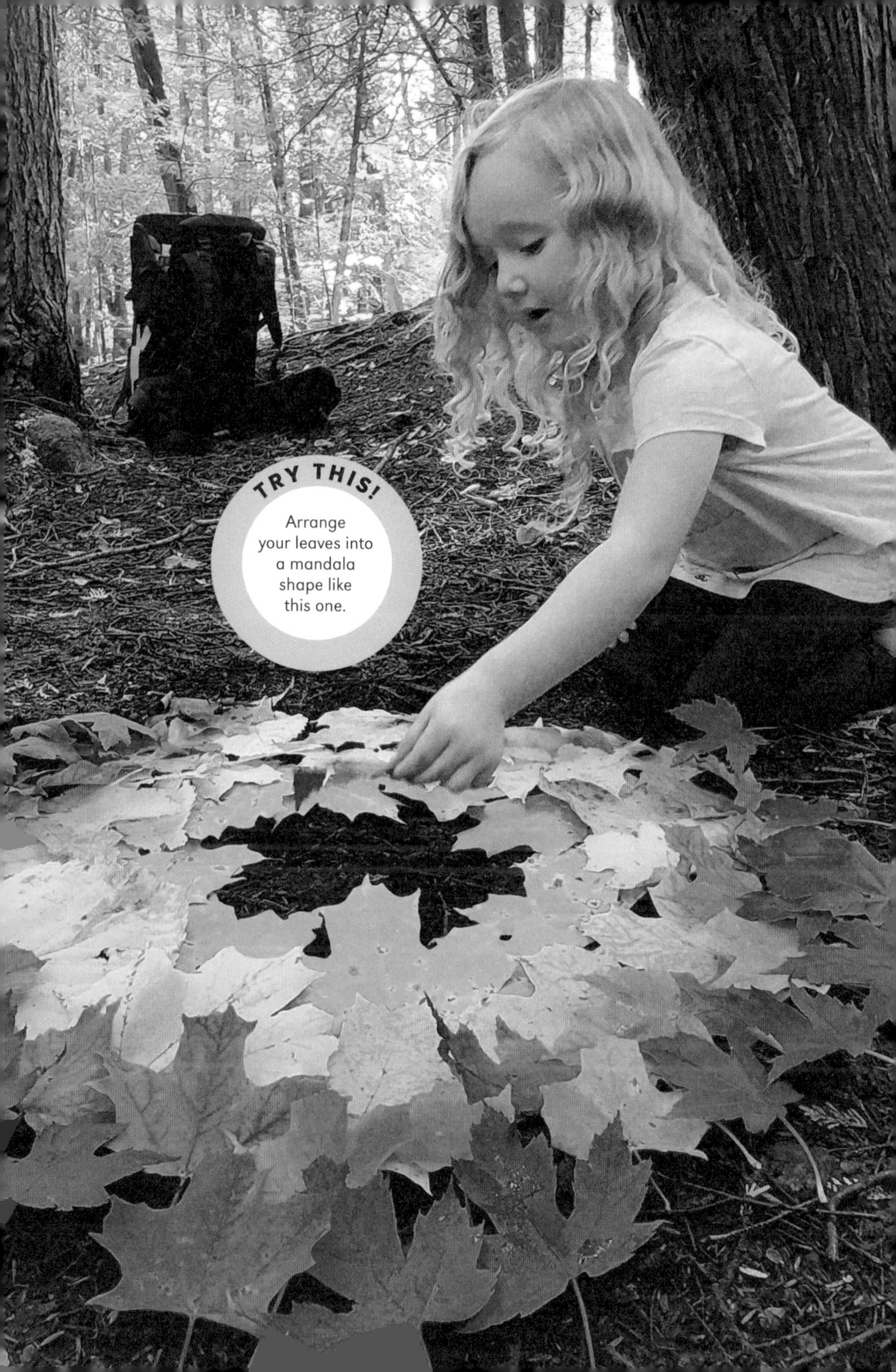
TRY THIS!
Arrange your leaves into a mandala shape like this one.

PUMPKIN VASE

1 hr

When summer fades and fall days creep in, it's sad to think of your summer garden disappearing. But displaying your summer flowers in a pumpkin vase blends the two seasons. Instead of waiting till Halloween, get a head start on using pumpkins for fun!

SUPPLIES

- Pumpkin
- Mason jar or medium-size glass for flower vase
- Pencil or pen
- Knife or carving tool (ask an adult for help!)
- Water
- Flowers

INSTRUCTIONS

1. Pick out a pumpkin that's similar in height to the jar that will be your vase.
2. Ask an adult to help you cut off the pumpkin's stem.
3. Place your jar on top of the pumpkin and trace around it with a pencil or pen to mark the hole. You want your vase to fit snugly in the pumpkin. Ask an adult to help you cut the hole.
4. Then it's time to scoop out the insides! If you've carved a pumpkin for Halloween, this will be familiar. Clean out the insides really well as that will prolong the life and usefulness of the vase.
5. Once the pumpkin is all cleared out, place the jar inside. Fill it two-thirds with water and add the flowers of your choice. This is a beautiful way to blend summer and fall together and a special activity to do with a friend or family member who likes flowers or pumpkins, or both!

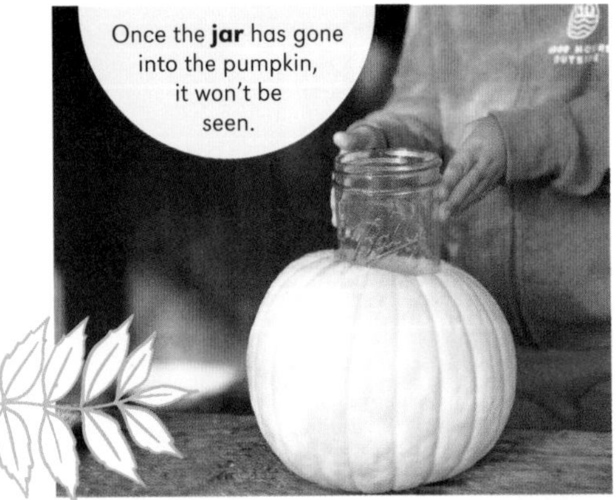

Once the **jar** has gone into the pumpkin, it won't be seen.

EXTRA TIME

- What's better than one pumpkin vase? Well, two, obviously! Create a **welcoming scene** for visitors by making a group of different pumpkin vases for your countertop or even near the entrance to your home.

TRY THIS!
Combine summery flowers with branches of leaves for a textured display.

APPLE TIME

It's thought that the very first apples came from Kazakhstan in Asia, and today about 7,500 varieties grow all around the world. Year-round there are so many fun activities you can do with a simple apple.

APPLE PICKING

Apple picking gives you the chance to learn about the broad varieties of apples and what they are best used for. Some like Granny Smith or Jonagold are great for apple pie. Honeycrisp and McIntosh are excellent for snacking, while using several types of apples is the best way to make applesauce.

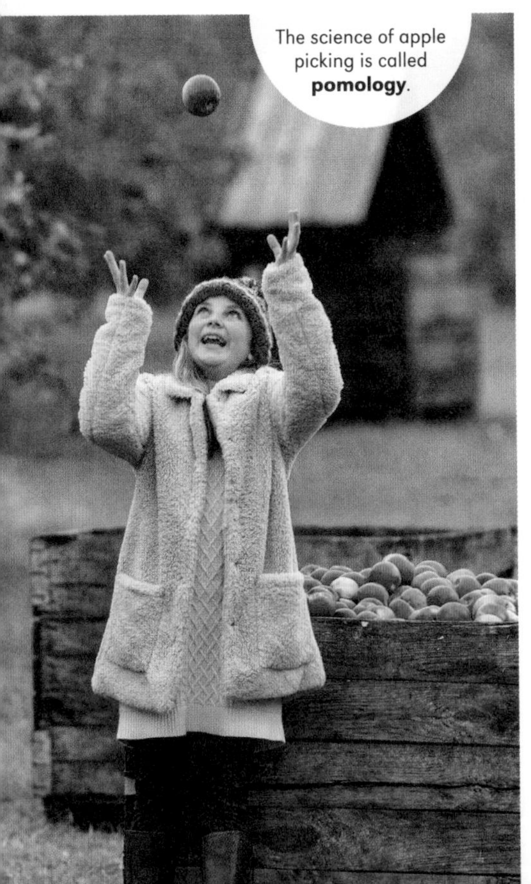

The science of apple picking is called **pomology**.

It takes about four to five years for an apple tree to **grow its first** apple.

APPLE GAMES

Bobbing for apples is fun, and you can also play apple stacking or an apple toss game with a basket. Or make an edible apple head: using melted caramel, stick on facial feature with nuts, chocolate chips, or marshmallows. Be careful because the caramel will be very hot.

EXTRA TIME

- Have an **apple tasting day**. Gather several varieties and cut them into slices so that everyone can have a wedge or two of each kind. Vote for your favorites type of apples and declare an apple winner!

APPLE CIDER

Cider is unfiltered apple juice and it's a great way to use up blemished fruit. An apple press allows you to make it by hand. You could rent a press or see whether a local farmer will let you come watch the process.

APPLE ART

Apples are the perfect size and firmness for printing, and, what's more, their seeds are in the shape of a star. Take two apples and carefully slice one in half vertically and one horizontally. Paint the faces and then gently press them onto a paper to make beautiful prints.

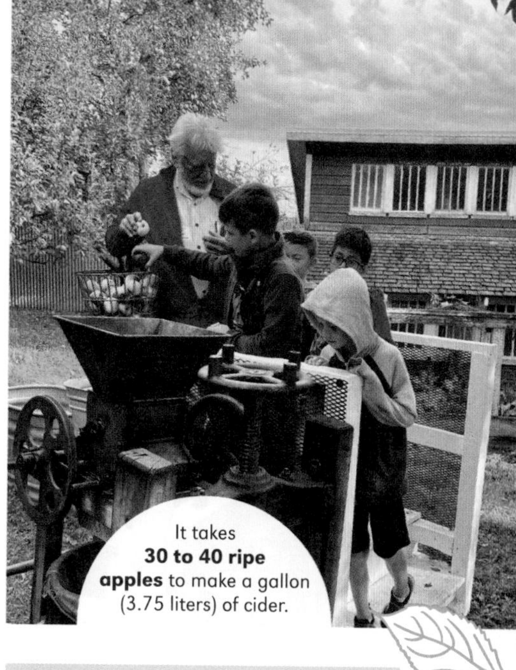

It takes **30 to 40 ripe apples** to make a gallon (3.75 liters) of cider.

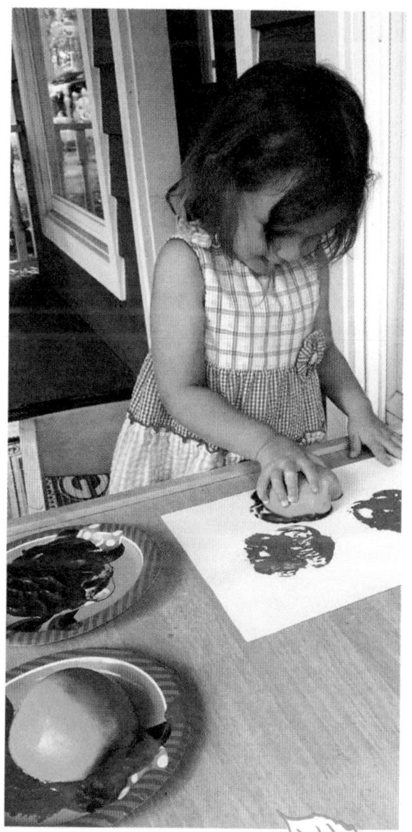

MORE IDEAS

- Stamp your apples onto an **apron or a T-shirt**.
- Draw or paint a **tree trunk** on paper and use your apple stampers to decorate the tree.
- Similarly, you could draw or paint a **basket** and fill it with apples using your stampers.

TIP

- The best way to pick an apple from a tree is to grasp it with the entire palm of your hand and then **twist** it rather than pull it.

Use a **paper plate** for each color of paint to keep the colors separate.

60–90 mins

ANIMAL FACES

Natural items around us offer all sorts of shapes, colors, and textures for capturing the expressive natural forms of animals. Leaves especially offer great variety. While collecting your leaves, notice their symmetry. Look closely to see if the veins extend out from a line down the middle or if they all begin at the base of the leaf.

SUPPLIES

- Brown paper bag or a piece of thin cardboard
- Markers
- Scissors
- Glue
- A collection of leaves and other natural materials

INSTRUCTIONS

1. Draw an animal face on your paper bag or cardboard and carefully cut it out. Consider making a lion face with leaves for the mane, a chicken or turkey face with leaves as feathers, or a goat face using grasses or leaves for the hair on the goat's chin—the goatee.
2. Turn your face over and put a layer of glue all around the edge.
3. Glue down your leaves and other objects, using extra layers of glue if you layer them.
4. Carefully turn your creation over and watch it come to life! It's exciting to see how much depth and character you've added with the items that you've glued on.

This **buck**'s whole face is built around a single large leaf.

MORE IDEAS

- Instead of a drawing a template, you could create the **entire face** from natural materials. Use objects like **walnuts** and **acorns** for the eyes, mouth, and nose.
- Cut eye holes in your animal face to turn it into a **mask** you can wear!

TRY THIS!
Match the colors of fall with the colors of a brown and fiery-maned lion.

1–2 hrs

NATURE JOURNALING

When you sit down to observe nature and recreate what you see with a drawing, it forces you to slow down and observe in a more intentional manner. But nature journaling isn't just about drawing. It's also about capturing in writing what you see—the sounds, smells, textures, and visual beauty that is all around you.

SUPPLIES

- Sketchbook
- Pencils—black and color
- Blender pencil
- Eraser
- Magnifying glass or bug box with lens (optional)
- Binoculars (optional)
- Clipboard (optional)

INSTRUCTIONS

1. Find a good spot in which to begin your nature journaling.
2. Spread your supplies around you so they are easy to reach.
3. Avoid wearing bright colors as this can scare birds away.
4. Try your hand at drawing a small bug first, or even a worm—write down some observations as well regarding how it looks, moves, and perhaps even smells. Did you learn something new? Write that down as well!

MORE IDEAS

- **Water colors** are fun to try when nature journaling—just make sure you use a thick enough paper.
- Using **binoculars**, see how far away you can see something and try to sketch it.
- Go nature journaling with a friend or sibling, choose the **same object** to write about and see how **similar or different** they are.

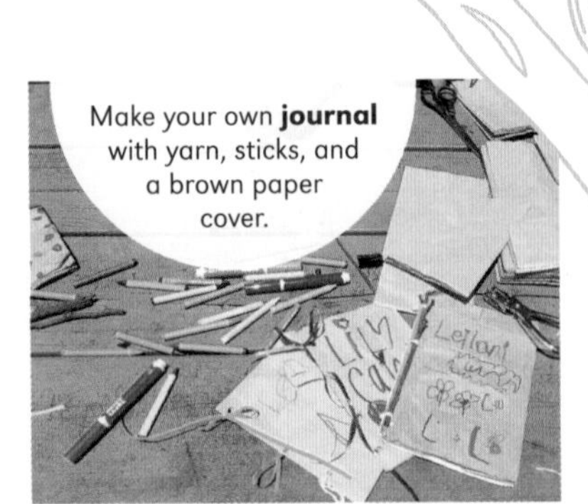

Make your own **journal** with yarn, sticks, and a brown paper cover.

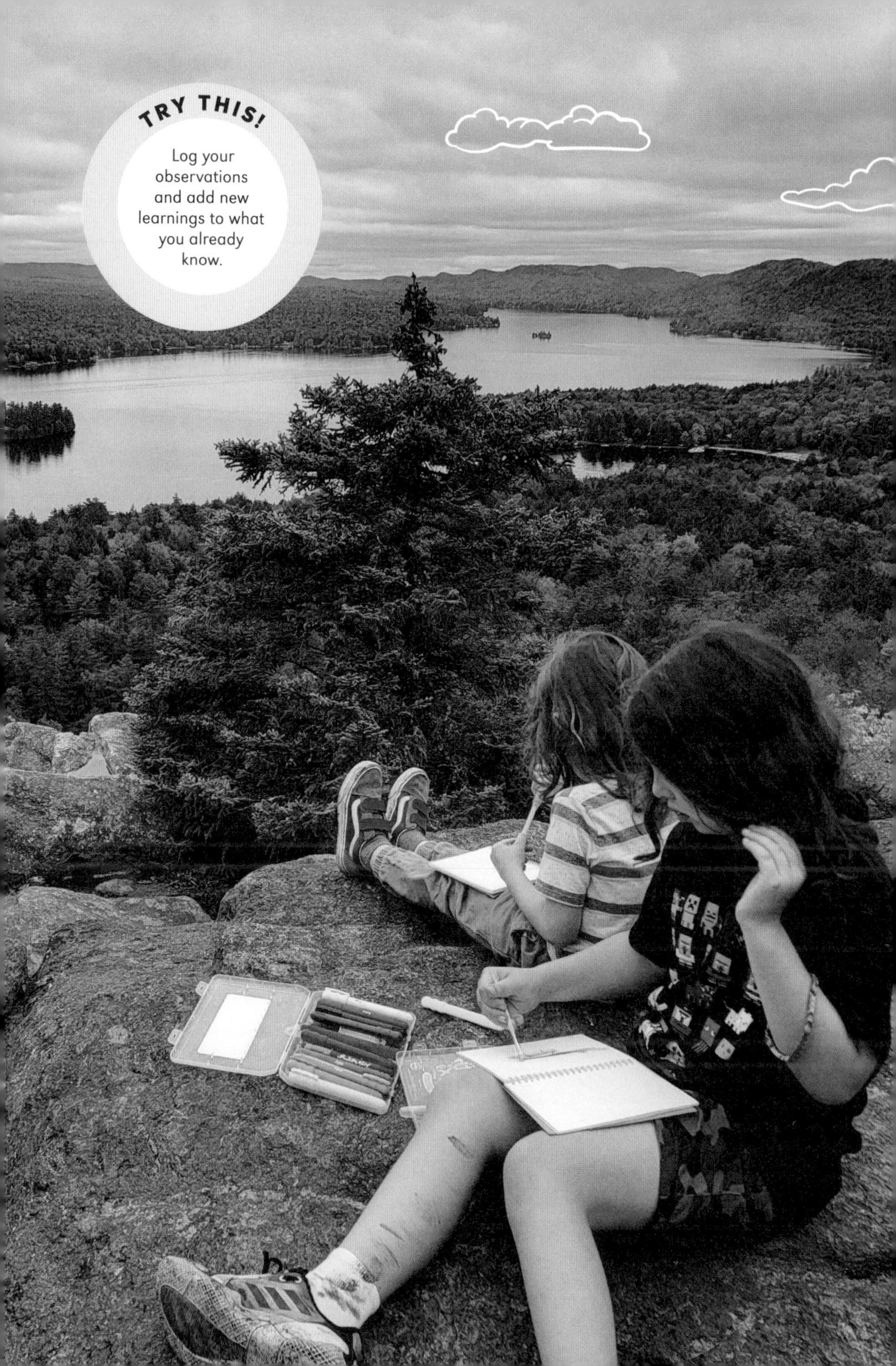
TRY THIS!
Log your observations and add new learnings to what you already know.

MUSHROOM HUNT

All over the world, a vast array of mushrooms can be found. It is so fun to search for mushrooms of different sizes, shapes, and colors, but remember not to pick or eat what you've found unless you have an expert with you.

CHICKEN MUSHROOMS

Chicken mushrooms—also named chicken of the woods—often look like bright orange and yellow fans growing on trees or stumps. There aren't any look-alikes for this mushroom so you can be fairly certain when you find them.

TIP

- Err on the safe side and search for what are known as the "**foolproof four**": chicken mushrooms, chanterelles, giant puffballs, and morels.

CHANTERELLES

Chanterelles are most commonly found in forests as they have a symbiotic relationship with the roots of trees and they love hot, humid weather. Look for orange (also called golden), red (also called cinnabar), or black trumpets. The mushrooms have a faint sweet smell of apricots.

The wrinkles on the underside of the cap are also called **gills**.

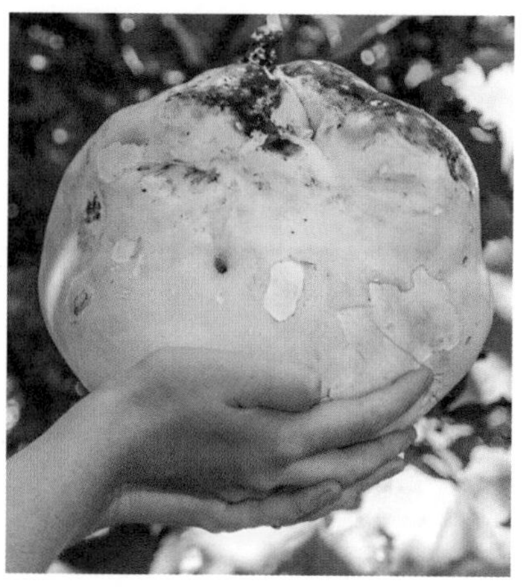

GIANT PUFFBALLS

Meadows and deciduous forests are great places to look for giant puffball mushrooms, but these can show up anywhere. Without a cap or a stem, these mushrooms can grow to be the size of a soccer ball, though they are not always perfectly round.

Depending on their size, giant puffballs can have up to a **billion spores**.

MORELS

Often popping up after a heavy rainfall, morel mushrooms are easy to identify due to their honeycomb-like appearance. Used in fancy restaurants due to their earthy and nutty flavors, morels are rather elusive and highly exciting to find. These don't pop up in predictable places so the hunt is on.

MORE IDEAS

- Keep a **journal** filled with drawings of the different types of mushrooms you find. Note things like size, shape, color, location, and time of year.

SAFETY FIRST

- Be **careful**—some mushrooms can be very **poisonous**, even if you only touch them. Go near only those mushrooms that adults say are safe.
- Sometimes adults make mistakes, so if they're unsure, they can check mushroom **guides** online.
- Look up any toxic mushrooms that are common in **your area** so you can recognize them and stay away from them.

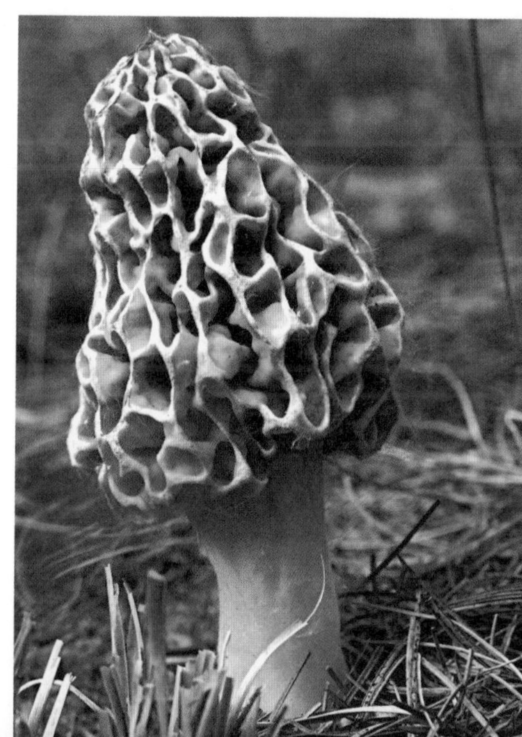

The crinkly, **honeycomb** mushroom is actually hollow.

STICK FORT

1–2 hrs

Forts are fun hideaways for imaginative escape. Building them out of pillows and blankets inside is always fun, but a great outdoors alternative is to make a stick fort. These secret rooms of wonder can start simple and grow over time into full-on shelters where kids can read books, play house, and retreat from battling dragons.

SUPPLIES

- Large branches of varying sizes
- A rake to clear the ground
- Leaves for the roof

INSTRUCTIONS

1. Start with finding a relatively flat, open space where you can clear the ground using your rake.
2. Search for fallen branches.
3. Use the thickest branches to make the frame, perhaps in a triangular shape like a tepee. Interlocking sticks at the point where they branch is a good way to help hold them in place.
4. Once your frame is stable, continue stacking and interlocking branches to fill out the walls, making sure they continue to lean in at an angle to form the roof.
5. Leave an opening in the front so you can easily get in and out.

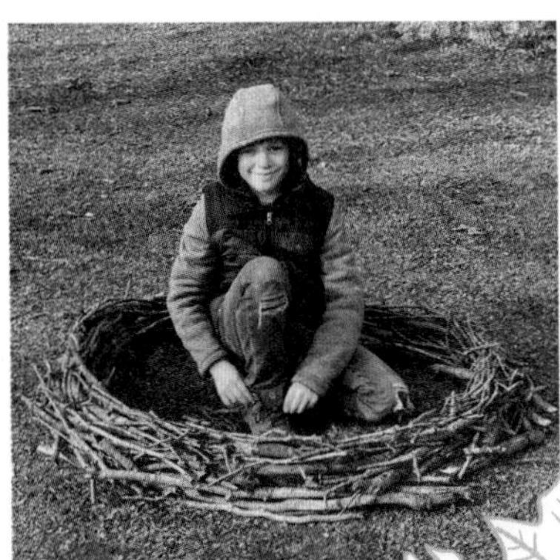

Stack and interlock sticks in a **circular pattern** to create a giant **nest**.

EXTRA TIME

- Angle the branches out on either side of the **doorway** to create a neat-looking entrance.
- Pad the structure with **dead leaves or moss** to create a more enclosed space.

TRY THIS!
Build against trees so they can help support your structure.

TRY THIS!

Make sure to choose items that will fit inside your egg carton.

1–2 hrs

EGG CARTON SCAVENGER HUNT

This open-ended activity combines the love of collecting with the love of searching for hidden things. The great thing is that it can be adapted to any geographical location or climate and can be geared for any season of the year. It also comes with its own closable carry case for all your goodies with a corresponding visual list.

SUPPLIES

- Sheet of paper
- Scissors
- Egg carton
- Ruler
- Pen or markers
- Glue

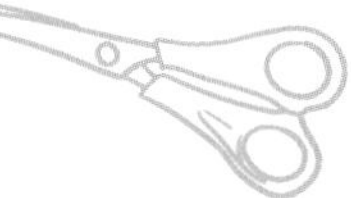

INSTRUCTIONS

1. Cut a sheet of paper so it's slightly smaller than the egg carton lid.
2. Using a ruler, divide your paper up into sections—the same number as in the egg carton.
3. Choose the same number of natural items that can commonly be found in your area.
4. Draw pictures of them for each section. Possible items include flowers, acorns, walnuts, pine cones, shells, bark, seeds, feathers, sticks, or leaves.
5. Glue your sheet to the inside of the lid.
6. Head out and see how many of the items you can find and place them in their compartments.

At the end, the egg carton serves as a **display case.**

EXTRA TIME

- Have everyone in the **family** create a hunt for each other.
- **Decorate** your egg carton before you head out. You could even color the inside of each compartment.

NATURE'S PLAYGROUND

Built play parks are fun, but nature sure provides its own variety of playgrounds that are always changing and evolving. There's never a shortage of things to play on when you head outside.

BALANCING

Fallen logs can be so many things: a dinosaur, a snake, a train, an airplane, or even a balance beam. Unlike indoor versions, nature's balance beams are diverse in their length and girth as well as their direction, elevation, and texture.

String up a **slackline** between two sturdy trees and practice balancing.

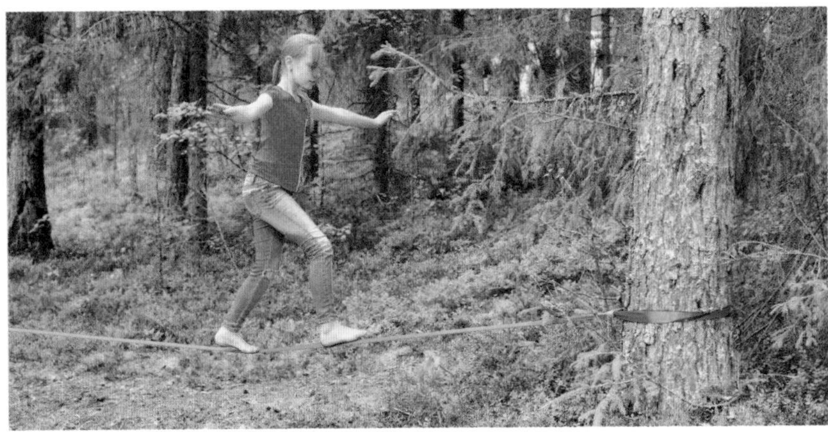

CLIMBING

When tree climbing, choose a large, sturdy tree with lots of limbs. Start small and learn to observe first, looking for any signs of rot or decay. Go only as far as you can reach by yourself. Going up can be easier than coming down. To come back, feel the way with your feet, and ask for help if you're not sure.

Tree climbing helps with making **micro assessments**.

Hay bales can provide hours of entertainment.

JUMPING

When you jump and land over and over, it strengthens your bones. Each impact provides the perfect amount of stress on the bones to increase their density. Nature provides all sorts of elements for jumping off or over.

SWINGING

Swinging allows you to feel like you're flying, and nature has found a way to help you swing even when there's no play set nearby. Vines such as grapevines can be cut and shaped into a swing or used where they are.

UPSIDE DOWN

Going upside down helps you regulate your central nervous system. Hang on tight with all limbs, like a sloth, and allow your head to invert in this gravity-defying feat.

Can you **crawl along** upside down?

Work up to **hooking your legs** over a branch.

LEAF CROWN

30 mins

Crowns are so much fun for pretend play! Make a quick crown and become the king or queen of the forest. These can have such different looks depending on the shapes and colors of the leaves you find in your area. Hunting for the most interesting leaves can be a fun activity for kids and adults alike.

SUPPLIES

- About 12 to 15 leaves, depending on their width
- Scissors
- Stapler and staples
- A strip of card or thick construction paper that is long enough to fit around your head.

INSTRUCTIONS

1. Carefully snip off all the stems of the leaves you've collected so that you won't get poked in the eye while wearing your crown.
2. Measure the strip of card or construction paper so that it will fit snugly around the widest part of your head without falling into your eyes.
3. Remove the strip, ask an adult to staple it, and cut off any excess paper.
4. Ask an adult to staple your leaves to your crown. Make sure they are positioned so they won't be covering your eyes. You can arrange them side by side or overlap them to give the crown a little depth.
5. Experiment with patterns and varying leaf sizes, such as putting a small leaf next to a taller leaf and so on.
6. If your little hands aren't strong enough to use a stapler, you can also attach the leaves using glue.

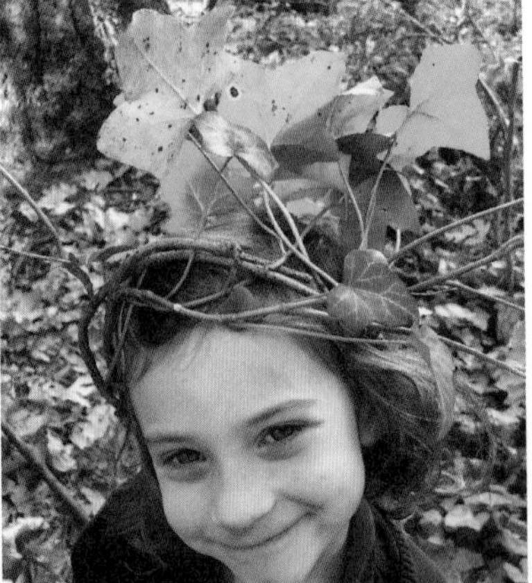

Flexible **vines** can be twisted into crowns. Weave extra leaves through, too.

MORE IDEAS

- Add extras to your crown like **wildflowers**, **seed pods**, or **feathers**.
- If leaves **aren't in season** right now, you can **draw** some. Color them and cut them out and then affix them to your crown with a stapler.

TRY THIS!
Color or paint your card first to create a more coordinated crown.

ACORN CANDLES

1 hr

Have you ever been outside and seen a squirrel run by with an acorn in its mouth? Guess what the squirrel left behind when snatching its treat—the acorn cap! And these are the perfect little items to collect in order to make floating acorn candles, which are a great way to bring nature inside. Make lots at once and display them in groups.

SUPPLIES

- Acorn caps
- Candle wax
- Metal spoon
- Candle and matches or lighter
- Wicks
- Bowl of water

INSTRUCTIONS

1. Head outside and collect acorn caps—the bigger, the better.
2. Place a small chunk of wax in a spoon, and ask an adult to hold it over a flame to melt the wax. Be careful because the wax will be hot.
3. Ask an adult to carefully pour the wax into the acorn cap.
4. Place the wick upright in the center of the acorn and hold it in place until the wax hardens.
5. Once the wax is solid, trim the wick if needed.
6. Fill a bowl with water, add the acorns, and ask an adult to light them.
7. Enjoy the show! But keep away from the candles once they're lit and never leave them unattended.

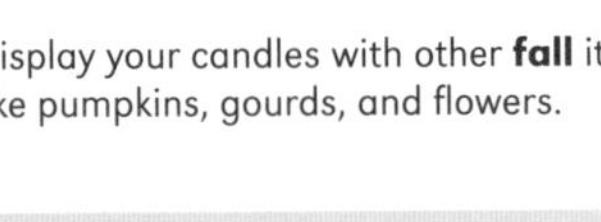

Display your candles with other **fall** items like pumpkins, gourds, and flowers.

MORE IDEAS

- You can add **food coloring** to the melted wax to make colored candles, but be careful because it can stain clothes, skin, and surfaces.
- These will look wonderful on your table as part of a **centerpiece**.

TRY THIS!
Put acorn candles on the table to light up your **meal** while you eat outside!

FOLLOW THE LEADER

The classic, beloved children's game "Follow the Leader" can be played year-round in a variety of ways. Some say you need at least four players, but out in nature even just a pair will enjoy this game of copycats.

FALL

When you play "Follow the Leader," one person is the leader, and the other players follow behind, mimicking the leader's path and actions. In the fall, when the heat of the day has lifted and many of the pesky bugs are gone, it's fun to play this through a wooded area.

Fallen logs help develop **risk assessment** as well as **balance skills**.

WINTER

The cold can make it harder to get out and get moving in winter. "Follow the Leader" is a motivational game for children to help keep their minds off the chilly air. This game is especially fun in the snow because kids can see the tracks they've made.

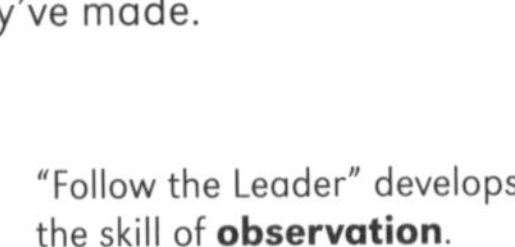

"Follow the Leader" develops the skill of **observation**.

SPRING

After a long winter, our bodies are ready to move and feel the sunshine. Melting snow and ice give way to many perfect places for "Follow the Leader," like across the rocks of a shallow creek bed.

Mimic movements but also **sounds and gestures**.

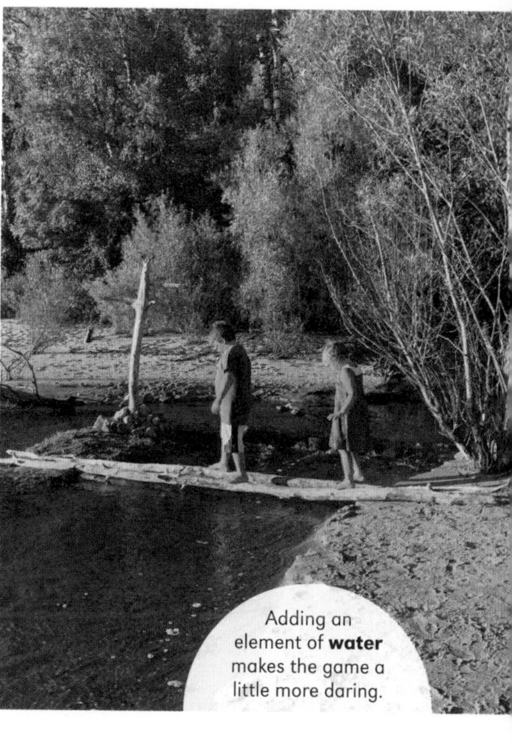

Adding an element of **water** makes the game a little more daring.

TIP

- In the classic game, anyone who fails to follow the leader is out and the last remaining follower becomes the **new leader**.

SUMMER

Add in summer toys and see whether you can still follow a friend. Can you bounce on top of a ball? How about bouncing a basketball? Can you toss a small ball into the air and still follow along?

Only play near or on a **road** with adult supervision.

MAGNIFYING GLASS

A magnifying glass allows you to see things you've never seen before, adding to the intrigue and wonder of your natural surroundings as well as improving your hand-eye coordination and focus.

FOCUSING IN ON PLANTS

It can be fascinating to zoom in on the unseen world like the details on the veins of a leaf. Magnification will show if a plant has any small hairs on it or if there are tiny bugs crawling about in it.

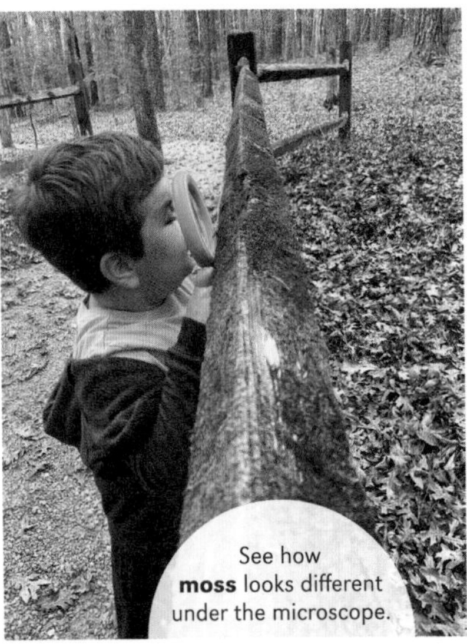

See how **moss** looks different under the microscope.

A CLOSER LOOK AT ROCKS

Hunt for rocks along hiking paths, rivers, or in gardens. Observe them under your magnifying glass when they're dry. Rocks can contain tiny amounts of minerals that might show up. Spray the rocks with a mist of water from a spray bottle and compare how they look now.

EXTRA TIME

- Play the magnifying glass **color game**. Announce a certain color and then find items of that color in your surroundings to look at under a magnifying glass. See how many different items you can find. When they're magnified, do they look how you expected?

Look deeper in between the scales of a **pine cone**.

ZOOMING IN ON BUGS

Using a net, bug tongs, or careful hands, gently set a few bugs in a tray. Good places to look are under plants and rocks or on tree bark. Magnify your bugs and talk about what you see. Then place them back in their natural habitats and wash your hands.

Your magnifying glass will make objects look **two to three times bigger** than they are.

MORE IDEAS

- With your magnifying glass, check out **the unexpected**, like the crystals inside of an ice cube, old keys, your hairbrush, and a feather.

Do objects look different up close when they're submerged in **water**?

MAKE YOUR OWN

If you don't have a magnifying glass available, you can make one. Fill a small, clear bottle with water and screw the cap on tightly. Glass works best, but clear plastic may also work. When you lay your bottle on its side, it will enlarge whatever is underneath.

TRY THIS!
Googly eyes give anything instant expression and personality!

LEAF ART

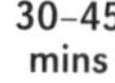

30–45 mins

Oak leaves, maple leaves, elm leaves—they're all so different and all so cool-looking! Each fall, however, every single one ends up on the ground. This presents us with a great opportunity to create art. Whether you use leaves as a canvas for silly faces, stamps, or writing, the options are endless—just like the number of fallen leaves.

SUPPLIES

- Leaves
- Paint
- Paintbrushes
- Glue
- Googly eyes (optional)
- Biodegradable glitter (optional)
- Metallic marker (optional)

INSTRUCTIONS

1. We can't do leaf art without leaves—so head outside and grab as many variations as you can.
2. Spread your leaves out on the ground and paint them however you'd like.
3. You could glue on googly eyes or biodegradable glitter.
4. You could draw faces, animals, or unique designs on the leaves using a metallic marker.

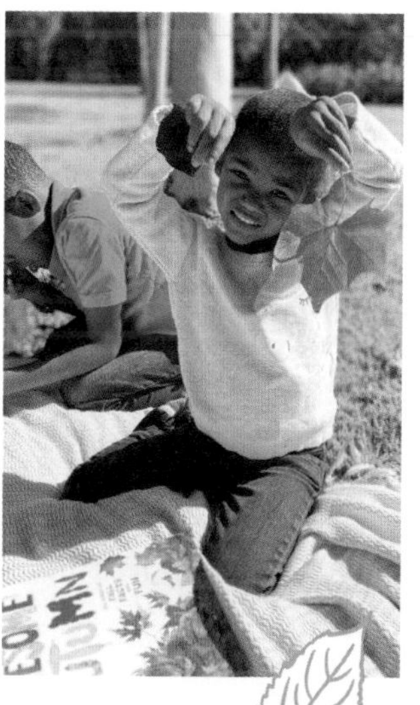

How many **different types** of leaves can you collect?

MORE IDEAS

- Make a **leaf mandala** by laying out your decorated leaves in a circular pattern.
- Once you've decorated leaves lots of different colors, glue them onto a large sheet of paper to make a **mosaic** leaf **picture or collage**.
- Write a **message** or your name by arranging your leaves to make big letters. It could be temporary on the ground, or you could make it more permanent by sticking it to paper.

CREEPY CRAWLIES

The earth is full of wonderful creatures, both big and small. Some are hairy, some are slimy, but all of them are important! Spiders, worms, slugs, and snails can all be found in many locations. Look around and see how many you can find, but always wash your hands after touching them.

SLUGS

Slugs have only one lung, and they can breathe through their skin! Thousands of species of these mollusks spend their time eating decaying things on the forest or ocean floors—a very useful job.

SNAILS

Slugs don't have shells, but snails do! Yet that's about where the differences end between snails and slugs—just the shell! They are basically the same creature otherwise.

The **largest slugs** can grow up to 10 inches (25cm)!

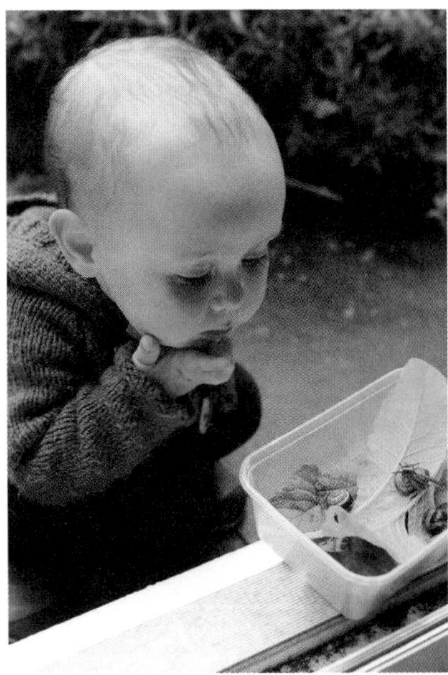

Snails have several **tiny rows of teeth** to eat their food with.

EXTRA TIME

- Make a small **temporary habitat** for your insects using old food storage containers so you can watch them up close. But make sure to put them back when you're done!

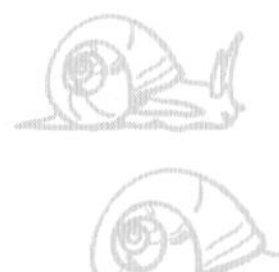

SPIDERS

While a few spiders are dangerous, most are harmless to humans and they do a great many things that are good, like eating other insects. Some spider silk is lighter than cotton and 1,000 times thinner than human hair!

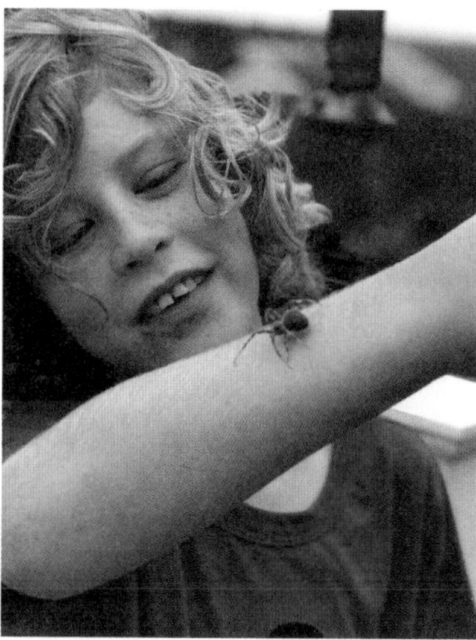

Have you ever let a large spider **crawl** on your arm?

TIP

- There's no reason to be afraid of creepy crawlies! If you are nervous, the more you explore and hold them, the more **comfortable** you will get.

WORMS

Earthworms are perhaps the most important living organism when it comes to soil health. They break down and decompose things, which makes the earth grow better food.

MORE IDEAS

- Gently place a piece of paper under a slug or snail so you can observe its **slimy trail**.
- Collect any empty **snail shells** for using in craft projects.
- See if you can **move** like a worm! How far can you go?

Earthworm bodies are made of sections of rings, which help them move.

25–40 mins

ROCK STACKS

Have you ever been walking along and seen a stack of rocks? Making them is as simple as it sounds—look for rocks and stack them as high as you can. Experiment with different shapes and the best ways to balance them. It's always a good idea to take the stack down when you're done with it and do your best to put the rocks back.

SUPPLIES

- Rocks
- Rocks
- More rocks!

INSTRUCTIONS

1. If you want to build a tall stack, you will need a large rock on the bottom—ideally one that can lay mostly flat and has a somewhat flat surface.
2. Now the fun starts! Keep looking for more flat rocks to stack. To build a stable structure, each rock you add should be no bigger than the one it's sitting on. Ideally, each rock should be slightly smaller than the previous one to get the maximum coolness effect of your rock stack!
3. As you add rocks, make sure the structure is still stable—if it falls, it could hurt someone. Watch out particularly for your fingers and toes!
4. Keep stacking until you are down to just a small pebble at the top and voilà! You have made yourself an awesome rock stack!

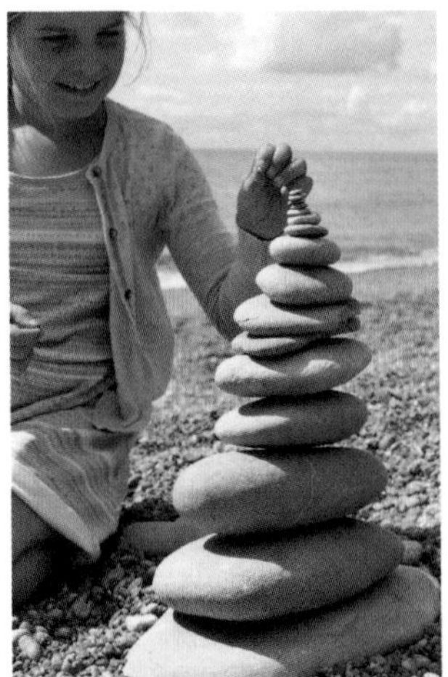

How many rocks can you balance?

MORE IDEAS

- Building stacks on a rock just below the surface of a creek or river is fun because it looks like the rock stack is **floating on the flowing water**.
- Have a competition to see who can stack their rocks the **highest** without them falling over.
- Even if you're just **at home**, you can use garden stones, bricks, and more to make your rock stack!

TRY THIS!
Make more than one stack and find flat rocks to link them like bridges.

BUG HOTEL

A bug hotel just might be what the tiny creatures in your area need for sanctuary during the coming cold months. You can buy an insect hotel at the store, but it can be more fun to make one yourself.

SELECT YOUR STRUCTURE

With an adult's help, carefully nail together a wooden frame. Or you could recycle something like a wooden drawer or a picture frame. Make sure it's at least 3 inches (8cm) deep. It's good if one side is deeper to shelter the box.

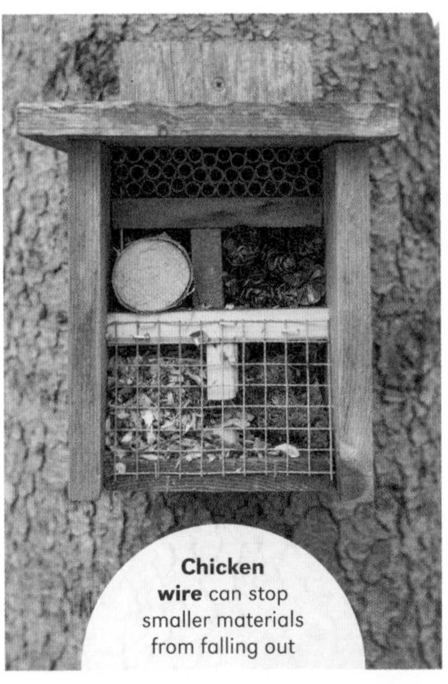

Chicken wire can stop smaller materials from falling out

GATHER YOUR MATERIALS

Stuff the frame with natural materials. Use hollowed-out stems, twigs, tree bark, pine cones, dried grass, and dried leaves to fill the bug hotel up. Create plenty of small crevices for insects to hide and nest in. Ask an adult to drill a hole in the back for hanging it up, or rest it in the garden near the ground.

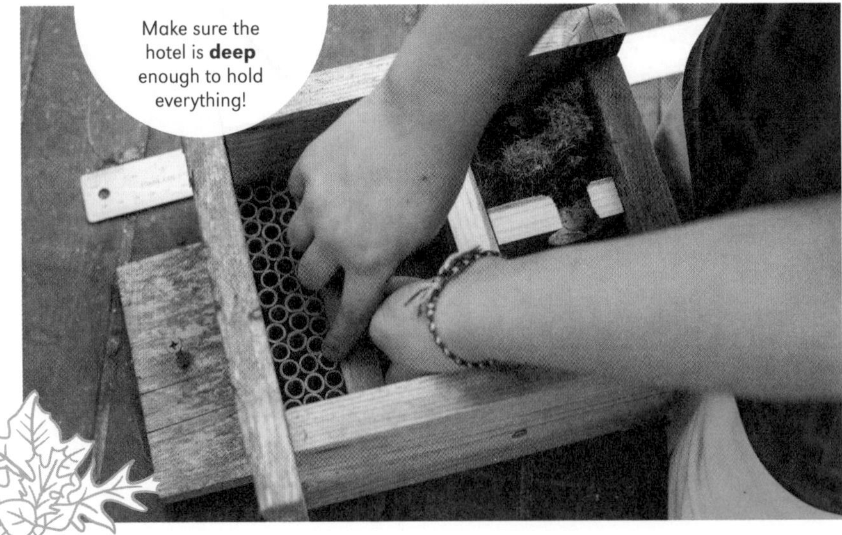

Make sure the hotel is **deep** enough to hold everything!

MORE IDEAS

- **Shreds of bark** make a good home for beetles, spiders, and millipedes.
- A bigger **wildlife stack** on the ground could also attract hedgehogs or frogs.
- Include **corrugated cardboard** for lacewings.
- Solitary bees like holes and nonplastic **tubes** in a sunny spot.

IT TAKES A VILLAGE

We need insects to live among us because they pollinate plants, make the soil healthier, and provide food for bigger creatures. They're an important link in the food chain. Bring together bug hotels, along with decorative rocks, plants, and pine cones to create an inviting village for your insect friends.

What would be a good name for your **bug village**?

TRY THIS!
Blow bubbles from various heights and see if your images look different.

30 mins

BUBBLE ART

This open-ended art activity never fails to fascinate people of all ages—even the adults! Blowing bubbles is already an enjoyable activity, but turning it into an art project makes it that much better. This activity works best on a day when it isn't very windy; otherwise, your colored bubbles will float off away from your paper.

SUPPLIES

- Tablespoon
- Bubble mix
- Small containers or a muffin pan (big enough to immerse the ends of the wands)
- Food coloring
- Plain paper, construction paper, or cardstock
- Bubble wands—different shapes and sizes add to the novelty

INSTRUCTIONS

1. Pour two tablespoons of bubble mix into each of your bowls or each section of your muffin pan. Use a different container for each color you plan to blow bubbles with.
2. Add a few drops of food coloring to each bit of bubble mix, being careful not to spill any—food coloring can stain clothes and skin.
3. Lay some paper on a flat surface that is protected from getting stained.
4. Put your bubble wand in one of the colored mixes so the whole ring is covered. Remove it and check that there's now a glistening film across the ring.
5. Blow bubbles in the direction of your paper.
6. As the bubbles hit the paper, they will pop and leave behind interesting patterns.
7. Repeat this process with the other colors.

EXTRA TIME

- Before you paint with bubbles, put pieces of masking tape on your paper. It could make letters or an image like a small house. Blow your bubbles, then when the paint is dry, carefully remove the tape to reveal your design.

MORE IDEAS

- Use bubble art to decorate the front of a **notebook**.
- Put your bubble art on long pieces of paper and use your decorated paper as **gift wrap**.

30–45 mins

LEAF WREATH

It's fun to decorate for the seasons, and natural materials make for cheap and easy decor. You can get involved with this project and be proud of what is hanging on your front door or around your home. When the season changes, you can make a new wreath that will look different, thanks to the varying bounty of each time of year.

SUPPLIES

- Large paper plate or cardboard
- Scissors
- A variety of leaves
- Glue
- Metallic markers (optional)
- Paint pens or acrylic paint and paintbrushes (optional)
- Hole punch
- Ribbon or twine

INSTRUCTIONS

1. Fold your paper plate in half and carefully cut out the center by cutting a folded-over semicircle. If you don't have a paper plate handy, you can make a ring shape using cardboard or sturdy construction paper instead.
2. If you want, you can decorate your leaves with metallic markers, paint pens, or acrylic paint. You can color and pattern each individual leaf before gluing them together or you can decorate the whole wreath after step 4.
3. Glue your leaves around the ring, overlapping some if you would like.
4. Wait for the glue to dry completely.
5. Decide which way up your wreath should be and then punch a hole near the outer edge of the top.
6. String some ribbon through the hole and tie a knot.
7. Hang your wreath up indoors or out and enjoy it for the season.

EXTRA TIME

- Once you have one layer of leaves and the glue has dried, add **another layer** of leaves to give more depth.

MORE IDEAS

- Your wreath could have some sort of **pattern** to it. You might **alternate** between different leaf colors or between different sizes or shapes of leaves.
- If you like the result, you could make more wreaths as gifts for **grandparents** or **teachers**.

TRY THIS!

Use your wreath to make a cute picture frame and snag a photo.

RAIN PLAY

There is a saying that there's no such thing as bad weather, only bad clothing, so a rainy day doesn't have to keep us inside! Enjoy the sensory experiences of the feel of raindrops, the sound, and the new smells.

UMBRELLA WALK

Go on a rain walk with an umbrella. Sing rainy days songs as you listen to the raindrops splash against the top of your umbrella. Umbrellas come in so many different sizes and colors. Choose a colorful one to brighten up the day or a clear one to see the world around you while still under a protective little shelter.

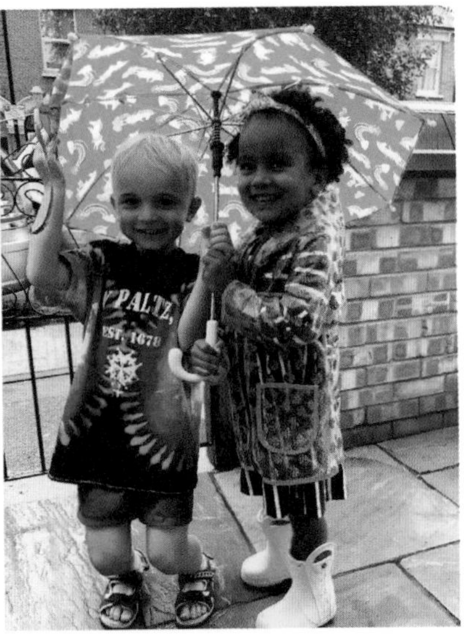

Sharing an umbrella works best with someone the same height.

CURBS AND PUDDLES

During heavier rainfall, curbs and puddles can be the perfect little spots to play with small plastic boats or watch leaves float away to nearby drains. Play only in driveways or on lawns and never on the actual road.

Look out for **worms** that need a little help after the rain and gently put them back on the grass.

UMBRELLA PICNIC

Sit on a waterproof mat, prop up an umbrella, and bring your picnic lunch outside. Enjoy your meal with the ambience of the surrounding rainfall. If it's a little chilly, choose foods that will warm you up inside like a bowl of soup or a grilled sandwich.

Set out a container while you eat to **measure** how much rain falls during your meal.

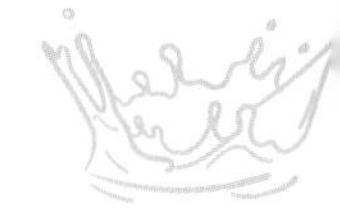

PUDDLE STOMP!

Puddle stomping is a grand experimentation where you can learn about the world of forces. Through sensory feedback, you see the differences between stomping lightly and hard and stomping faster and slower.

Petrichor is the name for the earthy smell when rain lands on dry soil.

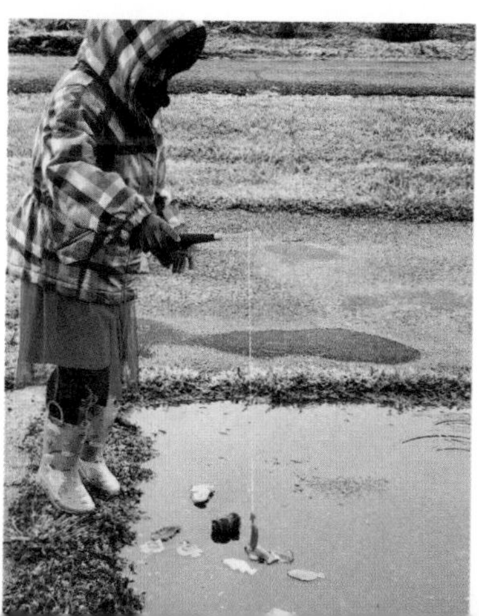

PUDDLE GAMES

Turn a rainy day puddle into a makeshift fishing spot with a magnetic fishing pole and any items that are magnetic. You could also use a puddle to play the game "Sink or Float," where you guess whether an object will sink or float and then test it out right before your eyes!

Bath toys are a good addition to your puddle play.

BIRD-WATCHING

Which birds you can see varies from place to place, but also with the seasons so it's an ever-changing activity. Set up food to attract birds to where you live or head out to see what you can find.

THE GREAT MIGRATION

Some birds travel from one place to another as the seasons change to find more resources. Some birds travel quite short distances, but some journey thousands of miles every year.

MORE IDEAS

- Try to provide birds a comfortable and plentiful yard with food, water, and space as they arrive back home.

Snow geese breed in the Arctic and some migrate south in fall.

HIBERNATION

Instead of migrating for winter, some animals hibernate. In a state of hibernation, a bat's heart rate drops from between 200 and 300 beats per minute to just 10 beats per minute, and it may go minutes without taking a breath. The bat's body temperature can also drop to near freezing.

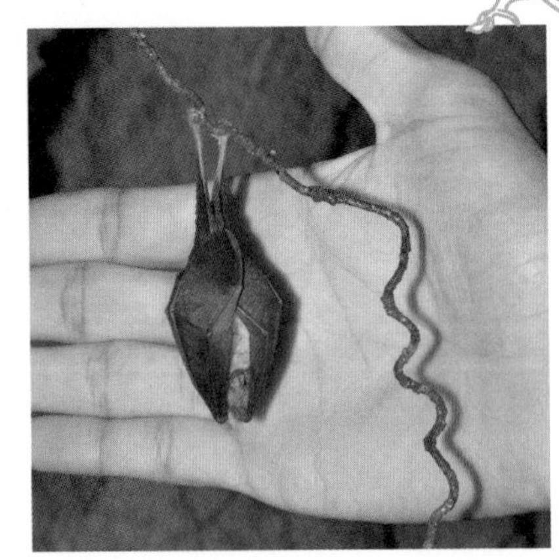

Some species of bats **hibernate** for up to **six months**.

The **pileated woodpecker** is a common sight (and sound) in many parts of North America.

BIRD SPOTTING

What kind of birds live near you? Woodpeckers can be found in many countries. Their tongue wraps all the way around their brain to protect it from the intense impact as they peck at hardwood trees to look for tasty insects.

BIRDING WITH BINOS

Binoculars are handy little devices that make things far away appear to be closer. They are a must-have for bird enthusiasts, and they allow you to see birds from further away, which prevents them from getting scared and flying off.

SIT-SPOT

A sit-spot is when you pick a place to settle and watch for something. Then you come back the next day to the same place and see whether you can see things that have changed, including the types of birds you do or don't see.

Going **deep into the woods** allows you to see birds interact with their surroundings.

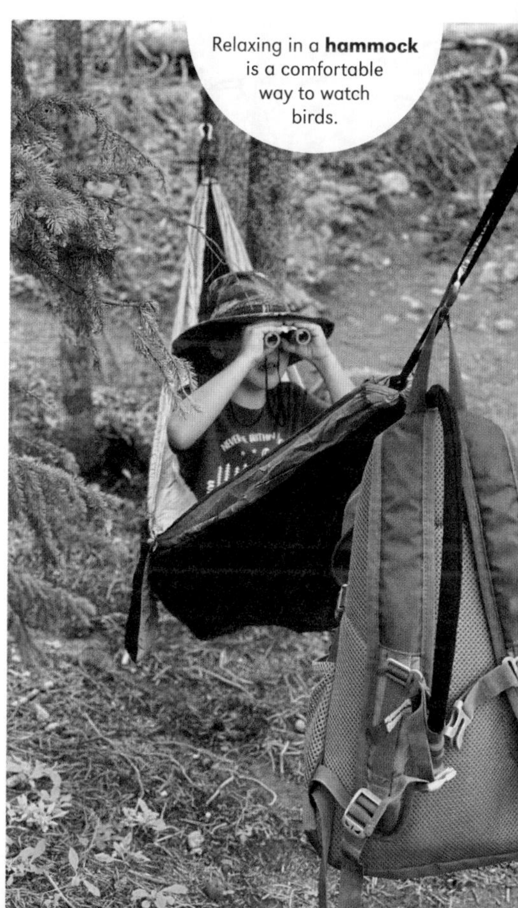

Relaxing in a **hammock** is a comfortable way to watch birds.

KITE FLYING

The feeling of getting a kite off the ground and soaring through the air is a triumphant one. Our eyes benefit from seeing both near and far, and you get to learn more about weather, ecology, and physics.

MAKE YOUR OWN KITE

For a simple kite, cross a long and a short stick and tie them with string. Carefully cut a garbage bag to fit the frame and tie it to the corners. Tie a loop of string to the short stick. Attach a large ball of string to your loop, and see if you can get it to fly!

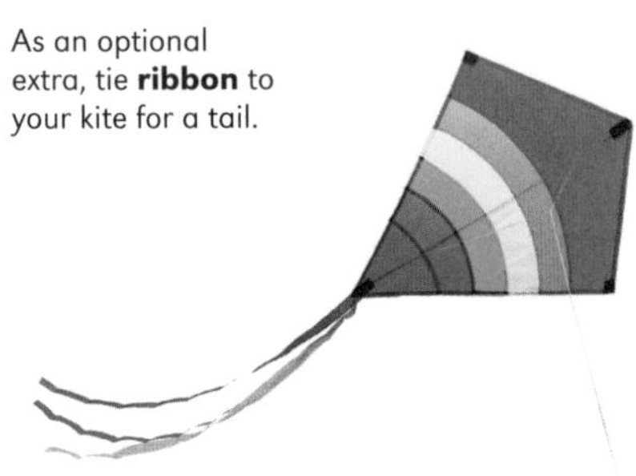

As an optional extra, tie **ribbon** to your kite for a tail.

BUILD RESILIENCE

Trying to get a kite soaring in the sky isn't always easy. Often you have to try and try again, and even when it seems like you've got it, the kite comes nosediving down to the ground. Repeated practice helps you build resilience, patience, perseverance, and self-confidence.

Flying a kite helps you learn **how to learn** new things.

EXTRA TIME

- Once you've got the basics of kite flying down and have no problem getting it high in the sky, learn how to do a few special **kite tricks**. With an adult, look at videos online for how to do the Lazy Susan, the 360, or the Backflip.

KITE LAUNCH

Launch a kite the easy way by having a friend hold the kite while you slowly back into the wind. Then have your friend let go while you let the string out. If you don't have a helper, you can set your kite on the ground and then run swiftly into the wind. Toss some dry leaves into the air or a few blades of grass to determine the direction of the wind.

Trees like to "eat" kites so fly your kite in open fields or on **beaches**.

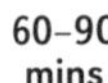

WEARABLE WINGS

60–90 mins

Playing dress-up encourages creativity and imagination. There are many places to buy dress-up clothes these days, but it's also special to make your own costumes. Creating your own set of wings is fairly easy and can be customized to your size, your favorite colors, and your favorite winged creature—either real or make-believe.

SUPPLIES

- Colorful flowers and foliage
- Tracing paper at least 2 feet (60cm) long
- Pencil
- Scissors
- 2 pieces of contact paper, each at least 2 feet (60cm) long
- Stapler or hole punch
- ¼-inch (0.5cm) wide elastic

INSTRUCTIONS

1. This craft works best with leaves or pressed flowers (see page 132). Fold your tracing paper in half so that your wings will be symmetrical.
2. Draw a single wing on one side of the paper, against the fold and carefully cut it out. When you unfold your paper, you'll see a shape with two wings.
3. Fold both sheets of contact paper in the same way.
4. Fold your tracing paper back in half, place it on one of the sheets of contact paper, matching up the folds, and trace around it. Carefully cut it out.
5. Repeat these steps for the other sheet.
6. Gently peel the backing off one sheet, lay it shiny-side down, and decorate the sticky side with flowers and foliage.
7. Peel the backing off the other set of wings and press the sticky side firmly to the other sticky side. Smooth out any bubbles.
8. Ask someone to hold the wings up to your body and mark where the arm straps should be.
9. Ask an adult to staple two elastic loops for arm bands or punch holes to tie the elastic through.

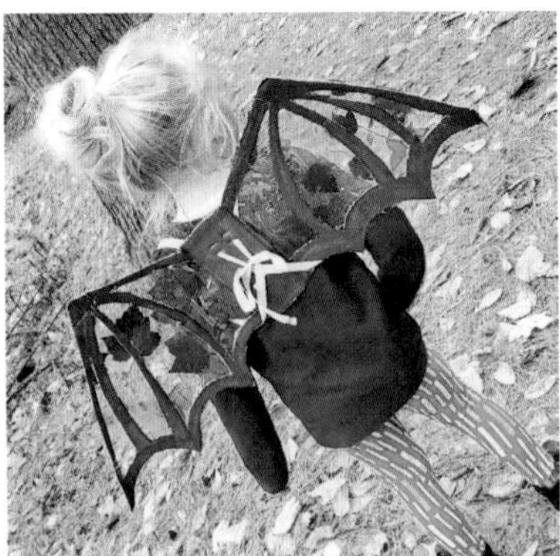

Cut your contact paper into different types of wings–like **bat wings**.

TRY THIS!
Go on a photo shoot with your gorgeous new wings.

PUMPKIN PICKING

A trip to the pumpkin patch will fill your day with the sights, sounds, and smells of fall. You could even make it an annual family tradition and invite friends to stock up on pumpkins together.

USE A WAGON

A big collection of pumpkins can get heavy to carry. Pushing or pulling a wagon instead builds strength and skill, as you learn to maneuver to where you want to go. Even young kids can join in with smaller wagons and pumpkins.

TIP

- Pumpkins can last up to **two to three months** so you have plenty of time for crafting, decorating, and baking with them all season.

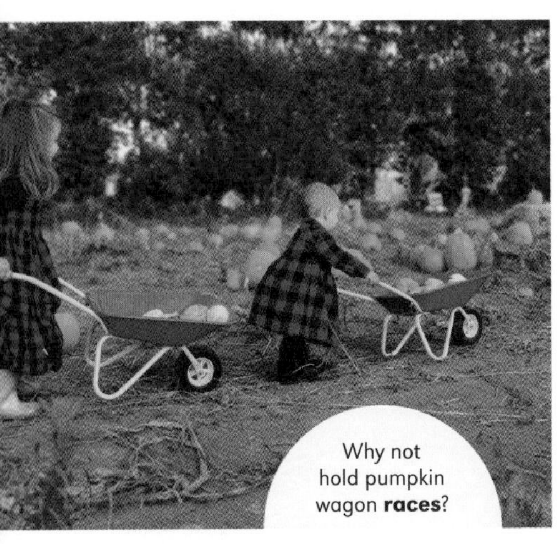

Why not hold pumpkin wagon **races**?

PUMPKIN SORTING

Gourds and pumpkins provide opportunities for sorting and being creative. Put bumpy gourds with bumpy gourds or striped pumpkins with striped pumpkins. For more ideas of how to use your pumpkins, see pages 224 and 280.

MORE IDEAS

- Use a pumpkin for **hammering practice**. Use real nails and a hammer or, for younger children, plastic golf tees and a wooden mallet.

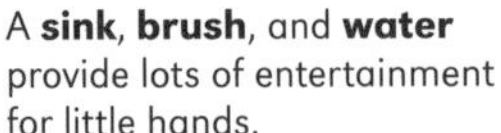

A **sink**, **brush**, and **water** provide lots of entertainment for little hands.

Get your
camera ready
for the stunning
colors and props
of fall.

TRY THIS!
Hunt for a **stick** to use for a handle or use a wooden skewer.

LEAF MASKS

30–60 mins

Leaves make food for trees. Isn't that neat? They use carbon dioxide from the air, water collected by the roots of the tree, and the sun itself to make sugar in a process called photosynthesis. Then they release oxygen that we humans need to breathe—thanks, leaves! They are also a brilliant material for craft—including masks.

SUPPLIES

- Leaves
- Scissors
- Paint (acrylic paint works best)

INSTRUCTIONS

1. First things first: it's not a good idea to go up to a healthy tree and start ripping its leaves off—ouch! Look for leaves that have fallen on the ground.
2. Once you find your leaf, carefully use the scissors to poke holes for the eyes, and any other features you want like a mouth, and then cut out the shapes.
3. Paint your leaf mask however you like—it could be plain colors, an animal face, or a mythical creature.
4. You can then hold your leaf over your face, like you're at a masquerade ball, and dance around the yard.

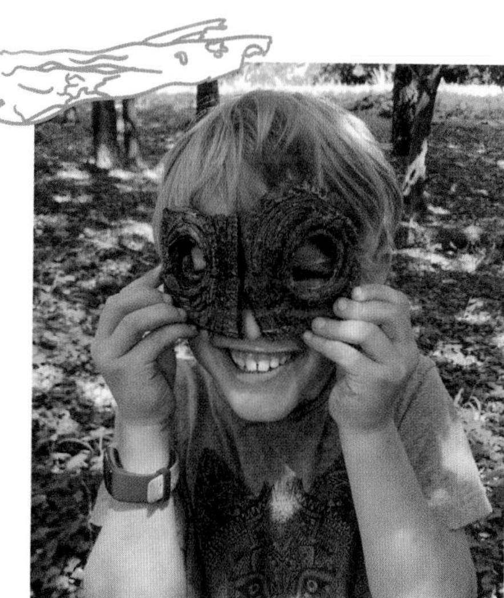

Pieces of **bark** from a dead tree can also make a really neat mask!

MORE IDEAS

- If you have only **small leaves**, you can glue several together to make a larger mask.
- To make a more **sturdy** mask, cut out a shape from cardboard and glue leaves on to it.

CORN HUSK DOLLS

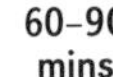

60–90 mins

There are many ways to add personal touches to these sweet homemade toys, which also make great gifts. As a bonus, the bending and twisting actions used to create the dolls are great for developing fine motor control. Plus this is a fun way to use corn husks that might otherwise find their way to the trash can or the compost heap.

SUPPLIES

- Corn husks—consider finding a variety of colors from ornamental corn
- Warm water
- String or twine
- Scissors

INSTRUCTIONS

1. If your husks are dried, soak them in warm water until they are flexible and bend without breaking. This usually takes around 10 to 20 minutes.
2. Choose four similarly sized husks and lay them on top of each other.
3. Fold them in half and tie string 2 inches (5cm) below the fold for a head.
4. Take a new single husk and roll it into a tube, tying twine at each end. This will be your doll's arms and hands.
5. Gently slide your husk tube up in between the front and the back of your doll. Using twine, tie underneath the arm where the waist will be.
6. If you'd like your doll to wear a skirt, you can cut your husks evenly across at the bottom. If you'd like your doll to wear pants, you can separate your husks into two separate legs and tie them with twine at the knees and at the ankles.
7. Allow your corn husk doll to dry in the sun for about 30 minutes and then add any extra decor.

EXTRA TIME

- Bring your corn husk doll with you on an outdoor **adventure**! Tuck your doll in a pocket, sit it in a stroller, or carry it around and show it all your surroundings.

MORE IDEAS

- Use extra bits of corn husk or silk to decorate your doll's **outfit**. Add accessories such as a headband or belt.
- Dress your corn husk doll in homemade clothes using **fabric** scraps. Attach the clothes to the doll with ribbon or glue.

TRY THIS!
Wrap fresh husks around your doll for green clothing.

PLAYGROUND HOP

Playgrounds are often a favorite part of childhood. Block off a few hours on your calendar, pack up some snacks and water, and don't just go to one playground—go on a tour, visiting several in one go!

TIP

- Use a **map application** with an adult to find your nearest playgrounds. Use pictures and reviews to choose which to visit.

HEAVY WORK

Whenever you lift, pull, or push, you're engaging in what is known as "heavy work." Heavy work puts pressure on joints and ligaments and helps you develop your proprioception sense and gives you a sense of body awareness.

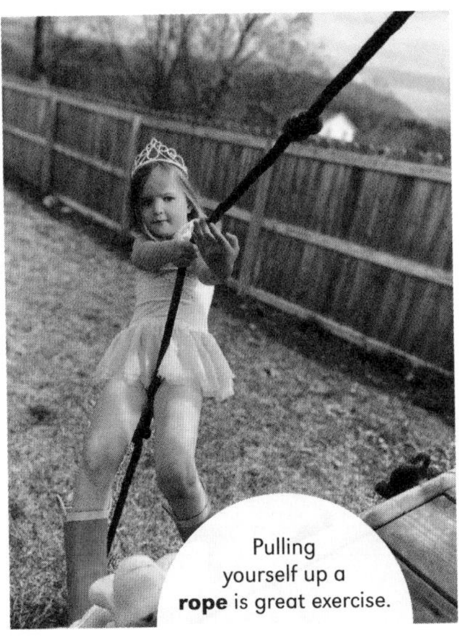

Pulling yourself up a **rope** is great exercise.

Inverting the head is one of the most powerful ways to stimulate the **vestibular system**.

VESTIBULAR SENSE

When you twirl, spin, roll, or spring, it activates your vestibular system and helps you have better balance and orientation to the space around you. Enjoy merry-go-rounds, swings, and any equipment that spins.

MORE IDEAS

- Do a breakfast, lunch, dinner hop. Eat **each meal** at a different playground.
- **Rate** all the playgrounds out of 10 for different criteria.

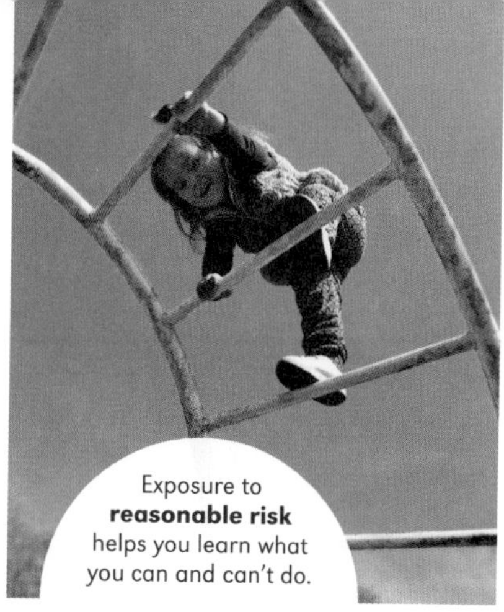

Exposure to **reasonable risk** helps you learn what you can and can't do.

MONKEY BARS

Monkey bars can be climbed over or swung under. These activities help you with your grip, arm, wrist, shoulder girdle, and core strength—all of which help tremendously with posture.

SLIDES

There are many benefits of slides beyond all of the high speed fun. Whether straight, spiral, or in a tube shape, slides entice you to head to the top again and again, helping you improve your upper and lower body strength.

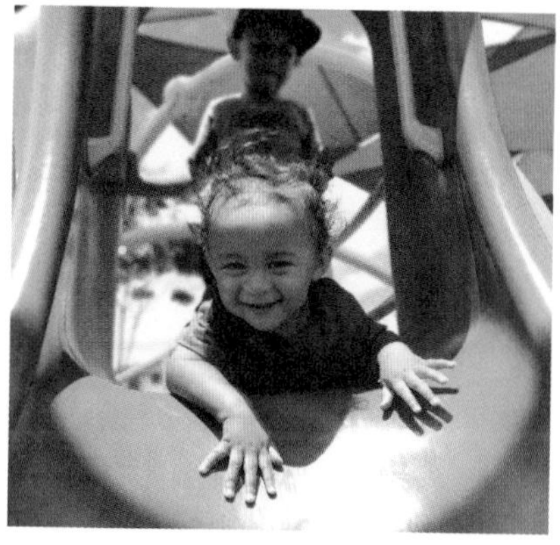

Mastering different elements in a playground improves **self-esteem** and **confidence**.

COMPLEX MOVEMENTS

Increasingly complex movements enhance brain function, so playground movements, while seemingly frivolous, actually help with academic pursuits. As you check out new playgrounds, know that you're helping your cognition in the long run.

Our brains are wired for **novelty**. Screens provide it, but so does a new playground!

30 mins

MUSHROOM ART

You may have heard it said, "there's a fungus among us"—and is that ever true! Did you know there are more than 10,000 different species of mushrooms? That's a whole lot of fungi, and one thing you can do if you're out and about and see mushrooms, either in the grass or growing out of a tree, is use them to create eye-catching art!

SUPPLIES

- Mushrooms
- Acorn tops
- Sticks
- Glue (a hot glue gun works best, but be careful)
- Markers (optional)

INSTRUCTIONS

1. First, you need to find mushrooms! The best places to hunt for them are on the outskirts of a wooded area near trees like oak, elm, or ash trees. Also look around and in dead trees or stumps. But be careful—some mushrooms are very dangerous. Touch only mushrooms that you know are safe.
2. Look for a variety of mushroom types and sizes.
3. Put your mushrooms together to make your art, using leaves, twigs, and acorns to dress them up. You could glue them together—ask an adult to help you if you use a hot glue gun.
4. If you make mushroom statues and they are sturdy enough, you could use them as puppets and perform a play.

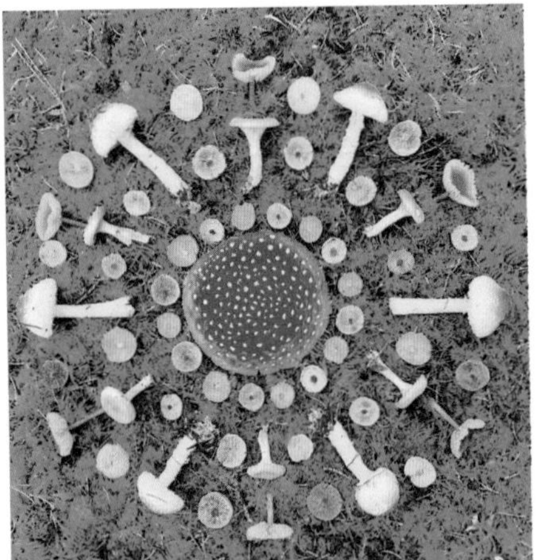

If you can find a large variety of mushrooms, make a **mandala** with them.

⚠ SAFETY FIRST

- Some mushrooms are very **poisonous**, even if you only touch them. Only go near those that adults say are safe.
- If adults are unsure, they can check mushroom **guides**.
- Familiarize yourself with any toxic mushrooms that are common in **your area**.

TRY THIS!

Use the natural markings on mushrooms for facial expressions—or draw some on.

NATURE COLLECTING

Nature is jam-packed with what are often referred to as "loose parts." These are materials that have no defined use and so they offer an endless amount of options for play.

RIVER TREASURES

A river or creek is a perfect place to kick off your shoes and look for treasures like smooth stones or crab claws. See what you can find when you're knee-high in the creek, but don't disturb any living creatures, and go in the water only with adult supervision.

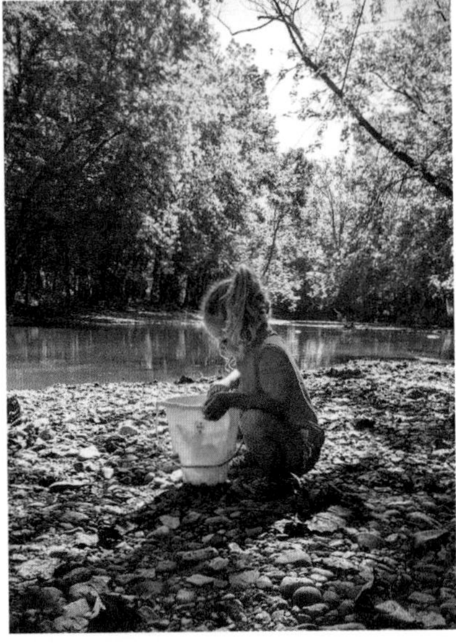

Bring **water shoes** so you can easily walk on the rocks in rivers.

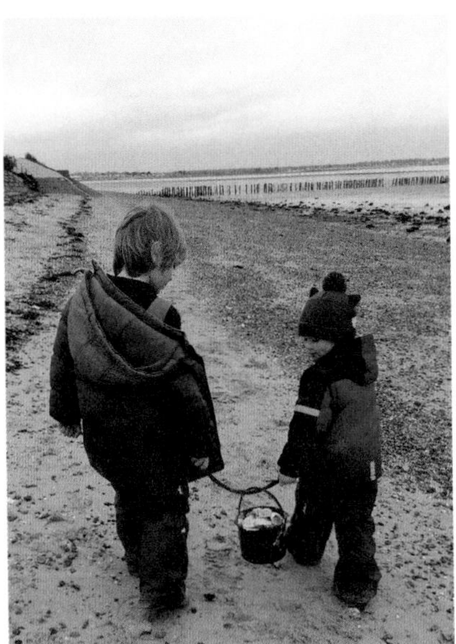

A bucket filled with beach **treasures** is a beautiful sight.

BEACH COMBING

Seashells, colorful stones, fish skeletons, seagull feathers, driftwood—the beach is full of amazing collectibles! Bring a bag or a bucket because you're sure to leave with a lot more than you came with.

EXTRA TIME

- You don't have to wait for warm weather to collect at the beach. Put on warm clothes and head there in the **winter**, too! Visiting after a windy storm is an extra good time to find treasures.

FORAGING

The forest holds all sorts of things to find—herbs, mushrooms, berries. Some people are so good at foraging that they sell hard-to-find goodies to restaurants. But don't eat anything without checking with an adult to make sure it's safe.

TREE BOUNTY

Pine cones, conkers, black walnuts, acorns, and other tree-related treasures are such neat forest floor treats and they're excellent things to add to your nature art.

NATURE DISPLAY

Bringing the outside to the inside is a way to embrace nature even when you're not out in it. Use an old shadow box or frame to arrange your nature treasures and collectibles in an appealing and festive manner in your home.

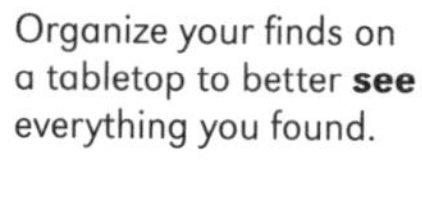

Organize your finds on a tabletop to better **see** everything you found.

What beautiful arrangements can you make with your **nature collectibles**?

2+ hrs

PUMPKIN NEIGHBORHOOD

Pumpkins are orange, right? Well, yes, a lot are, but did you know there are other colors, too? And many shapes and sizes. A fun way to make the most of this fruit (yes, it's a fruit!) is to build your own pumpkin village! Get super creative with different pumpkins and gourds to create a special play area like no other.

SUPPLIES

- Pumpkins
- Carving tools (ask an adult for help!)
- Paint and markers (optional)

INSTRUCTIONS

1. Variety is the spice of life, and that's never more true than when making your pumpkin village. Try to find different shapes, colors, and sizes. Pumpkins are green, orange, white, yellow, and black, and they grow short, tall, skinny, round—a mix will really make this special!
2. With the help of an adult, carefully cut holes in the tops of your pumpkins. Scoop out the insides so they last as long as possible.
3. Now it's time to get really creative—with an adult's help, carve windows, doorways, and chimneys, use sticks as chimney stacks, and add details with paint or markers.
4. Arrange all your pumpkin buildings into a neighborhood. Add your own toys or make your own characters with pine cones and paint to be the brightly colored citizens of Pumpkinville.

Pine-cone characters with wooden-ball heads and acorn caps live in this neighborhood.

TRY THIS!
Act out your characters' adventures in Pumpkinville!

LEAF PILE GAMES

This is a great one for parents because if the leaves are raked up into piles, it saves them a little work. Then you can use the same piles for games! A true win-win. Once leaves start falling, it's time to play!

Young and old love to watch leaves **flitter** and **flutter** back down to the ground.

LEAF PILE HURDLES

Create a series of small leaf piles, similar to hurdles in a track meet. Each runner races from one end to the other, being careful not to kick the leaf pile as they leap over it. See who finishes first or time each person separately to see who's quickest. You could penalize those who disturb the hurdles.

 **TIP**

- Have everyone pitch in and help rake so when you're done playing, you have a **clean yard**!

LEAF JUMP

Create a large leaf pile for "leaf pile long jump." Mark a take-off line with a stick so everyone jumps from the same point. See who can jump the farthest to land in the leaf pile.

Get your piles nice and **deep** so there's plenty of padding when you jump in.

LEAF OBSTACLE COURSE

Create multiple small leaf piles, intermittently spaced around the yard for an obstacle course. Small piles can be hopped over backward, run around in circles, and picked up and carried from one place to another.

Everyone loves **throwing** leaves and jumping in piles of them!

⚠ SAFETY FIRST

- Jump only into **freshly raked** piles of leaves. If left for an hour or so, they could become home to creatures who should not be disturbed.
- After playing in leaves, everyone should be **checked** for ticks, just in case any have been picked up. If you find one, an adult should carefully remove it with a tick remover. Don't just pull them off.

Burying yourself in leaves is just like **burying** yourself in sand at the beach, just less sandy and more leafy!

LEAF RUBBING

30 mins

Watch as a blank sheet of paper transforms to show you the beautiful form of a single leaf. You'll uncover its network of veins—the vessels that give structure and transport water, nutrients, and energy around the plant in a similar way to your own blood vessels. Both wax crayons and oil pastels work well—with different results.

SUPPLIES

- A variety of leaves of different shapes and sizes.
- Paper
- A clipboard or a hard surface
- Wax crayons or oil pastels

INSTRUCTIONS

1. Start by finding your leaves. Freshly fallen leaves work best as dried leaves may be brittle and prone to breaking. Make sure the leaves you choose are not wet or they will ruin your paper.
2. Place your leaf under your paper, with the veiny side facing upward. If you're using a clipboard, secure them both to keep everything from sliding around.
3. If your crayon has a paper wrapping around it, you can take it off and hold the crayon sideways, but this isn't essential.
4. Carefully rub the crayon or pastel back and forth over the leaf and watch the shape and the veins emerge through the paper. Rub over the edges of the leaf so its outline appears.
5. Once you are finished, remove the leaf from behind the paper.

MORE IDEAS

- Create a **collage** by overlapping leaves as you go.
- Do your leaf rubbings on a large sheet of butcher paper and use it as **wrapping pape**r throughout the year.
- Put one single leaf rubbing at the top of a sheet of paper and use it for **stationery**.

Play around with different colored crayons or oil pastels.

TRY THIS!
Take your materials out on a hike so you can make art right in the woods.

IMPORTANT SAFETY INFORMATION

Please take note and follow the guidance below before engaging in any of the activities in this book:

- Always ensure that children are supervised outdoors and/or when engaging in any of the activities suggested in this book.
- Children should always be supervised near water. Even very shallow water can be hazardous.
- Plants may be poisonous or protected by law from picking or uprooting.
- Fungi and berries should only be collected for consumption at the reader's own risk, since many fungi and some berries are poisonous.
- Wild animals may bite or sting, and some plants can cause allergic reactions. Take suitable precautions and a first aid kit.
- Ensure that no-one damages any nest or other shelter for a wild animal, and don't pick up eggs or touch or stroke wild animals.
- Some of the materials suggested by the author, such as food coloring, can cause damage such as staining. Always take appropriate precautions to avoid damage to personal items including clothing and furniture.
- Do not touch the batteries in any battery operated equipment, including tealights. Only adults should change the batteries where required.
- The recipes contained in this book have been created for the ingredients and techniques indicated. Be aware of potential allergies to any of the ingredients and of the health needs of any child following these activities, as the Publisher cannot be responsible for any reader's specific health or allergy needs, or any adverse reactions anyone may have to the recipes contained in this book.
- Be extremely careful when building a campfire. Follow the guidance on page 20, and ensure that you are permitted to build this in the location chosen. Certain areas may prohibit any fire due to the huge risk and loss to wildlife if it gets out of control.

ACKNOWLEDGMENTS

- My friends across the pond, Tori and Elly. Your guidance and leadership on this project made it all possible.
- The Fearsome Five for always being up for adventure.
- The global 1000 Hours Outside community for your enthusiasm and your incredibly inspiring photos that depict the grand and the every day—which is no less extraordinary.

Picture Credits

The publisher would like to thank the following for their kind permission to reproduce their photographs:

(Key: a-above; b-below/bottom; c-centre; f-far; l-left; r-right; t-top)

10 Dreamstime.com: Nadezhda Andriyakhina. **11 Dreamstime.com:** Nadezhda Andriyakhina. **14 Dreamstime.com:** Isssseeey. **15 Dreamstime.com:** Igor Sokalski. **27 Dreamstime.com:** Anastasiia Yanishevska. **39 Dreamstime.com:** Lubos Chlubny. **50 Dreamstime.com:** Steveheap. **51 Dreamstime.com:** Marcel De Grijs. **57 Dreamstime.com:** Chaoticmind. **64 Dorling Kindersley:** 123RF.com: Leonid Ikan. **78 Dreamstime.com:** Galina Barskaya (br); Montypeter (cl); Venkra (cr). **83 Dorling Kindersley:** Dreamstime.com: Prentiss40. **103 Dreamstime.com:** Famveldman (t); Varina And Jay Patel (b). **124 Dreamstime.com:** Maryia Kazlouskaya. **126 Dreamstime.com:** Robert Byron. **127 Dreamstime.com:** Robert Kneschke. **132 Dreamstime.com:** Vafina1980. **133 Dreamstime.com:** Eclypse78. **135 Dreamstime.com:** Punporn Aphaithong (cl). **141 Dreamstime.com:** Ecophoto (cl); Jill Lang (tl); Nikhil Gangavane (tr); Matthew Swartz (cr); Nikhil Gangavane (bl); Masezdromaderi (br). **158 Dreamstime.com:** Yvonne Bogdanski (cl). **167 Dreamstime.com:** Sasi Ponchaisang (tl). **192 Dreamstime.com:** Natpol Rodbang (bl). **193 Dreamstime.com:** Keith Brofsky (tl); Monkey Business Images Ltd (bl). **199 Dreamstime.com:** Florian Jung (b). **200 Dreamstime.com:** Agneskantaruk. **203 Dreamstime.com:** Josephine Julian Lobijin (cra). **213 Dorling Kindersley:** iStockphoto.com: SolStock. **215 Dreamstime.com:** Robert Kneschke. **232 Dreamstime.com:** Koldunova Anna (bl). **233 Dreamstime.com:** Jon Lamrouex (br); Yaroslav Shiyko (tl). **238 Dreamstime.com:** Dmitry Naumov (c); He Yujun (br). **239 Dreamstime.com:** Feverpitched (bl). **262 Dreamstime.com:** Remus Cucu (br); Ticomolafuera (cl). **264 Dreamstime.com:** Elisabeth Burrell (cra); Robert Kneschke (cl)

Cover images: (C) Imgorthand/Getty

The publisher would like to thank everyone from the 1000 Hours Community who submitted photos with their kind permission to include them in the book. DK would also like to thank: Methab Ali, Hollie Barber, Victoria Cochrane, Elizabeth Dowsett, Candace McManus, Dushana Pinfield, and Rachel Wilson.

Senior Editor Tori Kosara
Senior Art Editor Anna Formanek
Senior Production Editor Jennifer Murray
Senior Production Controller Lloyd Robertson
Managing Editor Paula Regan
Managing Art Editor Jo Connor
Publishing Director Mark Searle

Edited for DK by Elizabeth Dowsett
Illustrated and designed for DK by Rosamund Bird
Jacket designed by Rosamund Bird and Anna Formanek
Jacket illustrations by Rosamund Bird

Dorling Kindersley would like to thank Laura Barwick, Martin Copeland, Anne Damerell, Jennette ElNaggar, Adrian Low, Deepak Negi, Nicola Torode, and Nishani Reed.

First published in Great Britain in 2022 by
Dorling Kindersley Limited
DK, One Embassy Gardens, 8 Viaduct Gardens,
London SW11 7BW

The authorised representative in the EEA is
Dorling Kindersley Verlag GmbH. Arnulfstr. 124,
80636 Munich, Germany

10 9 8 7 6 5 4 3 2 1
001-332465-Dec/2022

Disclaimer

The activities in this book require some adult supervision. Always ensure that adults and children follow instructions carefully. The author has made every effort to set out basic safety guidelines as needed. However, it is the responsibility of every user of this book to assess any individual circumstances and potential risks and dangers of any activity they wish to undertake. The Publisher cannot accept any liability for injury, loss, or damage to any user or property following the suggestions in this book.

A CIP catalogue record for this book
is available from the British Library.
ISBN: 978-0-2415-7582-6

Printed and bound in China

For the curious

www.dk.com
1000hoursoutside.com

This book is made from Forest Stewardship Council™ certified paper—one small step in DK's commitment to a sustainable future.